THE
BIPOLAR DISORDER
Answer Book

Answers to More than 275 of Your Most Pressing Questions

CHARLES ATKINS, MD

SOURCEBOOKS, INC.®
NAPERVILLE, ILLINOIS

Copyright © 2007 by Charles Atkins
Cover and internal design © 2007 by Sourcebooks, Inc.
Cover photo © Jupiter Images
Sourcebooks and the colophon are registered trademarks of Sourcebooks, Inc.

All rights reserved. No part of this book may be reproduced in any form or by any electronic or mechanical means including information storage and retrieval systems—except in the case of brief quotations embodied in critical articles or reviews—without permission in writing from its publisher, Sourcebooks, Inc.

This book is not intended as a substitute for medical advice from a qualified physician. The intent of this book is to provide accurate general information in regard to the subject matter covered. If medical advice or other expert help is needed, the services of an appropriate medical professional should be sought.

All brand names and product names used in this book are trademarks, registered trademarks, or trade names of their respective holders. Sourcebooks, Inc., is not associated with any product or vendor in this book.

Published by Sourcebooks, Inc.
P.O. Box 4410, Naperville, Illinois 60567-4410
(630) 961-3900
Fax: (630) 961-2168
www.sourcebooks.com

Library of Congress Cataloging-in-Publication Data

Atkins, Charles
  The bipolar disorder answer book : answers to more than 275 of your most pressing questions / Charles Atkins.
      p. cm.
  Includes bibliographical references and index.
  ISBN 978-1-4022-1057-0 (trade pbk.)
  1. Manic-depressive illness—Popular works. I. Title.

RC516.A85 2007
616.89'5—dc22

                              2007027692

Printed and bound in the United States of America.
             BG 10 9 8 7 6 5 4 3 2

To Karen Kangas, EdD

Contents

Acknowledgments

In writing this book, I want to first thank all the people I've worked with over the years who have bipolar disorder and their families; whatever insights I've obtained came from them. I've also been fortunate to be able to tap into the wisdom of the experts at the Yale School of Medicine Department of Psychiatry, and elsewhere, who were willing to share their time, enthusiasm, and insights. With this project it was important to get everything right, and when I started to drift, having a strong network of consumers, family members, and experts to keep the ship pointed in the right direction was invaluable.

In particular, I'd like to thank Malcolm Bowers, Zubin Bhagwager, Steven Southwick, Ezra Griffith, Kim Yonkers, Robert Rosenheck, Betsy Smith, Gary Jayson, Tracey Violette, Elizabeth Fitzgerald, Al Zuckerman, Jeanine Sullivan-Wiley, Paul Morrissey, Paul Amble, Lori Sobel, Thomas Reinhardt, Doreen Elnitsky, Colette Anderson, Nassir Ghaemi, and Ronald Pies.

I'm deeply indebted to the medical librarians at Waterbury Hospital Health Center, Linda Spadaccini, and Kandace Yuen who made the research end of this project (which was a lot) a breeze. I'd also like to thank my colleagues at the Department of Behavioral Health of Waterbury Hospital for continuing to support my dual pursuits of writing and psychiatry. And to Waterbury Hospital for continuing to do that rarest of things—be a full-service community hospital while maintaining the academic rigor of a university-affiliated teaching hospital.

Finally to Shana Drehs, my editor at Sourcebooks, for ensuring that the final product was as good as it could be and accessible to all.

Introduction

I'm from a family with bipolar disorder; I grew up with it. I was frightened that I might develop it, and scared when someone I loved became so depressed that I worried that they'd take their own life. I was young at the time, but I remember the overall sense of confusion and fear in my family, of not knowing what to do or where to go for answers.

On a professional level, I'm a board-certified psychiatrist. I've kept a clinical faculty appointment at Yale University since I completed my residency there in 1994, and I've been working with people who have bipolar disorder and other major psychiatric and substance abuse disorders ever since. Currently I work in a hospital-based setting where I see people on an inpatient unit, in outpatient clinics, and in the emergency room and crisis center. But I could tell you stories about working with people with bipolar disorder that go back even further, from my years working as an EMT in Boston through my first job in psychiatry as a receptionist, where one man with mania and I decided that we could send the entire ward, including the staff, to Hawaii for what we were billing the insurance companies, and wouldn't that be a great study? When I interact with families on an inpatient unit, in emergency rooms, and in my office, I understand their anxiety, fear, anger, and all the other emotions they're going through. I've been there.

As a writer, I've published novels and well over a hundred articles, short stories, and columns. Much of my writing is focused on the subjective experience of mental illness, e.g., what it's like to have one, or to be the family member or significant other of someone who does.

My first novel, *The Portrait* (St Martin's Press, 1998), took this a bit further by introducing a hero, an artist with manic-depression, into a mainstream thriller.

I think a lot about bipolar disorder. I agree with the view that bipolar disorder represents a spectrum and is a part of the human condition, as opposed to something separate and disconnected from what we consider normal. After all, we're talking about the range of human emotions and moods. On one end of this continuum lies horrible depression that gets so bad death seems like merely an escape from unbearable suffering (10 to 20 percent of people with bipolar disorder commit suicide), and on the other pole is mania so severe that a person is non-functional, out of control, psychotic, and potentially dangerous.

I see the hard work that people with bipolar disorder go through as they learn to manage their symptoms and to not let the illness— or the treatments—overrun their lives. I believe that for most of those who are successful, their success is less about focusing on the disorder than it is about self improvement, self knowledge, managing stress, and building rich supports that will be there through the good times and the bad.

What I hope to achieve with this book, and what I've found in writing it, is a type of balance. I don't want to leave people with a politically correct picture in which all is good and cheerful on some romanticized road to recovery, or with a dire—and inaccurate— vision of bipolar disorder leading to a life of misery, substance abuse, destitution, and inevitable suicide. It's neither. What I believe to be true is that living with the different shades of bipolar disorder represents a unique set of challenges. Each person's path and better/best options are different and change over time. One person might find lithium to be a miracle in pill form, while for someone else the key will be a strong relationship with a therapist willing to balance low-dose or even no medication(s) with an understanding that symptom recurrence needs to be immediately addressed. And for many people with bipolar disorder the single most important thing may be finding a support group and peers who can constantly reinforce hope and the fact that you will get your life together.

I hope this book provides you with a useful and up-to-date tool for getting the information you need—whether you read it straight through or jump to the sections that are of immediate interest. I'll make it clear whether what we're discussing is a theory (what might be true or what we think is probably true) or a proven fact.

As with anything, knowledge is power. The more we understand the nature of bipolar disorder, the better equipped we are to help people get through the bad times and get on with their lives. For people with bipolar disorder, learning to manage—and hopefully eliminate symptoms—has everything to do with self-knowledge. For families and loved ones, it's learning how to be an effective support and having the tools and the resources you need.

Chapter 1

BIPOLAR BASICS

- What is bipolar disorder?
- What are mood disorders?
- When does a mood state become a disorder?
- Is there a cure for bipolar disorder?
- How long has bipolar disorder been around?
- How many people have bipolar disorder?
- Has there been a rise in the disorder in the last few years?
- What is a manic episode?
- What is hypomania and how is it different from mania?
- What is depression?
- What separates clinical (unipolar) depression from bipolar disorder?
- What is dysthymia?
- What is a double depression?
- What is a mixed episode?
- What are psychotic symptoms?
- If I have psychotic symptoms does that mean I'm crazy?
- Who gets bipolar disorder?
- At what age does someone develop bipolar disorder?
- Can children get bipolar disorder?
- Is bipolar disorder inherited?
- If one family member has bipolar disorder what are the chances that other members will have it?
- How do I know if I'm susceptible to bipolar disorder?
- Does bad parenting cause bipolar disorder?
- Can drug abuse cause bipolar disorder?
- Is bipolar disorder caused by something abnormal in the brain?
- Are people with bipolar disorder more likely to commit suicide?
- What are the risk factors for suicide?
- What can be done to decrease the risk of suicide?
- Are people with bipolar disorder at risk for harming others?
- If a person with bipolar disorder commits a violent act, who is most at risk?
- Are there specific factors that increase the risk of violence toward others?
- What can be done to decrease the risk of violent behavior during a mood episode?

What is bipolar disorder?

Bipolar disorder, which until the 1980s was called manic-depression, is a diagnostic term used to describe patterns of abnormal and severe mood swings, ranging from disabling depression to mania. For the sake of clarity, we're using the term "mood" to describe a sustained or prevailing emotional state. The term "bipolar" refers to extreme moods, from depressed on one pole to manic on the other.

There are four variants of bipolar disorder included in the current psychiatric diagnostic manual (the DSM-IV-TR), a book medical professionals use to diagnose patients.

- Bipolar I disorder
- Bipolar II disorder
- Cyclothymic disorder
- Bipolar disorder NOS (not otherwise specified)

These will be described in detail, along with their variants, in Chapter 2.

In the real world, what we find is that while these diagnoses are useful and provide a common language with which behavioral health professionals (psychiatrists, psychologists, social workers, counselors, therapists, and others) can communicate, the reality is that bipolar disorder represents a complex spectrum. Each person with bipolar disorder will have an array of symptoms unique to them and to their changing lives, circumstances, and moods. The range is vast, from people who will have multiple mood swings in a year to some who may go for years or even decades with the disorder lying dormant.

There is no one face to bipolar disorder, and because we're discussing moods—something everyone has—we'll need to define where normal ends and a disordered state begins.

What are mood disorders?

Mood disorders, also referred to as affective disorders, include the full range of depressive disorders (major depression, dysthymia, etc.) as well as the bipolar spectrum (bipolar I, bipolar II, cyclothymia, bipolar disorder NOS, and some would also include schizoaffective disorder). All of these are discussed and defined in Chapter 2. In practical terms, mood disorders are where sustained emotional states (days, weeks, months, or years as opposed to minutes and hours) are so extreme that they are out of proportion to the situation and cause impairment in major areas of a person's life (work, relationships, health).

When does a mood state become a disorder?

This is a fundamental question: when does a mood cross some imaginary line from normal to abnormal? Probably the best way to approach this is to look at disruptions and overall functioning in the individual's life. If someone gets by with four hours of sleep a night, has tons of energy, is extremely productive, feels rested, is getting on well with family, friends, and co-workers, does this make them hypomanic, or are they just energetic and happy? In this example you could argue that we're in the realm of normal, because there's no disruption being caused by the good mood and revved up personality; it's just the person's natural way of being.

In order for a mood state to cross the line into a disorder there must be—in addition to various symptoms and durations of symptoms that we will outline for each of the mood states (mania, mixed and depressed)—a significant disruption in overall functioning, at work, home, or in other settings.

Additionally, as is seen in depressed and mixed states, the presence of significant to severe and disabling emotional distress is what pushes a case of the everyday blues and occasional irritability that we all get into something that is a disorder.

Is there a cure for bipolar disorder?

Bipolar disorder, like many medical conditions, is treatable, although there is no known cure. People do recover, however, and by learning to manage their symptoms can have lives that are highly productive, rich, and meaningful.

How long has bipolar disorder been around?

The first recorded mention of mental illness of any sort dates back to Egyptian hieroglyphs. The ancient Greeks conceptualized various moods through the balance of four humors or biles (black, green, yellow, and red), which included melancholia or black bile to describe a depressed state. Mentions of a connection between depressed and manic states can be found in Roman writings of the second century.

The modern conceptualization of bipolar disorder/manic-depression is credited to the psychiatrist Emil Kraepelin (1856–1926), who coined the term "manic-depressive insanity." His careful descriptions of the natural course of the illness (before medications were around) still read true and laid much of the groundwork for current diagnostic thinking.

How many people have bipolar disorder?

According to the National Institute of Mental Health (NIMH), 2.6 percent of Americans age eighteen or older (5.7 million Americans) have bipolar spectrum disorder. Other sources place the incidence between 1 and 1.6 percent.

The broad discrepancy in reporting has a lot to do with how different researchers have looked at the disorder. Some include just bipolar I, while others include bipolar II, cyclothymia, and bipolar disorder NOS (not otherwise specified).

Has there been a rise in the disorder in the last few years?

The answer is both yes and no. The number of people with bipolar I—people who get both depressed and manic or mixed episodes—has remained relatively stable. But as the concept of a bipolar spectrum has expanded to include people who never become fully manic (bipolar II and cyclothymia—see Chapter 2), the actual number of individuals with bipolar diagnoses has increased.

What is a manic episode?

A manic episode is a sustained period of abnormally elevated mood. This can range from a glowing sense of euphoria to a pressured and agitated state, in which people feel as though they could jump out of their skin. When someone is manic he has seemingly boundless energy, and in the early phases may be quite productive. His speech becomes too rapid and the normal give-and-take of conversation is lost—you can't get a word in edgewise. The person with mania may become easily distracted and will describe his thoughts as having a racing quality. When listening to a person who is manic, the ideas that fly from his mouth seem to blossom one on top of the other (flight of ideas). Elaborate—and sometimes unrealistic and grandiose—plans are laid out. These take many forms, such as get-rich-quick schemes or religious revelations that he, and he alone, has discovered. If you attempt to reason with a person who is manic, he may become agitated, condescending, and openly hostile.

Psychotic symptoms, which include delusions, thought disorganization, and even hallucinations, can occur during a manic episode. The hallmark of a delusion is the belief in something unrealistic that cannot be shaken. People may believe that they have been chosen for a special mission, or that they have been imbued with magical abilities. If a person believes God is speaking to him, or that he makes all of the shampoo in North America, or that he has been chosen to save the universe, nothing you can say will alter his mindset.

Sleep becomes markedly diminished, or the person stops sleeping altogether. They typically will not complain of being tired, although as the sleeping pattern worsens, agitation and irritability often increase.

Problem behaviors develop. Generally these are pleasure-seeking in nature, and they may include:

- Out-of-control spending. This can take the form of draining bank accounts, maxing out credit cards, spending retirement accounts, and buying anything and everything in a highly impulsive manner.
- Risky sexual behaviors. These are common, and include multiple partners, unprotected sex, and random and impulsive encounters with strangers. Someone in a committed relationship might start an affair, or have a sexual encounter that is otherwise not typical for him, such as a heterosexual having a homosexual liaison.
- Gambling.
- Substance Abuse
- Impulsivity. This can include breaking off close relationships, leaving jobs, getting on a plane with no clear plan, and so forth.

Other types of behavior commonly seen in mania may center on specific goal-directed activities. Examples run the gamut from writing a novel or a symphony over the course of a few days to becoming involved in mystical or spiritual activities such as reading tarot cards for hours on end or saying thousands of rosaries. Still other people will turn to cleaning activities, often vacuuming through the night and getting down on all fours to pull lint from a rug.

For an episode to meet DSM-IV criteria for mania it must last at least one week, but this duration criteria goes away if the severity is such that hospitalization is required. Additionally, at least three of the previously mentioned symptoms (pressured or rapid speech, grandiosity, high-risk behaviors, etc.) should be present.

Finally, for the episode to be considered a true mania, it must cause severe impairment at work, at home, or in relationships. Likewise, mania is diagnosed if the symptoms rise to the level where the person is at imminent risk of harming themselves or others and requires inpatient hospitalization.

The following is an excerpt from "Chad," a short story about a mother and her recently diagnosed son, which illustrates many symptoms of mania.

She opens the door and looks at her twenty-one year old son, red hair spilling over his shoulders, naked behind his drum set.

"Listen to this. Listen to this," beating a lightening-fast cadence. "The world came out to play. I said I'd had enough. The man came down from Frito-Lay. I had to call his bluff. And so we sang and dance and played. The music man had run away. It gave me something to perceive, when all the others would not believe."

Mrs. Greene stands in the doorway, at a loss once again. What did Dr. Adams tell her? Where is she supposed to draw the line? Is he getting any better? She's scared to look him in the eye, their beautiful son. She shouts over the drums, "Chad, could you please get dressed, you're going to be late for your appointment."

His words shout out too fast and too loud, "I don't know if I want to go. You know you should wear more white, Mom. White is the color of purity, all the people in the world wearing white are joined by bonds of purity. I can see the rays connecting us. When I wear white we know each other. The only way they can know me is to be naked or wear white. That would be such a pretty song. I'm really making progress with the music, everything is so beautiful, check this out, check this out." The drumsticks fly over the skins.

"Chad! Look you promised," she's shouting to be heard as she wades through piles of dirty laundry. "You promised you'd keep your appointment with Dr. Adams."

He pivots abruptly, "Promise? Did I make a promise? Can't break a promise. One more song," beating down on the drums, eyes closed, his body fused to the music.

"CHAD!" she grabs a drum stick.

A rapid flash of anger crosses his face. She feels a different fear, the pulse of adrenalin and the single thought, *don't set him off*. She glances at the blank space over his dresser, the hook that held a mirror, his night of breaking glass . . .

What is hypomania and how is it different from mania?

Hypomania is similar to mania, but less intense. If a manic episode is a nine or ten on a scale of ten, a hypomania is a seven or eight. Psychosis (hallucinations, delusions, thought disorganization) is not present in hypomania and hospitalization is rarely required. Someone who is hypomanic has a persistently elevated, irritable, euphoric, self-important or grandiose mood for at least four days (DSM-IV-TR criteria). During this time they will also exhibit a number of the following symptoms.

- Rapid, or pressured, speech. In hypomania, people will talk more rapidly than is normal for them. But here, unlike in mania, you can break in and carry on more of a conversation. You'll likely have to interrupt a number of times, though.
- Decreased sleep. Often someone with hypomania will sleep just a few hours a night and feel rested.
- Increased goal-directed activities. These could include spending large amounts of time on work-related or school-related projects, cleaning, non-stop socializing, and talking on the phone for hours. Some people will describe how when they're hypomanic they will overbook activities and appointments, often enjoying the feel of racing from event to event.
- Pleasure-seeking behaviors, often with the potential for bad outcomes. These run the gamut from reckless spending and high-risk sexual activities to gambling and drugs and alcohol.

Some people with bipolar disorder view hypomania as a preferred state, where they feel energized, "high," or "the life of the party." They require little sleep and can be remarkably productive. At times, trying to achieve, or maintain, this state may prompt someone to discontinue or decrease the use of mood-stabilizing medications.

Figure 1: Comparison of Mania and Hypomania

SYMPTOM	MANIA	HYPOMANIA
Expansive, Euphoric, or Irritable Mood	Present +++ - ++++	Present ++
Rapid Speech and/or a feeling that one's thoughts are racing	Present and severe +++ - ++++	Present, but give-and-take of conversation can occur ++ - +++
Diminished Sleep	Present	Present
Increased Goal Directed Activities	Present and extreme	Present
Increased Pleasure Seeking Behaviors (Spending, Gambling, Sex, Substance Abuse)	Present and Extreme ++++	Present ++
Delusions (Paranoia, Grandiosity, Religious Delusions)	May or may not be present None - ++++	Not present
Hallucinations (Auditory or Visual)	May or may not be present None - ++++	Not present
Disorganized thought and behavior (speech patterns and behaviors have become illogical and bizarre)	May or may not be present None-++++	Not present
Duration	At least one week, unless hospitalization required	At least four days
Inpatient Hospitalization Required	Often	Seldom

Presence of symptoms 0=not at all, +=minimal or rare, ++=moderate, +++=considerable or common, ++++=severe or frequent, NA=not assessed

Still others have learned ways in which they can maintain a slightly hypomanic state—typically by keeping healthy and regulated daily routines, paying particular attention to getting adequate sleep, and avoiding drugs and alcohol

What is depression?

On the other side of the mood spectrum—or pole—from mania and hypomania is depression and a long-lasting depressed state called dysthymia. Unlike the passing blues we all get, an episode of depression is a sustained sad or unhappy mood. To be classified as clinical depression, it must persist for at least two weeks and have at least five of the following symptoms—you may find it useful to use a mnemonic (memory aid) taught in medical school, "sig e caps."

- Sleep. People who are depressed will often experience unwanted changes in their sleep pattern. This will range from difficulty falling asleep and middle-of-the-night-arousals to waking up earlier and earlier. In some types of depression, instead of sleeping less, some people will sleep excessively and feel constantly tired. In the depression associated with bipolar disorder, this increased tiredness is common.
- Interest. When depressed, people lose interest in things they usually enjoy. This can progress to a total lack of pleasure referred to as "anhedonia."
- Guilt. Here we're talking about guilt that is excessive and out of proportion to the situation. In some depressions this can actually assume delusional (psychotic) proportions: For example, someone who always pays her taxes on time and never cheats becomes consumed by the belief that the IRS is coming after her. More typically, a depressed person will ruminate about everything wrong they've ever done. Their self esteem is

at rock bottom, and they can feel worthless. You may hear them say things like: "It's all my fault" and "I can't do anything right."

- Energy. This is usually decreased. People feel run down, drained, tired. For some, depression has additional physical complaints that include generalized aches and an increased focus on medical concerns.

- Concentration. People with depression may have trouble focusing. They are easily distracted, and everyday tasks become increasingly difficult. As the depression worsens, even focusing on a television show or reading a short newspaper article may become too much.

- Appetite. Most commonly, people with depression lose their appetite, along with quite a bit of weight. Some, however, eat constantly and gain weight.

- Psychomotor agitation or slowing. This refers to how the person looks and feels. Sometimes people with depression can be markedly slowed, their speech diminished to one or two word answers and the expression on their face flat and unchanging. Or, they could be visibly anxious, worried, and jumpy—this could be called the 'hand-wringing' depression.

- Suicide. People who are in unbearable psychological pain often think of suicide as a way out. We'll talk more about suicide later in this book, but one of the key points to remember is that if someone says he has lost hope and no longer sees a future for himself, it's a serious red flag that he may be actively planning to kill himself. Expressed thoughts of suicide should always be taken seriously, as most people who kill themselves (over 90 percent) have told someone that they were thinking about it.

The following internal monologue illustrates many symptoms of depression.

Doug

It's so hard to find words. Everything inside of me feels dead. I don't want to write this, or think. I'd like to go away and be done with everything. I'm so sorry. I've screwed up everything. I don't want to do this to Peg or the kids, I can't shake this, and I know that they'll be better off in the long run.

I'm supposed to be looking for a job. John told me the layoff wasn't anything to do with my performance. Others got laid off—I know this—but how do you not take it personally? I'm such a total loser, failure. Like everything I've worked for all of these years didn't matter. You're with a company for twenty years and they tell you it's not personal, when you have two weeks to say goodbye, clean out your desk, and go for job counseling. What a joke that was.

I can't sleep. I lay there, the same thoughts over and over through my head, everything is coming undone. Two months of not paying the mortgage. I don't have the money for the taxes. No one's going to hire me, not for anything close to what I was making. I'm almost fifty. My whole life is unraveling and there's nothing I can do to stop it. I get up and even the television is too much. I can't focus. I hear Leno tell a joke, I used to think he was hysterical; it's not funny, even though I hear the audience laugh. I used to laugh all the time. People would come up to me and tell me what a happy person I must be because I'm always smiling.

Every day, every hour I think about the car in the garage and how easy it would be to do this. The weird part is that thinking about killing myself, of just turning the key and letting it run, doesn't feel bad, more like a relief, just be done with it. I think that's what I'll do. I'll do it in the morning.

What separates clinical (unipolar) depression from bipolar depression?

Unipolar depression (or major depressive disorder), which means that the person has never had a manic, hypomanic, or mixed (blend of depression and mania) episode, looks much the same as the depression associated with bipolar disorder. Studies trying to tease out subtle differences between the two have yielded little that is definitive. In bipolar depression people are likely to sleep more, rather than less. Also, psychosis is more common in bipolar depression. People with bipolar depression are more likely to have a family history of bipolar disorder. They also appear to have an earlier onset of symptoms and a greater number of depressive episodes. Unipolar depression has a higher incidence of insomnia, somatic (physical) complaints, and sadness.

Next, most treatments for depression have been studied only in unipolar depression. There have not been the same number of systematic controlled trials of antidepressants in the depression associated with bipolar disorder, although they are often used in the treatment of bipolar depression—an area of some controversy that will be discussed later.

One notable exception is that the antipsychotic medication Quetiapine (Seroquel) recently received FDA approval for the treatment of bipolar depression, as did the combination pill of Olanzapine/Fluoxetine (Symbyax)—the first medications to have this specific indication.

So the jury is still out on this question. From a clinical perspective, one of the reasons there is such a high miss rate on the diagnosis of bipolar disorder is that unipolar depression and bipolar depression look similar. Without reports of a manic or mixed episode, it can be hard to identify bipolar as such. If indeed these are two distinct entities, it would be wonderful to have some reliable way to differentiate between them.

What is dysthymia?

This is a diagnosis used to characterize a persistent depressed state—one that lasts for years (at least two years in adults, and at least one year if the diagnosis is in a child)—but does not quite meet the criteria for a depressed episode. Someone with dysthymia is chronically down (dysphoric) and will also have one or two of the other symptoms associated with a depressive episode, i.e., sadness, poor concentration, sleep disturbance, appetite disturbance, low self-esteem, excessive guilt, feelings of hopelessness. It is common for people with dysthymia to go on to have episodes of depression. The following diagram, or mood chart, gives a visual description of the course of dysthymia.

Figure 2: Dysthymia

Mania or Mixed	
Hypomania	
Normal	
Dysphoria	
Depression	

20 21 22 23 24 25 26 27 28 29
Age in years

Figure 3: Double Depression

Mania or Mixed
Hypomania
Normal
Dysphoria
Depression

20   21   22   23   24   25   26   27   28   29
Age in years

What is a double depression?

This is an old, and no longer used, term that refers to the development of a depressed episode on top of dysthymia. In other words, someone who has been chronically sad and down for the past few years develops a full-blown depression. (See Figure 3.)

What is a mixed episode?

A mixed episode of bipolar disorder is a mood state in which symptoms of both mania and depression are present at the same time for at least one week. Unlike the euphoria that is sometimes associated with a pure manic episode, people in mixed states are often highly agitated, angry, and miserable. The following table provides a useful checklist that can help determine if criteria for a mixed episode are met. What becomes apparent is that there's quite a bit of overlap of certain symptoms of depression and mania, such as changes in sleep and concentration. Additionally, in severe episodes of mania, depression, and mixed states, psychosis (hallucinations, delusions, and thought disorganization) can be present. As in a pure manic state, impulsive behavior, limited insight, and poor judgment are high. It is believed that 25 percent of the suicides associated with bipolar disorder occur during a mixed state.

What are psychotic symptoms?

Psychotic symptoms, which can occur in severe mood episodes, as well as in many other medical and psychiatric conditions, involve a person losing touch with some aspect(s) of reality. This can take a number of forms:

- Hallucinations. This is perceiving things that don't exist through one of the five senses.
  - Auditory—hearing voices, typically outside of the person's head.
    - Command auditory hallucinations—voices that instruct the person to do something. These can range from benign instructions like 'brush your teeth' to very scary orders to commit suicide or to harm someone else. The voice can be someone the person recognizes, such as an entity like God or the devil, a family member, or a celebrity, or an anonymous male or female voice. People may have a single voice or multiple different ones.
  - Visual—seeing things that aren't there.
  - Gustatory—tasting things that aren't there. These are often quite unpleasant.
  - Tactile—such as believing that there is something crawling on one's skin.

❑ Olfactory—smelling things that aren't there. Examples include smoke, feces, urine, and other foul odors.

● Delusions. These are fixed false beliefs that take many forms. Often these match the prevailing emotional state, and are termed mood-congruent. For example, a person who is depressed and psychotic may well have paranoid and persecutory delusions, while someone who is manic might be more on the grandiose side of things.

❑ Persecutory or paranoid
- Being pursued by the CIA
- Being secretly filmed
- Being conspired against by a secret society
- A belief that one's food or water is being poisoned

❑ Grandeur
- Having special powers
- Being the president (if in fact you're not) or some other important world figure or business leader
- Having vast quantities of money and/or property (when in fact you don't)
- Having dozens of children
- Being the messiah, a prophet, or some other religious or historical figure—often accompanied by having a special mission, such as rewriting the Bible, or needing to spread a message

❑ Somatic—the false belief that there is something going on with your body that is not reality-based
- Delusional pregnancies
- Aliens growing inside your body

● Thought disorganization—while not always included as a psychotic symptom (some experts include only delusions and hallucinations), when people became severely manic, their pattern of thought can reach a point where they stop making sense. Sentences and phrases no longer fit together, and the ability to think straight and to communicate through language is significantly impaired.

If I have psychotic symptoms does that mean I'm crazy?

By definition, psychotic symptoms relate to a loss of connection with reality, which is one of the dictionary definitions of "crazy." In bipolar disorder psychotic symptoms occur in the setting of a mood episode, and as the episode resolves, so too does the psychosis. So if you must use the word "crazy," rest assured that it's only temporary.

Who gets bipolar disorder?

Unlike major depressive disorder (unipolar depression), which occurs more frequently in women, bipolar I disorder affects men and women in equal numbers. It occurs in all nationalities and ethnic groups. bipolar II occurs more frequently in women, as does the rapid-cycling variant.

At what age does someone develop bipolar disorder?

Bipolar disorder most frequently manifests in the late teens through the twenties. Less commonly, bipolar can first appear when someone is in their thirties, forties, or beyond.

Can children get bipolar disorder?

The quick answer is yes, but the reality is that this is an area of ongoing confusion and some controversy. Up until recent years, it was thought that younger children were somehow immune to major

Figure 4: Overview of Manic and Depressed Symptoms

Symptom	Manic Episode (3 Symptoms Required)	Depressed Episode (5 symptoms required)	Mixed Episode (5 depressed symptoms and 3 manic symptoms) Present for at least one week
Mood	Expansive, euphoric or irritable	Sad, depressed, unhappy, irritable	Typically irritable
Sleep	Decreased	Decreased or increased	Decreased
Concentration	Decreased	Decreased	Decreased
Speech	Pressured/rapid	Not a diagnostic criteria	Typically pressured
Appetite	Not a diagnostic criteria	Decreased or increased	Decreased or increased
Energy	Increased	Decreased	Increased or decreased
Thought Patterns	Racing, grandiose, big plans, easily distracted	Sluggish and slowed, excessive guilt, feelings of hopelessness and helplessness, low self esteem	Similar to either depressed or manic, or a combination of the two.

(Continued on next page)

Figure 4—Continued

Behavior	• Increased goal directed behaviors (cleaning, schoolwork etc.) • An increase in pleasure-seeking behaviors (sex, drugs, gambling, spending etc.)	• Slowed or anxiously agitated • Loss of interest in usually pleasurable activities • Loss of interest in sex	Similar to either depressed or manic, or a combination of the two.
Psychotic Symptoms	Could be present	Could be present	Could be present
Suicidal Behaviors	Rarely present	Often present	Could be present

psychiatric disorders such as major depressive disorder, bipolar disorder, and schizophrenia. Part of the confusion has to do with the developing human brain; using adult criteria for children doesn't work well. Current thinking is that indeed younger children do develop these disorders, but that the symptoms look different from the adult forms (See Chapter 13).

Bipolar disorder in children may not manifest with the sustained disturbances of mood seen in adults. Rather they may develop rapid and extreme mood swings, often characterized by frequent tantrums and intense irritability and agitation. These episodes may last for days, or several switches from one extreme mood state to another can occur over the course of a few hours.

In dealing with children who may have bipolar disorder, it's important that medical professionals tease out other behavioral conditions and diagnoses, such as attention deficit hyperactivity disorder (ADHD), oppositional defiant disorder (ODD), conduct disorder (CD) and various forms of autism and Asperger's disorder.

Is bipolar disorder inherited?

There is a strong genetic (inherited) component to bipolar disorder, but that's not the whole story. This has been clearly demonstrated in studies of identical twins, in which one develops the disorder and the other does not. If genetics were the only factor, both identical twins would always have bipolar disorder. That said, if one identical twin has bipolar disorder, the chance that the other twin will also develop it is greatly increased (between 67 and 87 percent of the time). In fraternal, or non-identical twins, the likelihood that if one twin has bipolar disorder the other will as well goes down to between 22 and 39 percent.

So while it most definitely runs in families, it can also occur in people who have no family history. As the human genome (DNA) is mapped out by scientists, it seems likely that bipolar disorder is associated with more than one gene. One theory that has some evidence to support it is that the different variants of bipolar disorder, and the severity with which they affect a given person, relates to the number of "genetic hits" the individual has. In other words, multiple genes might be involved in a person who has severe bipolar I disorder, whereas a smaller number may predispose an individual to the less extreme bipolar II disorder, or cyclothymic disorder (these other diagnoses are discussed in Chapter 2). Additionally, it appears that even when this is teased apart, genetics will not provide a complete answer for who will and will not develop the illness. Environment, stress, and life circumstances will still factor into the equation.

Particular genes implicated in bipolar disorder are located on chromosomes 22 and 13. Interestingly enough, some of the implicated genes in bipolar disorder are also showing linkages to schizophrenia, a disorder discussed in Chapter 2

If one family member has bipolar disorder what are the chances that other members will have it?

Data shows that the risk increases the more closely related you are to the person with the disorder. If you have a first-degree relative (mother, father, sister, or brother) with bipolar disorder, you have roughly a 15 percent chance of developing it. If both parents have bipolar disorder the probability goes up to between 30 and 50 percent. If you also have brothers and sisters with the disorder, the likelihood increases. The chance of developing bipolar disorder diminishes the more distantly related you are to the family member who has it. The likely reason for this is that the further away you are, in terms of the direct blood line, the less genetic material (DNA) you have in common with a particular relative.

How do I know if I'm susceptible to bipolar disorder?

A family history of mood disorders is the only well-documented risk factor. That said, there is a growing interest in the possibility of environmental factors—such as stress and drugs—triggering or activating bipolar disorder, especially in individuals who may have a genetic susceptibility or vulnerability.

At present, with no tests that can positively determine who will and who won't develop bipolar, even in families with a history of it, the best we can say is that the risk increases—or decreases—depending on how many family members have mood disorders and how closely related they are to you.

From a practical perspective, if you think you are at greater risk for developing bipolar, it makes sense to avoid exposure to drugs, alcohol, and undue stress. While not studied, strategies discussed throughout this book, such as establishing and sticking to regular routines, maintaining healthy sleep/wake cycles, etc., might well be effective in helping a person with a genetic susceptibility from going on to develop bipolar.

Does bad parenting cause bipolar disorder?

The answer is no, and it's an important point to make, as for many decades parents of children with bipolar disorder and other biologically-based brain disorders have been saddled with the accusations and associated guilt that they were somehow responsible for causing the problem. The psychiatric profession had quite a lot to do with this. Nineteenth-century theories, many originating with Sigmund Freud, postulated that almost all psychiatric illnesses were caused by early-life events and traumas, and could be cured through intensive talking therapies. These theories took some interesting forms, and until the 1960s the concept of a "schizophrenogenic mother" (a mother who through erratic parenting could make her child develop schizophrenia), was very much in vogue. As science has progressed and it's become clear that these were biologically-based (nature rather than nurture) conditions, these earlier theories have been largely dropped.

While a parent cannot make his child have bipolar disorder, it is true that susceptible children who are severely abused and/or neglected are more likely to develop a host of psychological problems. Also, there is a connection between stress and the onset of mood episodes (especially the first ones), so a highly volatile and conflicted home environment will increase the chances of a susceptible person developing a mood episode.

Can drug abuse cause bipolar disorder?

This is a question that has been much studied, and until recently there has been no definitive answer. Many people with both bipolar disorder and schizophrenia and their families have told doctors that they believe their disorder was caused by heavy use of a variety of substances. Most frequently people will wonder if their use of hallucinogens (LSD, mescaline, peyote), marijuana, ecstasy, cocaine, amphetamines, etc., may have caused their bipolar disorder. Still others will notice distinct patterns between their mood episodes and their use of drugs and/or alcohol.

Part of what makes this question difficult to answer with a definitive yes or no is that the age of onset of bipolar disorder (most commonly in the late teens through early thirties) corresponds with the time when many adolescents and young adults are experimenting with drugs. So the question becomes, were they going to develop the disorder anyway and is it just coincidental that they were also using substances when this happened?

What is certainly true is that many substances can precipitate symptoms of bipolar disorder in a susceptible person. Stimulants and hallucinogens can set off a manic episode, and cocaine can both start a mania and trigger a crushing depression (especially after a heavy binge).

Beyond this, there is a new body of evidence that supports the theory that individuals who are genetically predisposed to certain psychotic disorders may have these brought on by the use of drugs. One particular gene variant that carries the code for an enzyme (catecholamine O-methyl transferase [COMT]) involved in the metabolism of dopamine appears to be triggered in susceptible people by the use of cannabis (marijuana). In other words, if people who have this particular sequence that runs in families smoke marijuana, they greatly increase their risk of developing a serious psychiatric condition.

Is bipolar caused by something abnormal in the brain?

Unlike many disorders of the brain, such as Parkinson's and Huntington's diseases, we have not yet identified a characteristic lesion or defect in the brains of people with bipolar disorder.

Current research using brain-imaging techniques such as PET and SPECT scans and Functional MRIs allow scientists to observe living brains and to try and identify differences between the brains of people with bipolar disorder and those without.

Are people with bipolar disorder more likely to commit suicide?

The unfortunate answer is yes. Between 10 and 20 percent of people with bipolar disorder will end their lives by suicide (some reports put this figure much higher, at 40 to 50 percent). Slightly less than 1 percent of people with bipolar disorder will commit suicide each year, or thirty to sixty times the rate of suicide in the general population.

Contrary to the popular belief that people who 'really intend to kill themselves don't talk about it, they just do it' research has shown that the vast majority do in fact tell someone in the weeks preceding their suicide. Additionally, it's well documented that between 80 and 90 percent of people who commit suicide have had some contact with a healthcare provider in the month prior to their death.

Times of greatest risk for suicide are when people are in a depressed or mixed episode. There is also greater risk for suicide early on in the illness—the first year after being diagnosed in particular.

It is critical, and potentially life saving, to remember that suicidal thinking, or any verbalization or visible behavior that indicates someone is thinking of suicide is a medical emergency that needs immediate attention.

What are the risk factors for suicide?

Each year in the United States, roughly thirty thousand people commit suicide, making it the ninth leading cause of death.

There are a host of risk factors that increase the likelihood that someone with bipolar disorder will commit suicide. Demographically speaking, older white men (eighty-five and older) carry the highest suicide rates. In general, men in every age and racial group are at a higher risk for committing suicide, although women will make a greater number of attempts.

Diagnostically, people with mood disorders, such as bipolar disorder, carry a greatly elevated risk of suicide. In bipolar disorder the periods of greatest risk are during depressed (75 percent) and mixed (25 percent) episodes. The active use of alcohol increases the risk five-fold. So too, can use of illicit drugs enhance the likelihood of an impulsive and fatal attempt. The symptom of "hopelessness" is particularly ominous, as the person who doesn't see any future might easily decide there's no reason to continue living. Other symptoms such as agitation, irritability, impulsivity and the presence of anxiety and panic attacks are associated with increased risk.

Access to lethal means must also factor into the equation. Over half of all suicides in the United States involve firearms. The largest numbers of suicide attempts, however, are by overdose. Therefore, it is critical to remove firearms from the home, and to lock away potentially lethal dosages of medications. While suicides involving

Figure 5

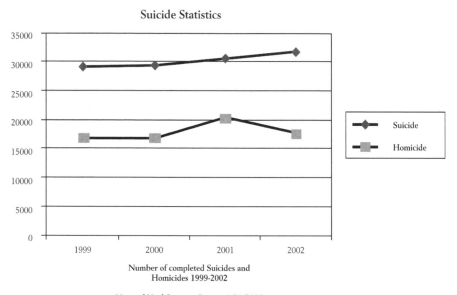

Suicide Statistics

Number of completed Suicides and
Homicides 1999-2002

-National Vital Statistics Reports 1/31/2006-

automobiles are reported as being relatively few, access to car keys should still be limited. For family members and practitioners this also means paying attention to how medications are managed, amounts of pills dispensed at any one time, access to potentially lethal doses of medication, and so on.

Social problems and acute stresses also factor heavily into the assessment of suicide risk. Marital/relationship conflicts, breakups, divorces, financial setbacks, school problems, bullying, legal problems, arrests, admission to a convalescent facility, and recent diagnosis of medical and/or psychiatric problems all significantly increase the risk of suicide.

What can be done to decrease the risk of suicide?

There's a large literature devoted to this topic. So at the risk of being overly simplistic, let's refer to the previous question and turn it around. That is, certain risks such as age, gender, genetic makeup, family history, and so forth cannot be changed. They are static. On the other hand, active psychosis, mania, depression, hopelessness, panic attacks, and alcohol and substance abuse are all things that can be targeted and treated with social interventions, therapies, medications, etc. They are dynamic and can change. So too can social stresses, such as legal problems, marital conflict, a school bully, or a sadistic boss be addressed. Access to lethal means can also be limited—although probably not eliminated.

Figure 6

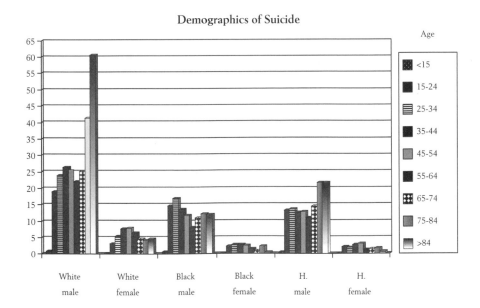

Suicide rate/100,000 by age, gender and
ethnicity CDC 2000 statistics

Figure 7

Means of Suicide 2002

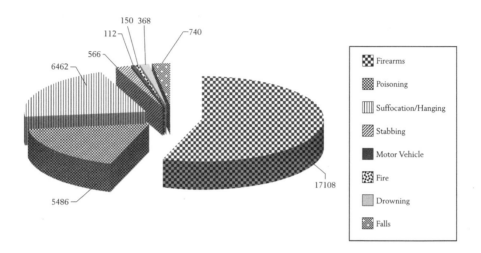

If we think about risk in terms of an equation, there are many things you can do to decrease the overall risk of suicide. Many people with bipolar disorder will have active suicide-prevention plans that might include friends and family they can be with around the clock, having someone else monitor their medication, or ensuring that they don't have access to a vehicle in the midst of a mood episode.

Are people with bipolar disorder at risk for harming others?

For many years, it was argued that people with major mental illnesses were no more likely to commit violent crimes than anyone else. This has been shown to be false in numerous studies completed over the past twenty years. There is an increased incidence of violent crimes in people with mood disorders, including bipolar disorder. In many of the studies specific diagnoses were not separated out, so it's difficult to come up with a consistent number that correlates directly to bipolar. It appears that without additional risk factors for violence—most notably the use of drugs and alcohol—the risk associated with bipolar disorder is real, but small. The overwhelming majority of people with bipolar disorder do not commit violent acts. Furthermore, just as with suicide, the desire to do harm to others is typically a state that eventually passes. With appropriate intervention, this critical period can be safely managed.

Verbalizations or actions that indicate someone is thinking of harming or killing another person represent an emergency that must be taken seriously. It's quite natural for family and loved ones to downplay the seriousness of a situation, thinking things such as: "Oh, he doesn't mean that; he wouldn't hurt a fly" or "she's just being hot headed." There is too much at risk when someone is actively manic, with or without psychosis, and expressing thoughts of wanting to harm another person; it's important to err on the side of safety and seek emergent help until the crisis passes.

If a person with bipolar disorder commits a violent act, who is most at risk?

Family members and significant others are at the greatest risk.

Are there specific factors that increase the risk of violence toward others?

There are numerous factors that increase the risk that one person will do harm to another, and not surprisingly, many of these are the same risk factors we saw for suicide. When talking about bipolar disorder, we need to pay attention to a number of important red flags, including:

- Currently in a manic or mixed state, and may also be experiencing psychotic symptoms
- History of violent acts toward others, possibly including:
    Arrests for assault
    Domestic violence
    Violence while intoxicated
- Verbalizations of intent to hurt—or kill—another person
- Active use of alcohol and/or other drugs
- Auditory hallucinations instructing the person to do a violent act (referred to as command auditory hallucinations)
- Paranoid delusions
- Access to firearms
- Impulsivity

What can be done to decrease the risk of violent behavior during a mood episode?

As we did in looking at suicide risk, we can divide the risk factors for harming someone else into those things that can be changed (dynamic) and those that remain the same (static). If someone has a history of violent behavior toward others, that's a strong predictor that he has the capability to commit violence again in the future. Similarly, it's well known that young men are at the highest statistical risk for committing a violent act. Because a person's history, gender, and age cannot be changed, these are static factors.

Dynamic factors include the current mood state—if someone is severely depressed, manic, or in a mixed episode, treatment is critical. So too can the use of drugs and alcohol, psychotic symptoms, ready access to weapons, an unstable living environment, and homelessness be addressed. The single greatest risk for committing violence—and this holds true whether or not a person has bipolar disorder—is the active use of alcohol and/or drugs.

Chapter 2

THE BIPOLAR SPECTRUM: ONE DIAGNOSIS DOES NOT FIT ALL

- Are there different types of bipolar disorder?
- What is bipolar I?
- What is bipolar II and how does it differ from bipolar I?
- What does *rapid cycling* mean?
- What is cyclothymia?
- What is bipolar disorder not otherwise specified?
- What is schizoaffective disorder?
- What is schizophrenia?
- What is seasonal affective disorder and how does it relate to bipolar disorder?
- What is the DSM-IV-TR?
- How important is a person's history in making a diagnosis?
- What is a mood chart or life chart?
- How do you make a mood chart or life chart?
- Are there laboratory tests that can determine if someone has bipolar disorder?
- Why should the diagnosis of bipolar disorder be left to professionals?
- Is bipolar disorder difficult to diagnose?
- Why is there so much misdiagnosis?
- How important is an accurate diagnosis?
- Why is even an accurate diagnosis sometimes a bad fit?
- Are there questionnaires or screening tools for bipolar disorder?
- Who makes the diagnosis of bipolar disorder?
- What is a multiaxial diagnosis?
- What does a multiaxial diagnosis look like?
- What is a personality disorder?
- What medical conditions can mimic bipolar disorder?
- What medications and drugs can mimic bipolar disorder?
- Can herbs and nutritional supplements mimic or precipitate bipolar disorder?
- What laboratory tests are done to rule out medical conditions that can mimic bipolar disorder?
- Is there a role for brain imaging in the diagnosis of bipolar disorder?
- Is a physical examination important in the diagnostic assessment of bipolar disorder?

Are there different types of bipolar disorder?

There are four delineated variants of bipolar disorder.
- Bipolar I
- Bipolar II
- Cyclothymia
- Bipolar disorder NOS (not otherwise specified)

These categories get further broken down by severity, presence or absence of psychosis, length of time between cycles, and whether a person is currently in a manic, mixed, depressed, or asymptomatic (symptom free) state.

What is bipolar I?

Bipolar I, sometimes referred to as classic bipolar, involves the presence of at least one manic or mixed episode (descriptions of these can be found in Chapter 1) and at least one episode of sustained depression. When a psychiatrist, psychologist, or other qualified professional makes the diagnosis of bipolar I using the DSM-IV-TR, they will go on to specify:
- Is this a single episode or have there been multiple occurrences?
- What is the current mood state (manic, hypomanic, mixed, or depressed)?
- How severe are the symptoms (mild, moderate, or severe)
- Are psychotic symptoms present (hallucinations, delusions, disorganized thought processes)?

In bipolar I, the frequency and pattern with which any person will cycle from depression to a normal mood to mania to a mixed episode or to a hypomania is highly variable. Some individuals may experience years, even decades, between episodes of a major mood disorder. For others, a mania can end with a crushing depression, which if left untreated may drag on for six months, a year, or longer.

What is bipolar II and how does it differ from bipolar I?

Bipolar II is characterized by recurrent episodes of major depression and at least one hypomanic episode. This is the distinguishing feature between bipolar I and bipolar II. In bipolar II, the "ups" never make it to a frank mania or mixed episode. In evaluating people with recurrent depression, one of the questions clinicians must tease out is: Has there ever been a hypomanic episode? On the surface this appears to be a simple question, but many people who suffer from recurrent depression may view hypomanic episodes as times when they actually felt good.

One way to distinguish this is to evaluate whether the individual has ever had a period of time in which they found themselves needing less sleep for days on end, having greatly improved energy and/or being highly productive. If these periods have lasted at least four days, then they meet the criteria for hypomania according to the DSM-IV. But again, it's important to remember that the DSM-IV is a guideline, so if someone has had multiple hypomanic episodes that don't make the four-day criteria, they could still receive a diagnosis of bipolar II.

It's also helpful to ask questions specific to the person's life circumstances and occupation. If she is a truck driver it could be finding out how long she can drive at a stretch without needing sleep (It's important to ask whether she's using stimulants). For students it could be habitual all-nighters and week-long cram sessions. For others, including police, firefighters, doctors, and nurses it would be important to ask about periods where they've picked up multiple extra shifts and have gone for days on end with little sleep.

It's important to find out about spending patterns, bankruptcies, problems with credit cards, and gambling. The sexual history may also help elicit a period of hypomania, as many people with depression experience a loss or decrease of libido (sex drive). If someone has periods where they've rapidly fallen in love; impulsively gotten engaged, married, or divorced; had an extramarital affair; been uncharacteristically promiscuous; or had a different-for-them sexual liaison, this is significant. Because while this behavior may not rise to the level of symptoms characteristic of mania, it may represent a period of hypomania, and have significant ramifications when selecting what treatments might be most effective for this person.

Figure 8: Bipolar II

Mania or Mixed	
Hypomania	
Normal	
Dysphoria	
Depression	

1   6   12   18   24   30   36   42   48   54
Months

What does *rapid cycling* mean?

This term is used to further differentiate the diagnosis of either bipolar I or bipolar II. If someone has rapid cycling bipolar he will have at least four—and often quite a few more—separate episodes that will meet criteria for a depressed, manic, hypomanic or mixed episode within a one-year period.

The same diagnostic criteria apply for distinguishing between bipolar I rapid cycling and bipolar II rapid cycling—that is, someone with the latter will need at least four separate episodes of depression or hypomania, but none of these can rise to the level of a manic or mixed episode.

What is cyclothymia?

Cyclothymia is a bipolar variant that involves (1) recurrent episodes of hypomania that don't meet criteria for a manic or mixed episode and (2) recurrent bouts of depressive symptoms that don't meet criteria for a major depression. It's helpful to think in terms of mood symptoms having amplitude. In cyclothymia, neither the highs nor the lows ever make it to the level of a manic, mixed, or depressed episode.

People with Cyclothymia cycle through their moods rapidly, and part of the diagnostic criteria is that they go for at least two years without a two-month symptom-free stretch. Many people who are first diagnosed with cyclothymia in their late teens and twenties will eventually progress to either bipolar I or bipolar II.

In older texts, cyclothymia was often referred to as cyclothymic neurosis, and was believed to be more in the realm of a personality disorder. This belief changed partially in response to the observation that many of these people do progress to have a more classic bipolar presentation and the realization that mood-stabilizing medication can be helpful in diminishing the mood swings associated with cyclothymia.

Figure 9: Rapid Cycling Bipolar I

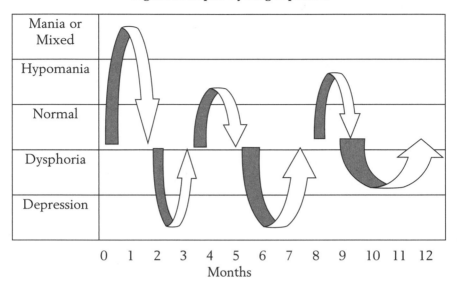

What is bipolar disorder not otherwise specified?

This is a broad diagnostic term that speaks to just how variable severe mood symptoms can appear.

In this category, we'll find people who rapidly cycle through severe mood states that will meet criteria for mania or mixed or depressed states—but whose episodes don't have the duration necessary for classification as one of the other variants.

This is also the diagnosis that would be used with someone who has recurrent bouts of hypomania without depressive episodes.

Or this could be the best-fit diagnosis for someone who has had hypomanic and some depressed episodes, but not severe enough to meet criteria for a major depressive episode or with the frequency needed for a cyclothymia diagnosis.

Figure 10: Cyclothymia

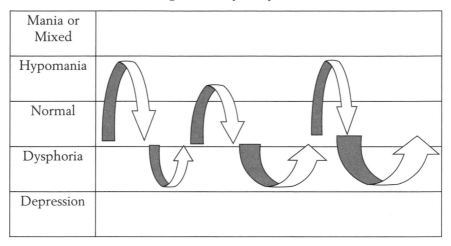

0 2 4 6 8 10 12 14 16 18 20 22 24
Mood swings over a two-year period (in months)

Right now, this diagnosis speaks to all that is not yet known about the bipolar spectrum. It's often a useful diagnosis in the early stages of working with someone, in which not enough of the history is known, or where coexisting conditions (such as anxiety, personality traits, or substance abuse/dependence) cloud the overall picture.

What is schizoaffective disorder?

The term schizoaffective relates to conditions in which a person has mood episodes that will meet criteria for a diagnosis of bipolar disorder (mania, mixed and depressed) but in addition has symptoms of schizophrenia—typically psychotic symptoms such as hallucination, delusions, and disorganized thought processes—that persist after the mood episode has resolved.

Whether or not schizoaffective disorder, like all of the diagnostic labels we've been using, is truly a separate entity is a matter of debate and study. What may pan out to be true, or close to it, is that schizoaffective disorder is another twist on the notion that bipolar disorder—and schizophrenia as well—represents a continuum of illness, and the presence of persistent psychosis after the mood state has resolved is a variant. Genetic studies have found overlap between genes involved in schizophrenia, schizoaffective disorder and bipolar disorder. Family trees where these conditions, along with unipolar depression, are found at an increased frequency add support to the continuum theories.

What is schizophrenia?

Schizophrenia is a diagnostic category covering a broad range of disorders that have at their core a combination of psychotic symptoms, such as hallucinations, delusions, and thought disorganization (often referred to as positive symptoms, not because they're good things to have, but because they're extreme and readily apparent) and a type of blunting and flattening of emotion often accompanied by extreme apathy and lack of motivation (negative symptoms).

As with bipolar disorder, people with schizophrenia can appear many different ways, and there can be a great deal of overlap when someone is in an emergency room in a psychotic state. Being able to differentiate the psychosis of schizophrenia from that which can accompany a mania or depression is not easy. What ultimately makes the difference is that in bipolar disorder, if psychosis accompanies a mood episode, it resolves when the mood returns to a normal state. In schizophrenia, regardless of the person's mood, the psychosis may persist.

What is seasonal affective disorder and how does it relate to bipolar disorder?

Seasonal affective disorder (SAD) refers to a condition in which a person becomes depressed as the days grow short in the fall and winter and happier when the days get longer in the spring. Some people with bipolar disorder will find their mood swings follow this pattern, in which they become clinically depressed in the fall and winter and return to a normal, hypomanic, or mixed state in the spring and summer.

What is the DSM-IV-TR?

DSM-IV-TR stands for *The Diagnostic and Statistical Manual of Mental Disorders, Fourth Edition Text Revised*. It was published in 2000, as an update to the DSM-IV (1994). The DSM-IV-TR represents the latest in an evolving series of attempts to group observable behaviors and symptoms into diagnostic categories. It is published by the American Psychiatric Association and represents the work of hundreds of leading experts, who attempted to further clarify what does, and does not, constitute a particular disorder (inclusion and exclusion criteria). The next version—the DSM-V—will not be released until 2010, or later.

The DSM-IV—TR serves a few purposes:

- By standardizing diagnostic criteria, it allows for mental health professionals to use a single language when talking about a specific disorder. This not only helps clarify diagnoses, but is useful when selecting therapies that are likely to benefit a particular condition.

- The diagnostic criteria in the DSM-IV-TR are used heavily in research. So if someone is doing a study of bipolar I disorder and a particular treatment or medication, everyone is clear on what condition is being studied.
- The DSM-IV, along with a second manual that covers all medical conditions (*The International Classification of Diseases and Related Problems*, or ICD-9), provides the codes used by insurance companies, hospitals, and others to generate bills and to calculate statistics.

How important is a person's history in making an accurate diagnosis?

Personal history—often mapped out on a mood chart or timeline—is of prime importance in making a diagnosis of bipolar disorder. The various diagnoses in the bipolar spectrum will be based on the presence and frequency of abnormal mood episodes of depression, dysthymia, mania, hypomania, or mixed.

A point to stress here is that family involvement in the early diagnostic phases—especially around the giving of the history—greatly increases the chances of receiving an accurate diagnosis.

What is a mood chart or life chart?

Mood charts, sometimes called life charts, are tools that can be used both to diagnose and to help people learn about their symptoms and what works and what doesn't. In its simplest form, a mood chart is a way of tracking emotional changes over time. They can be extremely basic or as complex and detailed as a person wants.

Along with learning how to chart out moods, it's helpful to begin identifying the severity—or amplitude—of a particular mood. One approach is to use a rating scale: "On a scale of zero to ten, with zero being no depression whatsoever and ten being the most hopeless and suicidally depressed anyone could be, where are you right now?"

How do you make a mood chart or life chart?

We'll start with a simple mood chart that can be useful in making a diagnosis, as well as in helping people construct meaningful relapse-prevention plans. As we move forward in this book we'll return to this illustration and see how it can be used to evaluate medications, stress reduction and relapse-prevention strategies, therapies, etc. The simplest approach is to put the moods on the left (the Y axis) and time on the bottom (the X axis). Basically, you're constructing a timeline of your life, paying particular attention to abnormal shifts in your mood, when these occurred, how many episodes there have been over time, and so forth. See if you can track how long the moods lasted and if they were associated with particular things, such as a change in the seasons, menstrual cycle, the birth of a child, a major loss, or a major family event, and whether there are possible connections between the use of substances or medications, including going off medications.

Family/significant other/friends can be extremely helpful in completing an accurate mood chart, as many people with bipolar disorder will remember the depressed episodes far more than the manic, hypomanic, or mixed ones. Bringing a completed mood chart to your practitioner—especially early in the diagnostic process—will aid him in reaching a diagnosis and tailoring interventions. There's no single correct way to complete these; some people find it helpful to do both a chart and a descriptive narrative:

Figure 11: Sample Mood Chart

Mania or Mixed	
Hypomania	
Normal	
Dysphoria	
Depression	

Time (can be in days, months or years)

My Narrative:
"Thinking back I was very active through most of high school, got very little sleep, but didn't seem to need it. I played two varsity sports, was on the honor roll, and had a part-time job on the weekends. The real problem started when I went off to college. I thought it had to do with moving away from home and my girlfriend breaking up with me, but I became severely depressed. I was unable to focus and had to drop out my second semester. I also started to smoke marijuana and I drank more than I should have; I had a horrible time trying to sleep at night and I think I used alcohol to help me pass out. I saw my medical doctor and she started me on Fluoxetine (Prozac) that didn't seem to do anything, other than make me feel more irritable, and my thoughts felt like they were racing. I stopped the medication, didn't tell my doctor and smoked pot heavily. I tried to work during this time, but ended up either not showing up for work, or getting fired because I couldn't focus. On my twenty-first birthday I decided I couldn't take it any

Figure 12: My Mood Chart

Mania or Mixed	
Hypomania	
Normal	
Dysphoria	
Depression	

Age   10 11 12 13 14 15 16 17 18 19 20 21 22 23 24 25 26 27 28 29 30 31 32 33

longer. I wrote a note for my parents and went out to the woods behind our house with a bottle of vodka and every pill I could find. I woke up in the Intensive Care Unit and was then sent to a psych ward. They started me on two different antidepressants and referred me to a day program—I didn't go and I didn't take the medication. Around this time I stopped sleeping all together, decided that I wanted to be an artist, and began painting around the clock. I felt like I was flying and I wasn't using any drugs at all. I had limitless energy and believed that my paintings were incredibly important and would transform the world; it felt amazing. My parents tell me that I was talking non-stop, that they couldn't understand half of what I was saying. They tried to get me to go to the hospital, but I wouldn't. One night we got into a really bad fight and I started to break things. They called the cops and I was back in the hospital. This time they started me on Lithium and an antipsychotic medication, it made me feel very sluggish, but they were able to get the dose down to where I can handle it and I've been dong pretty well since. Just lately, maybe because I got a promotion, I've noticed my sleep is starting to get bad again."

Are there laboratory tests that can determine if someone has bipolar disorder?

While there is active research in understanding the genetics of bipolar disorder, there is to date no laboratory test that can be run that will determine if someone has Bipolar Disorder or is likely to get it. There are exciting advances in the field of brain imagery, such as PET (Positron Emission Tomography) scans, SPECT (Single Photon Emission Computed Tomography) scans, and Functional MRIs (Magnetic Resonance Imaging), that allow us to glimpse the working human brain. (This is different from older imaging techniques like X-Rays, CT (Computed Tomography) scans, and regular MRIs, which gave a non-moving picture—a snapshot versus a movie.) While these largely experimental tools show promise, and while the journals are filled with findings that indicate subtle differences in the brains of people who are manic and depressed from those of normal subjects, there is not yet a high enough degree of accuracy to make any of these studies useful in general practice.

Why should the diagnosis of bipolar disorder be left to professionals?

There's a truism in medicine that "the physician who treats him/her self has a fool for a patient." The diagnosis of bipolar disorder, like any medical condition, involves systematically ruling out other conditions that can mimic it. While it might be perfectly clear to you that your son/husband/self has bipolar disorder, it's important for the individual to be thoroughly assessed so that some other underlying condition, such as a thyroid abnormality, infectious process, tumor, etc., doesn't get overlooked. As you'll see throughout this chapter, many conditions can look a bit, or a lot, like bipolar disorder.

Is bipolar disorder difficult to diagnose?

It's estimated that 70 percent of people with bipolar disorder will receive at least one inaccurate psychiatric diagnosis. On average they will see four doctors before receiving the appropriate diagnosis. The time between the onset of symptoms and receiving an accurate diagnosis may be ten years or more.

Why is there so much misdiagnosis?

One reason is that bipolar disorder is easily misdiagnosed as depression. This makes sense, as when people are depressed they will often go to their primary care doctor looking for an antidepressant medication (80 percent of antidepressants are prescribed by non-psychiatrists). During the visit, symptoms of mania, hypomania, or mixed states are easily overlooked by the doctor or not mentioned at all by the patient. For many with bipolar disorder, unless the mania or hypomania is so severe that family or friends intervene and bring them to a crisis center or emergency room, they may not remember these episodes, or perhaps recall them as positive experiences or nothing out of the ordinary—"I just had so much energy, I could go for days with very little sleep; it was wonderful!"

Other common misdiagnoses include schizoaffective disorder and schizophrenia—discussed earlier in this chapter. This also makes sense, because if someone presents with delusions, hallucinations, and/or mania, their condition can be indistinguishable from psychotic disorders, such as schizophrenia.

How important is an accurate diagnosis?

As more is known about the bipolar spectrum, there is more evidence to support that the use of antidepressants, without mood-stabilizing medication, can not only precipitate manic, hypomanic, and mixed episodes, but may worsen the overall course of the illness. Because bipolar disorder is so often misdiagnosed as major depression, it's common for people to be prescribed antidepressants without a mood stabilizer. If they are not closely monitored, it's possible that a manic or mixed episode could develop.

And that brings us to the importance of the diagnosis: Since the risk of suicide is increased in mixed episodes, it's easy to see how serious—and tragic—a missed diagnosis can be. Some experts speculate that the increase in suicidal behavior for some people taking antidepressants may relate to this phenomenon of triggering a mixed episode.

Why is even an accurate diagnosis sometimes a poor fit?

It's important to remember that manmade diagnoses are approximations of what actually occurs in the real world. This topic of diagnostic accuracy is one that frequently comes up among the experts. Essentially the DSM-IV diagnoses are boxes into which we try to make all, or at least the majority, of a person's symptoms fit. Sometimes this works, but more often than not we find that people don't quite meet the criteria or have multiple other conditions. As we go through this book, we'll look at various issues related to dual diagnoses, and to the strong relationship between alcohol and substance abuse and bipolar disorder. But there are many other conditions, both psychiatric and medical, that will impact on a given person's overall symptoms. So while the DSM-IV diagnostic boxes work well for some, for others it's less clear where bipolar symptoms start and stop and other co-occurring conditions, such as personality disorders, other psychiatric disorders, substance abuse issues, trauma, etc., begin.

This is not to say that the current system of diagnosis is a bad one. It reflects the current state of the science and art of psychiatric diagnosis; it's a work in progress that has come a long way and has a long way to go.

Are there questionnaires or screening tools for bipolar disorder?

There are a number of questionnaires and screening tools that can be helpful in making the diagnosis of bipolar disorder. Two are included in this book: The Mood Disorder Questionnaire (MDQ) and the Bipolar Spectrum Diagnostic Scale (BSDS). The thing to remember with screening tests is that they can't be used alone to make a diagnosis, as they're not 100 percent accurate. What they do is help to rule out—or rule in—the likelihood that someone has a given condition.

The Mood Disorder Questionnaire (MDQ) is one that is widely used and is especially helpful in teasing out the presence of past manic or hypomanic episodes. It was developed by Dr. Robert Hirshchfeld and his team, and is reprinted here, along with the scoring, with permission of the author. (For the complete citation, see Appendix C.)

The Mood Disorder Questionnaire (MDQ)
Instructions: Please answer each question as best you can.

1. Has there ever been a period of time when you were not your usual self and . . .

Place a check in each appropriate box	YES	NO
. . .you felt so good or so hyper that other people thought you were not your normal self or you were so hyper that you got into trouble?		
. . .you were so irritable that you shouted at people or started fights or arguments?		
. . .you felt much more self-confident than usual?		
. . .you got much less sleep than usual and found you didn't really miss it?		
. . .you were much more talkative or spoke much faster than usual?		
. . .thoughts raced through your head or you couldn't slow your mind down?		
. . .you were so easily distracted by things around you that you had trouble concentrating or staying on track?		
. . .you had more energy than usual?		
. . .you were much more active or did many more things than usual?		
. . .you were much more social or outgoing than usual, for example, you telephoned friends in the middle of the night?		
. . .you were much more interested in sex than usual?		
. . .you did things that were unusual for you or that other people might have thought excessive, foolish or risky?		
. . .spending money got you or your family into trouble?		

2. If you checked YES to more than one of the above, have several of these ever happened during the same period of time?(circle one)   Yes   No

3. How much of a problem did any of these cause you—like being unable to work; having family, money or legal troubles; getting into arguments or fights? (Please circle one response only)

No Problem   Minor Problem

Moderate Problem   Serious Problem

Have any of your blood relatives (i.e., children, siblings, parents, grandparents, aunts, and uncles) had manic-depressive illness or bipolar disorder? (circle one)   Yes   No

Has a health professional ever told you that you have manic-depressive illness or bipolar disorder? (circle one)   Yes   No
Scoring the MDQ

The screen is considered "positive" if:
You answered "yes" to seven or more of the 13 items in question number 1:
    And
"Yes" to question number 2;
    And
"Moderate" or "Serious" to question number 3.

A positive screen, according to the authors, carries roughly a 70 percent chance that the test-taker does indeed have a bipolar spectrum disorder. A negative screen carries a 90 percent chance that the person does not have a bipolar spectrum disorder.

A second screening tool, The Bipolar Spectrum Diagnostic Scale (BSDS), created by Ronald Pies, uses descriptive sentences to help identify bipolar disorder.

The Bipolar Spectrum Diagnostic Scale (BSDS)
Instructions: Please read through the entire passage below before filling in any blanks.
Some individuals notice that their mood and/or energy levels shift drastically from time to time____. These individuals notice that, at times, their mood and/or energy level is very low, and at other times, very high____. During their "low" phases, these individuals often feel a lack of energy; a need to stay in bed or get extra sleep; and little or no motivation to do things they need to do____. They often put on weight during these periods____. During their low phases, these individuals often feel "blue," sad all the time, or depressed____. Sometimes, during these low phases, they feel hopeless or even suicidal____. Their ability to function at work or socially is impaired____. Typically, these low phases last for a few weeks, but sometimes they last only a few days____. Individuals with this type of pattern may experience a period of "normal" mood in between mood swings, during which their mood and energy level feels "right" and their ability to function is not disturbed____. They may then notice a marked shift or "switch" in the way they feel____. Their energy increases above what is normal for them, and they often get many things done they would not ordinarily be able to do____. Sometimes, during these "high" periods, these individuals feel as if they have too much energy or feel "hyper"____. Some individuals, during these high periods, may feel irritable, "on edge," or aggressive____. Some individuals, during these high periods, take on too many activities at once____. During these high periods, some individuals may spend money in ways that cause

them trouble____. They may be more talkative, outgoing, or sexual during these periods____. Sometimes, their behavior during these high periods seems strange or annoying to others____. Sometimes these individuals get into difficulty with co-workers or the police during these high periods____. Sometimes, they increase their alcohol or non-prescription drug use during these high periods____.

Now that you have read this passage, please check one of the four following boxes:
( ) This story fits me very well, or almost perfectly
( ) This story fits me fairly well
( ) This story fits me to some degree, but not in most respects
( ) This story does not really describe me at all

Now please go back and put a check after each sentence that definitely describes you.

Scoring the BSDS

Scoring: Each sentence checked is worth one point. Add six points for "fits me very well," four points for "fits me fairly well," and two points for "fits me to some degree."

Total Score	Likelihood of Bipolar Disorder
0–6	Highly unlikely
7–12	Low probability
13–19	Moderate probability
20–25	High probability

A score of 13 or above on the BSDS is considered a positive screen. With both of these tools, a positive screen should be followed by a medical evaluation for bipolar spectrum disorders.

Who makes the diagnosis of bipolar disorder?

Formal diagnosis is the realm of physicians—both medical doctors (MDs) and doctors of osteopathy (DOs). Licensed clinical psychologists (PhDs) can also make diagnoses. Depending on a particular state's statutes and/or healthcare agency's policies, advanced practice registered nurses (APRNs) can also make psychiatric diagnoses.

What is a multiaxial diagnosis?

The DSM-IV utilizes a particular style of diagnosis that attempts to capture a more complete view of the person being evaluated. This style of diagnosis will show up on formal psychiatric evaluations, insurance paperwork, and so on. The five axes (this is the plural of "axis" and not the tool used to chop wood) are as follows:

AXIS I: Major psychiatric disorders including substance abuse diagnoses. Axis I is where a mood disorder, such as bipolar, would be placed.

AXIS II: Personality disorders and mental retardation

AXIS III: Medical conditions

AXIS IV: Major active sources of stress in the person's life. These range from problems with work, finances, and housing to marital conflict and difficulty obtaining medical care.

AXIS V: The global assessment of functioning. This is a number from zero to one hundred that attempts to incorporate overall social, occupational, and psychological functioning. The lower the number, the more impaired a person will be.

What does a multiaxial diagnosis look like?

To illustrate this point we'll use the following case.

Chad is a twenty-one- year-old college junior who was brought to the emergency room by the police after his mother called 911. According to Chad's mother, her son, who was hospitalized last year for two weeks following a serious suicide attempt by hanging, has been phoning home multiple times a day for the past week and a half and speaking in a loud voice at a very rapid rate. He becomes easily angered, and his speech and thought processes are rambling and disorganized.

In the emergency room, Chad is found to be disheveled and unshaven. He talks without stopping and any attempt to interrupt him is met with angry outbursts. His roommate reports that Chad stopped attending all of his classes two weeks ago, has not been sleeping, and for the past week has been spreading copies of the stock market report on the floor of his room stating that he has discovered a secret conspiracy involving the president and CEOs of several Fortune 500 corporations. He refuses to answer most questions, but angrily shouts that he has no thoughts of harming himself or anyone else.

His past history is significant for two episodes of depression, and he has a paternal grandmother who had bipolar disorder.

Blood tests and urine tests obtained in the emergency room show no presence of drugs or alcohol and no acute medical processes are occurring. He has no allergies and is currently taking no medication.

Using Chad's presentation, his five axes diagnosis would be as follows.

Axis 1: Bipolar I Disorder, most recent episode manic, severe with psychotic features

Axis 2: No diagnosis

Axis 3: No medical problems

Axis 4: Educational problems (stopped attending classes)

Axis 5: Global assessment of functioning: 21 (this out of a possible 100)

What is a personality disorder?

People with personality disorders have long-standing (over many years) and problematic patterns of behavior and ways of perceiving and misperceiving the world and those in it. The personality disorders are grouped into three categories and include such conditions as:

- Antisocial personality disorder—no sense of empathy and a blatant disregard for the rights of others.
- Borderline personality disorder—women and men who become emotionally triggered or dysregulated quite readily, often resulting in self-injurious behaviors (cutting, burning) and frequent thoughts of suicide. People with borderline personality disorder may describe their emotions as going from zero to a thousand in the blink of an eye.
- Narcissistic personality disorder—an inflated sense of self importance, but not rising to the level of grandiose delusions.
- Paranoid personality disorder—people who misperceive the intentions of others and are highly suspicious but not to the level of becoming delusional.

There are a number of other personality disorders, but for the sake of our discussion of bipolar disorder, the above represent the ones that most frequently co-occur with bipolar.

What medical conditions can mimic bipolar disorder?

This is a long list, as many acute medical problems can manifest with large fluctuations in mood and mental status. This is one reason why it's important not to jump to conclusions as far as diagnosis goes. There have been tragic instances in which someone appeared manic but was actually in a hypoglycemic state (low blood sugar) and rapidly heading toward a diabetic coma. Likewise, disorders of the thyroid gland, which produces hormones that regulate the body's metabolism, can mimic both depressed and manic states. The following list touches on a number, but not all, of the medical conditions that can present with serious mood symptoms.

- Hyperthyroidism and hypothyroidism (too much or too little thyroid hormone)
- Hypoglycemia, hyperglycemia, diabetes (abnormalities in blood sugar)
- Cushing's syndrome (a hormonal disorder involving excessive cortisol)
- Anemia and other blood disorders, including porphyria
- Traumatic brain injuries—both open and closed head injuries
- Brain tumors, aneurysms, or cranial bleeds
- Strokes
- Dementia (Alzheimer's disease and other variants)
- Epilepsy (especially the confusional—post-ictal—state following a seizure)
- Parkinson's disease
- Huntington's disease (a hereditary neurological disease)
- Multiple sclerosis (an autoimmune disease that affects the nervous system)
- Wilson's disease (a disease in which the body accumulates copper)
- Syphilis
- Systemic lupus erythematosus (SLE) (an autoimmune disease)

- Meningitis (inflammation, often caused by infection, of the tissues that cover and protect the brain and spinal column)
- HIV/AIDS infection, including opportunistic infections of the brain, and HIV-associated dementias
- Pancreatic and bladder cancers
- Withdrawal from alcohol
- Withdrawal from benzodiazepines (the valium family of drugs, which includes, klonopin, xanax, halcion, restoril, and librium)
- Delirium (This broad term refers to a confusional state that can be caused by many things from high fevers and infections to drug reactions to organ failure to tumors.)
- Severe nutritional deficiencies (vitamin B12, thiamine)
- Electrolyte imbalances (sodium, calcium)
- Sleep disorders such as sleep apnea, narcolepsy, and severe sleep deprivation

What medications and drugs can mimic bipolar disorder?

Because bipolar disorder covers a vast range of emotional states, we need to consider medications and other substances of use and abuse that can cause both abnormal elevations and dips in a person's mood. Many substances can become toxic in the body and lead to a delirious state. If not discovered, the result could be permanent damage, coma, and even death. This is why it's so important to not jump to conclusions when someone is in a manic or psychotic state—even if she has a well-documented history of bipolar disorder.

Medications implicated in causing significant mood changes (this is not meant to be an all-inclusive list.):

- Steroids (e.g., cortisone, prednisone)—can cause psychotic symptoms and precipitate both depressed and manic states

- Interferon—(used to treat hepatitis C and multiple sclerosis and to prevent rejection of organ transplants) carries a high rate of depression
- Thyroid hormone—if too much can mimic mania, too little can present as depression
- Some heart and blood pressure medications, beta-blockers (propranolol [Inderal], metoprolol [Lopressor] etc.)—associated with depression
- Antidepressants—can precipitate a manic state in susceptible individuals
- Stimulants (amphetamines, Ritalin, etc.)—can mimic mania, with and without psychosis
- Levodopa—a medication used in treating Parkinson's disease
- Anticholinergic medications (medications, such as benztropine [Cogentin], trihexyphenidyl [Artane] and diphenydramine [Benadryl]—often used to counteract side effects of older antipsychotic medications
- Antihistamines—this includes many over-the-counter cold and allergy products, such diphenhydramine (Benadryl), pseudophedrine (Sudafed) etc..

There are many substances with abuse potential that can mimic or precipitate symptoms of bipolar disorder:
- Alcohol
- Marijuana
- Hashish
- Cocaine
- PCP
- Hallucinogens, including LSD, Ecstasy, ketamine, peyote, mescaline
- Opiates
- Ephedrine

Can herbs and nutritional supplements precipitate or mimic a manic episode?

Any medication, nutritional supplement, or herb that has antidepressant properties can trigger a manic episode in a person with bipolar disorder. Substances that are stimulants can conceivably mimic a manic episode. Nutritional supplements and herbs that have been reported to either precipitate or mimic mania include:

- St. John's Wort
- S-adenosly 1-methionine (SAMe)
- Asian Ginseng
- Rhodiola rosea
- Ma Huang (Ephedra)

What laboratory tests are done to rule out medical conditions that can mimic bipolar disorder?

Routine tests are typically ordered when a person first presents with serious mood symptoms. The tests run are used to either rule in or rule out medical conditions that might be causing the symptoms. These tests might include:

- Complete blood count
- Electrolytes
- Liver enzymes and proteins
- Blood urea nitrogen (BUN) and creatinine (measures of kidney functioning)
- Thyroid function tests
- Tests to rule out specific infectious agents such as HIV, syphilis and hepatitis
- Urine and/or blood and/or hair analysis to rule out active substance abuse

Is there a role for brain imaging in the diagnosis of bipolar disorder?

At present, there has not been a specific brain lesion identified with bipolar disorder. Researchers are making headway in the use of functional imaging studies that do show some differences in the brains of people who are depressed, manic, psychotic, and normal. None of these studies currently have direct applicability to the diagnosis of bipolar disorder.

However, in someone currently experiencing an acute mood or mental status change, especially for the first time, it is often worth the effort and the expense to obtain a CT scan or MRI of the brain to be certain that there is no acute medical problem, such as a hemorrhage, aneurysm, infectious process, or tumor, which might manifest with mood symptoms.

Is a physical examination important in the diagnostic assessment of bipolar disorder?

As discussed, many physical ailments can first present with mood symptoms. A good medical history, review of organ systems and physical examination should be part of any workup of bipolar disorder. The physical examination is not typically performed by the psychiatrist (although it could be), but rather by the individual's primary care physician, an internist, or a hospitalist. In the case of someone being admitted to a hospital in the midst of a severe mood episode, a physical examination will be performed early in his stay (within the first twenty-four hours). This is on top of a more cursory examination performed in the emergency room (medical clearance). Information from the examination and medical history is incorporated into the overall diagnostic picture. In an outpatient setting, a recent physical examination and communication with the patient's primary care physician, if there are active medical issues and medical medications, is a recommended part of the overall evaluation.

Chapter 3

GETTING INTO TREATMENT

- When should someone go for treatment?
- What things are important to know when selecting a mental health professional?
- How important is the fit between a person with bipolar disorder and the mental health professional(s) she works with?
- Why do some people with bipolar disorder not see that they're manic or psychotic?
- What is noncompliance?
- Why do so many people with bipolar disorder stop their medications?
- What constitutes a behavioral crisis?
- How does one manage a behavioral crisis?
- What if the person refuses to go to the hospital to be evaluated?
- How does someone advocate for a person with bipolar disorder in an emergency room?
- What happens if the emergency room discharges someone while he is still gravely disabled, suicidal or homicidal?
- When is an inpatient hospital stay needed?
- What happens when someone is admitted to a hospital?
- What happens if someone refuses to go into the hospital?
- What happens if someone refuses to take medication at home?
- What happens if someone refuses to take medication when he leaves the hospital?
- What is outpatient mandated treatment?
- What is a partial hospital program (PHP)?
- What is an intensive outpatient program (IOP)?
- How do you know when someone is ready to move to a less intensive treatment?
- What is a treatment plan?
- What is a recovery/wellness plan?

When should someone go for treatment?

There's a vast range of reasons that will cause a person with bipolar disorder to first seek—or be brought to—treatment. Clearly, if someone is experiencing protracted mood symptoms that are causing emotional distress and/or an inability to function at work, home, school, or in social situations, this is a time to seek professional help. This is easier said than done, and accounts for the fact that the vast majority of depression and bipolar disorder goes untreated or undertreated in this country. Or, people turn to other sources, such as drugs and alcohol, in an attempt to dampen their emotional pain.

It can take years to seek help, and indeed the majority of people with bipolar disorder will go years after the onset of symptoms before they first interact with a mental health professional. The most common first presentation to a practitioner will be with symptoms of depression. In other cases, the first contact with a mental health professional may be triggered by a severe mood episode that results in a psychiatric emergency, such as a suicide attempt, or a manic or mixed episode with out-of-control behaviors that involve a call to 911. In other instances family/friends will convince a person experiencing serious mood symptoms to be seen in the emergency room, local clinic, or crisis center, or by a private practitioner.

What things are important to know when selecting a mental health professional?

When selecting a mental health professional there are a few questions that will help guide you:

- Will medications be required? If the answer is yes—and it most certainly will be with bipolar I—you'll need someone who is licensed to prescribe medication. This will include psychiatrists, who can be MDs (medical doctors) or DOs (doctors of osteopathy), and APRNs (advanced practice registered nurses).

In the state of New Mexico, some psychologists (PhDs) can also prescribe psychiatric medicines if they've obtained additional training and DEA (Drug Enforcement Agency) licensure to do so.

- Will psychotherapy be included in treatment? Here your options open up a great deal, and when we discuss various therapeutic choices in Chapter 9 this will guide your choice. While many prescribers, such as psychiatrists and APRNs can provide the therapy component, most do not, and will work with other professionals who do, such as licensed social workers, psychologists and licensed professional counselors.

- How are you going to pay for treatment? For many this is a major question that will need to be resolved, and we will go into this in more detail in Chapter 15. But to start you'll need to evaluate what—and which practitioners—your insurance may, or may not, cover, what you can afford out of pocket and what other resources may be available in your community that accept sliding scale payment, or even free treatment, as is sometimes found in training programs or state-operated agencies.

How important is the fit between a person with bipolar disorder and the mental health professional(s) she works with?

Some see this as the single most important factor in whether or not an individual will progress in treatment and with recovery, and studies looking at this factor have consistently demonstrated the benefits of a positive relationship between the person in treatment and his therapist. Without getting technical, it comes down to trust, comfort level, and whether or not you like your doctor or therapist as a person.

You want to know that your doctor and/or therapist is competent to treat bipolar disorder. You want to know that if you're in a crisis there is a way to reach them, or that they have a backup system—such as access to a crisis center, or an on-call system—that you can use in an emergency. Finally, there's the very important human element. Is your doctor/therapist working with you as one person helping another, or is there a 'trust me, I'm a doctor' attitude? We all want physicians and other practitioners who will take our concerns seriously and who will foster and nurture hope.

Why do some people with bipolar disorder not see that they're manic or psychotic?

It's common for people who are actively psychotic and/or manic to lack insight into their disturbed state. The term for this is anosognosia. The reasons for this lack of insight have everything to do with our brains being the organ through which we perceive the world. If someone's brain is making her hear voices, see visions, or experience delusions, such as the belief that she's being videotaped by the CIA or has been imbued with magical power, it is entirely real to that person. It's as though she's been tuned into a station that the rest of us can't get. In the past this lack of insight into the illness was mostly viewed as a form of denial, of avoiding the truth. Increasingly, it's now understood that anosognosia is part of the disordered state—a brain that is not working right.

Beyond that, for some people who have a euphoric mania, there's the issue of why they would want to let anyone take away their wonderful, giddy, super-productive, and top-of-the-world feeling. If somebody truly believes he is Jesus Christ out to spread the word, the thought of taking medication to change that doesn't make sense to him.

When confronted, the person who is manic or delusional may view the other person as the one having the problem. This response can run the gamut from the person becoming demeaning and condescending to open hostility and, in worst-case-scenarios, violence. This standoff is one of the most challenging to negotiate for all involved— the person with bipolar disorder, her family, her friends, and her treators. The best approach is not to directly confront the person but to listen, be empathic, and if possible, find an acceptable middle ground that will allow everyone to win. For example: "Perhaps the medication might help you get a bit of sleep?"

What is noncompliance?

Noncompliance is a word used to describe any and all ways a person is not following doctor's orders. This term can give the impression that people are being bad and conceal the reasons why someone has missed his appointments or stopped taking potentially life-saving medications. Among the consumer movement (people with bipolar disorder and other serious mental illnesses actively seeking to improve treatment and protect the individual's rights) there is a growing desire to see this term eliminated and replaced with accurate descriptions of why someone is not following various treatment recommendations.

Why do so many people with bipolar disorder stop their medications?

To start, we need to lose the assumption that people take medications just as the doctor orders them. We don't. Studies show that roughly 25 percent of medications are not taken as prescribed. When we head into psychiatric medications, this number doubles.

In bipolar disorder, one in two patients will stop her medication in the first twelve months of treatment. It is quite common for people to have several episodes in which they will experiment with their dosage and/or go off their medications altogether.

But the big question remains: If the medications can help control the mood swings, why would someone stop?

As we'll see when we hit the chapters on medications, these are not benign substances. Here's a list of commonly cited reasons why people stop their medications:

- Don't believe they have an illness—This could be both a lack of insight (anosognosia), and/or something more existential
  - ❏ "I don't have bipolar disorder, Doctor! You do!"
  - ❏ "Maybe my mood swings are just a little bigger than other people's. I don't want to medicate away my true feelings," or "The medication dampens my creativity."
- Side effects—Feeling over-sedated, sluggish, or slowed down. Weight gain and sexual dysfunction are often-cited reasons for stopping medication, but each medication has its own list of common and more rare side effects.
- Financial issues
  - ❏ Lack of insurance that covers medications.
  - ❏ Medicaid "spend downs"
  - ❏ Access to medications—no transportation and/or pharmacy doesn't deliver
- Stigma and shame—Wanting to see what will happen if they go off the medication
  - ❏ "Maybe I don't really need them."
  - ❏ "I was feeling better and thought I could come off of them."
- Using drugs or alcohol
  - ❏ "I wanted to get high and didn't think I should mix the medication with [drug of choice]"
- Concerns about long-term health effects

❏ "I heard that lithium is bad for the kidneys and the thyroid gland, I got scared and stopped taking it."
- Pressure to not take medication from friends, family, or other social contacts
  ❏ "My church doesn't believe in taking medications."
  ❏ "Someone at AA told me that taking medication is just another addiction."
  ❏ "My father/mother/girlfriend/sister told me I don't need to take it."
  ❏ "My father said it's a sign of weakness to take medications. He said I should be able to kick this on my own."
- Pregnancy-related concerns
  ❏ "I'm trying to get pregnant and don't want my baby to be adversely affected by medications in my system."
  ❏ "I just found out I'm pregnant and stopped all my medications."
  ❏ "I want to breastfeed and was told I couldn't if I'm on psychiatric medications."
- Performance-related concerns
  ❏ "I can get a lot more done when I'm manic."
  ❏ "I'm more creative off of the medication."

This list covers many of the common responses and should underscore the variability of why people will go off medication. Why a particular person does is vitally important to understand, so we can address the reason through education, adjustment of medication, and various therapeutic means.

What constitutes a behavioral crisis?

Behavioral crises in bipolar disorder can take a number of forms. In one typical situation, a person who is hypomanic and highly energized progresses to mania and psychosis, and thus represents an imminent risk to himself or others. Or perhaps someone in a mixed or depressed episode is so highly agitated and miserable he seeks out the means to kill himself. Here are some more examples, but this is by no means an exhaustive list:

- Expressions of suicidal or homicidal intent
- Dangerous impulsive behaviors, such as wild spending—mortgaging homes, cashing out retirement accounts, gambling large quantities of money—sexual promiscuity, placing oneself or others in dangerous situations
- Active psychosis, especially if the person's behavior is based on delusional beliefs or in response to command auditory hallucinations
  - ❑ Someone who believes the CIA is out to get him, and hears a voice telling him to "free America," and has begun stockpiling firearms.
  - ❑ Someone depressed and paranoid believes her food is poisoned and stops eating entirely.
  - ❑ A person with the belief that he is on a mission from God to rid the world of devils goes after local politicians with a shotgun.
- Post-Partum Psychosis. Women with bipolar disorder are at very high risk for serious mood episodes toward the end of pregnancy and in the days to months following delivery. Immediate intervention is a must, as the risk for both suicide and infanticide (killing of the baby) is high.
  - ❑ A woman with bipolar disorder who shortly after delivering her baby has the delusional belief that she was impregnated by the devil and her child is the antichrist.
  - ❑ A woman in a depressed episode toward the end of her pregnancy decides that her family would be better off without her, and reveals that she intends to kill herself after she delivers.

- Out of control behavior, such as dangerous and reckless driving, getting on the freeway in the wrong direction, fire setting, or barricading oneself inside a room or a home.
- Out of control use of narcotics and alcohol. Here we're talking about severe situations, in which the person is at imminent risk of serious injury or fatal overdose.
- A catatonic state. Catatonia refers to an extreme state in which the individual becomes totally, or almost totally, immobile, sometimes with what is referred to as a *waxy flexibility*, in which if a limb is placed in a particular position it can remain in that position for an indefinite period. Or in its other extreme, catatonia is a state of disabling disorganization and psychosis, often accompanied by elevated temperature and bizarre behavior, such as parroting every word that is said or making odd repetitive gestures.

How does one manage a behavioral crisis?

The quick answer is get help. If your community has a crisis number, call it. If they don't, or if you don't get the immediate response you need from your crisis center, call 911.

In the midst of a crisis it's helpful to think of things in the simplest manner possible. Perhaps the most important question to ask to get through the worst of things is, "does this person need to be in a secure environment to maintain her safety or the safety of someone else?" If the answer is "yes," then you're likely looking at an inpatient hospitalization to stabilize the situation.

The reason for this somewhat cool approach has to do with the intense emotions that are typical in the midst of a crisis. The person with bipolar disorder may be saying everything possible to avoid being admitted, but if there's evidence to support the fact, for example, that she's been actively planning her suicide and has assembled the means to accomplish it, getting her into a safe setting may save her life.

What if the person refuses to go to the hospital to be evaluated?

Call your area crisis center or emergency service number (in most areas, 911). It's important to let the operator/dispatcher know exactly the nature of the behavioral crisis, that is, what the person is saying and doing. Do not get off the phone until told to do so: the dispatcher will need enough information from you to know the appropriate level of response:

- Can the situation be handled by a crisis team? In areas that have these, a service called mobile response or crisis outreach can go to an individual's home and assess the situation.
- Does an ambulance need to be dispatched?
- Is the person so out-of-control and/or dangerous that a police response needs to be added?

If the determination is that the person should go to the hospital, keep in mind that every state has specific rules around when people can be brought to an emergency room—against their will if necessary—for psychiatric evaluations. For involved friends and family this will mean giving clear histories that document the severity of the situation to the professionals who will be involved in transportation (paramedics, EMTs, crisis clinicians, and possibly police).

How does someone advocate for a person with bipolar disorder in an emergency room?

Emergency rooms and crisis centers are hectic and pressured places almost by definition. Decisions need to be made fast, and definitively. Perhaps the single-biggest decision that gets answered is whether the person being evaluated needs to be admitted to an inpatient facility or could be safely treated in a less-restrictive setting, such as a partial hospital program (PHP), intensive outpatient program (IOP), or by her own clinician in a regular outpatient or clinic setting.

This is where family and friends can make all the difference. Even though professionals in an emergency room may not be able to give you information about your family member or loved one (due to patient confidentiality and more stringent rules through the Health Insurance Portability and Accountability Act (HIPAA)), they can most certainly take in any information you have to give them. It is important that you do not hold back. If someone has been talking about hurting himself or someone else, you need to let the psychiatrist, social worker, or crisis clinician know exactly what has been said and done. Likewise, if he's been refusing all food and lying in bed for days, this needs to be communicated.

Where someone is acutely psychotic, manic and/or depressed, you, as a family member or friend, might be able to supply critical information about past treatments, medications the person is currently taking, and whether or not he has been using alcohol or other drugs. It's this vital information that can make the difference between someone getting admitted to the hospital or not. If you must leave the emergency room or crisis center, be sure to give your phone numbers to the staff who are working with your family member or friend. By communicating critical information to treators you are helping your loved one, not betraying him.

What happens if the emergency room discharges someone while he is still gravely disabled, suicidal, or homicidal?

Many families have had the frustrating experience of going to the emergency room with someone who is agitated and manic, or severely depressed, and having them "pull it together" while they are being evaluated. The net result is that the crisis clinician or doctor sees someone who is in good control and is denying any thoughts of wanting to hurt themselves or anyone else. In the absence of other information, that person will be released. Then the family is right back where they started—with someone who is dangerously impulsive, behaviorally out-of-control, severely disabled, suicidal, or homicidal, and now also angry at you for having brought them to the emergency room.

Each state has specific criteria to determine when and how someone can be admitted to an inpatient facility against his will. These typically center on the person being imminently suicidal, homicidal, or so disabled as a result of his psychiatric symptoms that he cannot provide for his own basic needs (food, clothing, shelter). If someone is manic, in a mixed state, psychotic, or suicidally depressed, he will often try to keep this hidden from an evaluating clinician. Corroborating information that family and friends can provide may make all the difference in getting the appropriate care.

Another point that figures heavily into the real world of emergency rooms and crisis centers is that if a person is discharged and the crisis is still severe and ongoing, you need to call 911, the crisis center, or your area's emergency number and start again. This is no time to be complacent. Just because one emergency room doctor thought the patient was "fine to go home," if his behavior is telling you otherwise, don't let up, and don't leave him alone. The emotional toll on all involved can be huge, but getting help, at times being the squeaky wheel and insisting on it, may save a life. It is common to have more than one emergency room visit—often to the same hospital—before finally getting admitted to an inpatient unit.

When is an inpatient hospital stay needed?

Since the closure and downsizing of most large state hospitals in the past few decades, inpatient hospitalizations have become increasingly brief (a few days to a few weeks)and crisis-focused. Recent statistics from the Centers for Disease Control (CDC) place the average length of stay for a psychiatric admission between seven and ten days. But those numbers are a bit misleading, because they include people who've been admitted to state hospitals for extended periods (months to years). In reality, an admission could be as brief as a day to a few days.

The major reasons why someone will become hospitalized—either voluntarily or against their will—are because she is believed to be actively suicidal, homicidal, or so disabled as a result of her psychiatric condition that she cannot provide for her basic needs. If one of these conditions is not met, even if a person is willing to be voluntarily admitted for stabilization of active symptoms, insurers may argue that *medical necessity* has not been met and may refuse or question paying for the admission.

What happens when someone is admitted to a hospital?

Each inpatient unit/ward or hospital is structured somewhat differently. But the overall approach is of a multi-disciplinary treatment team that consists of a doctor (MD or DO), nurses, a social worker, therapists (possibly occupational therapists, art therapists, and recreational therapists), aides, and possibly a psychologist. It is common for a patient to be assigned a daily contact person, or primary clinician, to help coordinate his overall care.

With inpatient hospital stays being quite brief, the goal is to rapidly stabilize the person's symptoms in a safe environment. If the person is in a manic or mixed state, stabilization is usually achieved through the use of tranquilizing and sedating medications combined with a mood stabilizer such as lithium, lamotrigine or valproate (see Chapter 5).

Typically, medications to regulate sleep will also be made available. In all of the mood states a good night's sleep can be helpful in moving things in the right direction.

For a person who is severely depressed, treatments might include mood stabilizing medication, antipsychotic medication if psychosis is present, and possibly an anti-depressant.

In situations where the depression, mania, or mixed episode is severe and not responding to medication, electroconvulsive therapy (ECT) might be considered. (See Chapter 8.)

Apart from medications and the secure setting, inpatient treatment teams will also work quickly to address major stressors (marital conflict, financial problems, lack of insurance, legal issues, etc.) and pull together discharge plans so that the treatment initiated in the hospital has the greatest possibility of being continued in a less-restrictive community setting. This connection to outpatient care—discharge planning—is crucial.

For family, getting acquainted with the treatment team is important. As there are many rules around confidentiality, one step that needs to happen early in the admission is for the patient to agree to have his family and/or significant other be allowed to participate in treatment. This is done through the signing of a form (Release of

Information) that gives hospital staff permission to talk to the designated people.

When a patient is determined to no longer be at imminent risk of harming himself or others and to be able to provide for his basic needs in a less-restrictive setting, he will be discharged. Typical next steps in treatment may include:

- Partial hospital programs
- Intensive outpatient programs
- Private psychiatrists and therapists
- Outpatient clinics

What happens if someone refuses to go into the hospital?

Each state has specific rules determining when and how a person with a psychiatric disability can be hospitalized on an involuntary basis. In general, the goal is to offer treatment in the least restrictive setting that is safe and appropriate. This is not just a treatment philosophy but is backed by federal laws such as the Olmstead Act that seek to protect the individual's constitutional rights.

Because of the variability between states, different processes need to be followed when seeking involuntary hospitalization. Because we're talking about taking away a person's freedom—even if for just a brief period—each state has written into law various safeguards that ensure multiple evaluations and sometimes even the involvement of a judge before an involuntary admission is approved. In most states, however, a physician has the ability to admit a person on an involuntary basis to a psychiatric ward or hospital.

What happens if someone refuses to take medication in the hospital?

There is a great deal of state-to-state variability on when and how a person can be medicated against his will.

Typically, in an emergency situation (such as a person being so out-of-control or so combative that he's at risk of being forcibly put into restraints or seclusion), laws allow for the administration of tranquilizing medications (often as an injection) without the person's consent.

Once the emergency has passed, however, the rules change. People have the right to refuse treatment—even necessary treatment. There's active debate—and court cases—around whether or not someone whose judgment is seriously clouded by psychosis, mania, or depression is able to give informed consent to refuse treatment. Each state will have specific statutes around what processes must be followed in non-emergent situations to medicate a person with a psychiatric disorder against his will. Often this will involve legal hearings, typically at the psychiatric hospital or ward, where a judge (not a physician) will determine if the use of involuntary medication should be allowed. These statutes will also specify what kind of legal representation (an attorney) must be made available to the patient.

What happens if someone refuses to take medication at home?

It's quite common, especially when someone first receives the diagnosis of bipolar disorder, for her to discontinue treatment, especially medication. It's also common for someone to be hospitalized two or three times—or many more—before coming to terms with the need to continue on medication.

For some people who lack insight into their bipolar disorder, the situation may go like this: They will take medication while in the midst of a crisis or while hospitalized. On the inpatient unit they will reassure their doctors and family that they will continue to take their medication when they go home. Frequently, however, they stop the medication soon after leaving the hospital. So ultimately it becomes a question of finding reasons that make sense to the person with bipolar disorder why there is benefit in taking medication. The reason may have nothing to do with having an illness, but could range from, "they keep me out of the hospital" to "they help me sleep at night" to "they help my nerves."

For people who do have insight perhaps the most important thing is to become educated about every aspect of the illness, the medications, available treatments, etc. Often the people who manage their bipolar disorder the best are the ones who have fully accepted the reality that this is a condition they have to deal with. They're the ones who steer their treatment, they've assembled natural supports (friends, family) and professionals they can trust, and in general they've gotten to where their bipolar disorder does not define who they are—it's just a part of them.

While this notion of acceptance may seem simplistic, it's critical, because without it the possibility for change and moving forward with treatment is poor.

What is outpatient mandated treatment?

In the majority of states—but not all—there are laws concerning mandated treatment in the community. These are used with people who, as a result of their history, are unlikely to accept treatment that is necessary for them to survive in the community. These go by various names and perhaps the most well-known is New York State's Kendra's Law or assisted outpatient treatment (AOT).

With AOT, various people (family members, psychiatrists, psychologists, etc.) can petition the court to have treatment provided in the community on an involuntary basis, if needed. AOT orders involve a clear demonstration that the person with the mental disorder has consistently refused treatment and are unlikely to manage in the community without it. If the person under an AOT order continues to refuse treatment, the law allows for the person to be brought to a hospital and admitted. Again, there is great variability between the states and a good place to get this information is through your own state's Department or Division of Mental Health Services [See Appendix B for a state by state listing].

AOT programs are a source of a good deal of controversy and conflict. Many patients' rights advocates believe these infringe on the individual's constitutional rights, while family advocacy groups more typically are in support of AOT programs.

What is a partial hospital program (PHP)?

A partial hospital program is an intensive level of outpatient treatment that can be thought of as one step down from an inpatient stay. PHP is a frequent treatment for people who have either just been released from an inpatient stay or are very symptomatic and likely to go inpatient if something is not done quickly. The intensity is so high that PHP is part of Medicare's inpatient benefit (Medicare A). Again, one overriding principle throughout treatment is to provide the appropriate level of care or service in the least restrictive way.

An individual enrolled in a PHP will attend groups four to seven days a week for at least four hours a day. She will be evaluated by an MD or APRN and will participate in the treatment-planning process, in which goals are set with specific target dates and interventions. Groups will focus on education, symptom identification, strategies to decrease stress, coping skills and so forth. Because substance abuse is so prevalent in bipolar disorder, many PHPs offer a dual-diagnosis track so that treatment for the chemical abuse/dependency is incorporated into the overall plan and treatment. Couples' work and family sessions may also be part of the treatment, and many programs offer a weekly group in the evening for families to come together and receive support and education.

Similar to an inpatient unit, the PHP utilizes a multidisciplinary approach (psychiatrist, nurses, social workers, psychologists, and various therapists) so that all aspects of a person's recovery can be addressed (psychological, social, occupational, and spiritual).

Length of stay in a PHP is typically brief—on the order of one to four weeks. The goal is to stabilize symptoms, often with further adjustment of medications, and to look toward transitioning the individual to less intensive, less restrictive treatment options.

What is an intensive outpatient program (IOP)?

An IOP shares a lot of features with the PHP but with fewer meetings per week and for fewer hours (on average three days a week for three hours a day). Similar treatment groups are offered using a multidisciplinary approach. Length of stay is again on the order of a couple of weeks to a couple of months. Medication management, overseen by a psychiatrist and/or APRN, is generally included in the program.

How do you know when someone is ready to move to a less intensive treatment?

This question is best answered by another question: How is the person doing?

After answering that we proceed to several more specific questions, which guide us in finding a good fit for treatment:

- What is the individual's goal(s) for treatment? Are things on track?

- If she was manic and psychotic, have those symptoms resolved, or mostly resolved?
- If she was having thoughts of suicide, have these thoughts gone away?
- How stable does she feel with her current medication(s)?
- Is she actively abusing substances?
- If there were high-risk behaviors while in a manic or mixed state, have those stopped?
- Are there major stressors that need to be resolved (housing, job, finance, relationship issues, looming legal problems) ?

While it's unlikely that all of the above will be fully resolved over the course of PHP admission, most major issues and symptoms will be improved so that the person can progress to a less intrusive level of care.

In general, you want to provide the help someone needs, but not do for them what they can do for themselves.

What is a treatment plan?

Ideally, treatment plans are documents created collaboratively between people with a particular condition—in this case bipolar spectrum disorders—and their treatment team. A treatment plan is a blueprint of the work to be done. It's also a mandatory require-ment for most insurers, including Medicare and Medicaid. Organizations, such as the Joint Commission (JC) (previously the Joint Commission on the Accreditation of Healthcare Organizations (JCAHO)), as well as Medicare and Medicaid, maintain guidelines as to what must be on a treatment plan and how it needs to be worded. Agencies and practitioners that provide healthcare need to do regular treatment plans with all of their clients. This includes home-health agencies, hospitals, clinics, and private practitioners that bill

Medicare, Medicaid, and other insurers that require a written plan of care.

Treatment plans include specific long- and short-term goals—also referred to as goals and objectives. Each long-term goal (typically something that can be achieved within six months) is broken down, and specific interventions, such as therapy, medication, social interventions, etc., are slotted in to help move the person toward the stated objective. Every goal and objective needs to be worded in such a way that progress is measurable—something that can be counted or quantified in some manner. They must be behavioral, i.e., something that can be observed, and they must be realistic and desirable.

Evidence of the patient's involvement in the treatment plan is also a requirement for the JC. In order for agencies to be reimbursed for services provided, the treatment plan must also be under the direction of a physician (MD or DO) and signed by him.

What is a recovery/wellness plan?

In response to the very medical nature of treatment plans, the mental health consumer movement has advocated for a more user-friendly and person-centered style of treatment plan. These are often homegrown documents, written in plain language that speaks directly to the person working on her own recovery. Nationwide, a number of mental health organizations and state agencies are attempting to integrate—or have already implemented—various recovery/wellness plans. The actual plans may be a part of a much larger shift in treatment approach and philosophy.

There are many similarities between treatment plans and recovery plans; both have explicit short- and long-term goals, specific interventions to get there, etc. A couple of key differences are that in recovery plans, the goal is whatever the person says it is—get a job, find a wife, become president. There is no attempt to mold the person's stated goal into what professionals might consider appropriate or even realistic. Another difference is that recovery plans focus on the individual's strengths, whereas treatment plans, because they must document ongoing "medical necessity" for billable services, are written from a medical or illness-based approach.

Recovery/wellness plans are ideal for people to do themselves, or with the assistance of a friend, peer, family member, or someone on their treatment team. Treatment plans are mostly written by the professional or paraprofessional and then reviewed and/or signed off by the individual in treatment.

In general, recovery/wellness plans serve to empower the individual and recognize her own expertise—after all, she's the one living with the particular symptoms, medications, etc. Recovery/wellness plans help people identify strategies and techniques that will improve their overall sense of well-being and move them in the direction of their hopes, dreams and aspirations.

Chapter 4

MEDICATIONS: USEFUL TOOLS ON THE ROAD TO RECOVERY

- How important is medication in treating bipolar disorder?
- What does it mean if a medication is used "on label" or "off label"?
- What do I need to know about advances in the pharmacological treatment of bipolar disorder?
- What are the risks of not taking medication?
- What types of medications might be prescribed?
- How much do the drug companies influence the prescribing of medications?
- How can someone get unbiased information about medications used in bipolar disorder?
- If it's hard to get unbiased information about medications, how do I know what medications are best?
- What is a black box warning?
- How long will someone need to be on medication?
- What is meant by acute, continuation, and maintenance treatment?
- How long do medications stay in the body?
- How do medications get excreted or broken down and what does this have to do with drug interactions?
- What is medication potency?
- Do medications dampen creativity?
- Will the medication turn me into a zombie?

How important is medication in treating bipolar disorder?

Most experts agree that medication is important in the treatment of bipolar disorder. Before the discovery of the first effective mood stabilizer—lithium—it was common for people with bipolar disorder to spend years of their lives in psychiatric hospitals. Manias and depressions—as described by pioneers like Emil Kraepelin, or in first-person accounts like that written by Clifford Beers—could last months and even years. Partially as a result of effective treatments, these types of long hospitalizations are rarely needed today. Mood episodes can be shortened, and their severity and frequency diminished, through the use of medication, especially when combined with therapy and relapse-prevention strategies.

Certain medications, such as lithium, have also been demonstrated to decrease the likelihood that a person with bipolar disorder will end his life by suicide.

These are compelling reasons to take medication, but what is more important to people has to do with getting back on track. It's not all about the symptoms of bipolar disorder, but about functioning and having a life worth living, about moving forward and having successful relationships, meaningful work, and a rich social and spiritual life. Medications, either as single agents or in the combination that works best for an individual and his symptoms, can be powerful tools in that person's recovery.

What does it mean if a medication is used "on label" or "off label"?

"On label" means that a medication has received FDA approval for the prescribed usage. In order to receive an on-label indication a medication must be shown to be better than a placebo (sugar pill).

FDA approval in no way implies that the medication is better—or worse—than other medications used for the same condition(s).

Some examples: Lithium and lamotrigine have FDA approval for the treatment of the mania and depression associated with bipolar disorder, as well as for maintenance (ongoing) treatment for mood stabilization. Other medications, which some studies have found to be effective in the treatment of mood swings, such as oxcarbazepine (Trileptal), and carbamazepine (Tegretol) are frequently used in an off label manner in treating bipolar disorder. And, to further confuse things, some medications have specific FDA-approved indications (uses) in bipolar disorder—such as for the treatment of acute mania—but do not have the indication for maintenance therapy; valproic acid (Depakote) is one example.

What do I need to know about advances in the pharmacological treatment of bipolar disorder?

The research and understanding of pharmacological treatments in bipolar disorder is rapidly changing. The American Psychiatric Association's (APA) *Treatment Guidelines for Bipolar Disorder, Second edition*, published in 2002, are already substantially out of date as it applies to medications. For example, sweeping statements made about the benefits of the newer antipsychotic medications (atypicals) over the older ones (typicals) need to be revised in light of recent research that shows that the differences and advantages are not as great as previously thought.

At the same time, pharmaceutical companies have been actively seeking new indications (on-label uses) for the atypical antipsychotics and other medications. Since the publication of those guidelines, a number of medications have received FDA approval for use in the maintenance treatment of bipolar disorder as well as specific indications for either mania or depression.

The good news is that bipolar disorder is receiving significant attention, and with this burgeoning in research will hopefully come more effective treatments that can lessen the severity of mood episodes and improve overall functioning.

The challenge is that in research no one study is usually considered the be all and end all. Being able to replicate a study and get the same—or at least close to the same—findings is tremendously important, and it's only after replicating a finding that one can have a degree of confidence in the results.

So with the excitement of all the new research, and new options, come a few cautionary words. With the exception of some important federally funded studies, most of the new research is underwritten by the pharmaceutical companies; these are for-profit corporations looking to bring new compounds to the market or find fresh indications for existing medications that will generate a profit.

So what we need to know about the advances in the field is: what are the latest studies showing, how strong are the results, and have those results been replicated in other studies by different researchers? It becomes a balance of keeping up to date and keeping in mind the medications that have been around for a longer time, that have an established track record and multiple studies to back up their usefulness.

What are the risks of not taking medication?

The quick answer is that it all depends on who we're talking about. If it's someone with bipolar I who historically becomes manic, depressed, or psychotic once medications are stopped, the risk is obvious—She is at high risk for going into a mood episode. In fact, the most common reason a person with bipolar disorder is hospitalized is because she stopped taking her medication and went into a serious mood episode.

Depending on the individual, behavior while manic, psychotic, or in a mixed state can have devastating financial, legal, and social consequences. It can take years to pull out of the debt from maxing out credit cards and draining savings accounts. Diseases contracted while in a hypersexual state may not be responsive to medications (HIV, hepatitis), and/or a spouse or significant other may decide that this is the last straw and important relationships can be broken forever. Impulsive and illegal acts committed while manic and/or psychotic may mean years of legal headaches, and there is an unfortunate and growing trend in this country to incarcerate people with serious mental illnesses. The risk of suicide is also greatly increased when someone is actively depressed or in a mixed state.

On the other hand, if we're talking about someone with bipolar disorder who has had very few mood episodes, it becomes a different gamble. And for readers looking for 'yes' or 'no' answers, here's where we get fuzzy. There are people who go years, and even decades, between episodes. Some of these people will decide the risk of being on medication outweighs the risk of being off of it. If this is something you, or someone you care about, are contemplating, it's vitally important to have a strong support network and a good handle on the warning signs that a relapse is coming (such as disrupted sleep patterns, increased spending, impulsive behavior, increased alcohol intake, etc.). As with other disorders that go into remission, such as multiple sclerosis and lupus, it's sometimes easy to think—or to wish—that the illness is gone altogether. Unfortunately it's not; it's just sleeping.

What types of medications might be prescribed?

In the following chapters we'll go into the major classes of medications that are commonly prescribed in bipolar disorder. These include:

- Mood stabilizers: Lithium, and lamotrigine (Lamictal), and other medications that are frequently used "off label" for the treatment of serious mood episodes, as well as for maintenance treatment or prophylactic treatment, when someone is not experiencing symptoms.
- Antipsychotic medications: These includes a large number of both older medications such as chlorpromazine (Thorazine) and haloperidol (Haldol) and more recently approved medications such as risperidone (Risperdal), quetiapine (Seroquel), and aripiprazole (Abilify).
- Antidepressants
- Medications for anxiety
- Medications to help with sleep

How much do the drug companies influence the prescribing of medications?

Extensively, and more so than most people—including practitioners—realize. The pharmaceutical companies have a financial interest in seeing their drugs prescribed. These are for-profit corporations that invest heavily in bringing a new medication to the market; it's estimated that the cost of developing a new drug is between $100 million to $800 million.

To insure profitability, the drug companies market extensively to physicians and, more recently, the general public through television and other forms of direct-to-the-consumer advertisement. In addition, the drug companies sponsor numerous events, often under the guise of providing continuing medical education (CMEs). Up until the federal government began to scrutinize some of these practices, it was common for drug companies to sponsor "educational" cruises, trips, and other expensive promotions for physicians and their spouses.

While the rules on what drug companies can offer to prescribers have become increasingly stringent thanks to the Office of the Inspector General (OIG), there are still an incredible number of free dinners, lunches, and tickets to sporting and cultural events and sponsored symposia, where speakers—paid for by the drug company—will present material often prepared by the drug company. Many universities, healthcare organizations, and state agencies are drafting, or have implemented, ethics policies to put caps on what can be accepted from the drug companies.

This is just the tip of the iceberg. Most professional journals are indirectly funded by the pharmaceutical companies—often in the form of multipage advertisements. When you read the articles in those journals, it's clear that the bulk of new research is funded by the pharmaceutical industry. The influence doesn't stop there, and recent court cases have brought to light disturbing practices wherein results of entire studies have been suppressed because they did not support a particular medication's usefulness. To address this practice, new guidelines for research have gone into effect, requiring that all drug studies be registered and the results be made available. Additionally, all professional authors and speakers must disclose any/all financial ties to pharmaceutical companies.

Another factor that influences prescribing patterns has to do with not just what is being aggressively marketed and promoted, but what is not. Drugs that are no longer under protection of patent (a patent generally runs out after twenty years) are less likely to be funded for study and promoted. In bipolar disorder this raises interesting questions regarding older medications, such as lithium and the first generation of antipsychotic medications. Lithium in particular has an extensive literature with proven benefits, yet its use has been declining in recent years to where many new trainees no longer view it as a first-line strategy in bipolar disorder, opting instead for newer and less fully understood treatments.

Finally, most pharmaceutical companies provide physicians with free samples of newer medications to give to their patients. On the surface this appears to be a win-win-win situation. But again, if there are two—or more—drugs of equal merit and you don't have free samples of both (and no one is giving away samples of older and off-patent medications) then it's more likely that the newer and more costly medication will be the one prescribed.

How can someone get unbiased information about medications used in bipolar disorder?

Realistically, it is nearly impossible to get data that is entirely free from pharmaceutical company, or other, bias. That said, there are independent sources of medication information and reviews that actively strive to be free from bias. These include *The Medical Letter* and *The Therapeutics Letter*, which are produced by non-profit organizations (The Medical Letter, Inc., and the Department of Pharmacology and Therapeutics at the University of British Columbia). There are a number of websites, such as healthyskepticism.org and nofreelunch.org (operated by non-profit organizations) that strive to counter misleading drug promotions. Also, the consumer magazine *Consumer Reports* has a public education program called "Best Buy Drugs" and an excellent web site, crbestbuydrugs.org, that includes free downloadable reports on various medications.

There are also large studies sponsored by the National Institute of Mental Health and others, which should be relatively free of pharmaceutical company bias. Notable current studies include ones comparing the newer antipsychotic medications to the older ones.

Indeed, the early findings from these studies show that with the exception of clozapine's (Clozaril) repeatedly demonstrated superior efficacy in treating resistant psychosis, the others come out all about the same. A notable difference is the price, with older off-patent medications costing a fraction of what the newer on-patent ones cost. Another important source that evaluates the evidence for or against various treatments is the Cochrane Library through Wiley InterScience at www.interscience.wiley.com.

If it's hard to get unbiased information about medications, how do I know what medications are best?

In the absence of a cure for bipolar disorder and lacking bias-free information around medications and other therapies, it becomes increasingly important for the person with bipolar disorder and her practitioner(s) to have an open and honest communication about what's working, what's not working, and everything in between. We refer to this as an empiric approach, where observation and experimentation guide the treatment. This doesn't mean we're throwing out what the literature is telling us, just that it is another information stream. Ultimately it is the individual's response to a given treatment that is of the utmost importance. An example of an empiric recommendation might be, "I'm going to prescribe compound 'X' to help you sleep; let me know if it was useful or not. Start with a single pill; if you're not asleep in thirty minutes, take a second, and then let me know if it worked."

What is a black box warning?

A black box warning occurs when the FDA determines that a medication carries a serious risk of a severe adverse reaction. When this occurs, a heavy black box is placed around the specific warning in literature produced by the pharmaceutical company that manufactures the specific medication. Included in the black box (literally a dark black line drawn around the warning) are often recommendations for increased monitoring when a person is on these medications, which might include more frequent visits, lab work, and other studies. Examples of black box warnings that might pertain to medications prescribed for bipolar disorder include:

- Lithium toxicity, and the need to be able to monitor lithium levels in the body.
- Increased risk of suicidal thoughts and behaviors with antidepressants in children and adolescents.
- An increased risk of death in elderly patients with dementia who are taking atypical antipsychotic medications.

How long will someone need to be on medication?

For many with bipolar disorder, medication will be an ongoing part of treatment. This is because at present there is no known cure for bipolar disorder. With a cure—like taking an antibiotic for pneumonia—there is a definitive end to taking the medication; the infection clears up and you stop. With many other medical conditions, such as hypertension, diabetes, and bipolar disorder, treatments are used to keep the symptoms under control. When the medications are stopped the underlying condition is still there.

Key factors that will impact how long people need to remain on medications, and which medications they'll need to take, are their history and symptoms. It's quite typical for someone who is manic to use both a mood stabilizer and an antipsychotic. As the mania goes away, the antipsychotic is frequently tapered off over the course of a few months, while the mood stabilizer(s) will be continued to prevent a recurrence of symptoms. For some, maintenance therapy will involve the ongoing use of multiple medications.

What is meant by acute, continuation, and maintenance treatment?

These terms describe stages of treatment. When somebody is currently experiencing a mood episode, he is said to be in the acute stage. Here the goal is to get the most severe symptoms of mania or depression under control. Once the individual is somewhat stable, the continuation phase of treatment, the next six to twelve months, is a time to address residual symptoms and functional impairments—such as conflicted relationships, work, housing, and so forth. The continuation phase is also a period of high risk for a relapse, so frequent clinical contacts and a tolerable medication regimen are important.

The maintenance phase of treatment occurs after the symptoms have resolved. Medications are now used to decrease the likelihood of recurrence, and other treatments, such as psychotherapy, are geared toward maintaining and improving overall functioning and quality of life.

How long do medications stay in the body?

Every medication is unique in terms of how long it stays in the body. The term "half-life" is used describe the length of time it takes the body to clear/eliminate/metabolize 50 percent of a dose. This concept leads to the goal of a "steady state," which is where the daily dose equals what the body eliminates over the course of a day. Half-life is also important to take into consideration when stopping a medication, because it takes roughly five half-lives to eliminate more than 90 percent of a medication from the body.

The half life of a medication can be very brief—on the order of minutes as is often seen in anesthesia—or it can be days and even weeks. The antidepressant fluoxetine (Prozac) is a good example, as it has a half-life on the order of seven to ten days. This is neither a good nor a bad thing, but it is important to know. So if someone needed to be off Prozac and have it out of her system (five half-lives) it would take over a month, possibly longer in an older person. On the flip side, you can see that if someone has been on Prozac for a long time and is at a steady state, missing a dose or two will have little effect on her blood level.

The half-life of a medication can be seriously shortened or lengthened when someone is taking another medication that impacts its elimination from the body. For people with bipolar disorder this becomes especially pertinent with mood stabilizers such as lithium, valproate (Depakote), and other medications whose half-lives can be significantly altered (increased or decreased) when on multidrug regimens. The result is that levels of a medication can become either dangerously high or too low to work. This is one of the reasons it's important to maintain an accurate list of medications that can be reviewed anytime a drug is being added, adjusted, or discontinued (an index card in your wallet or pocketbook works well).

How do medications get excreted or broken down and what does this have to do with drug interactions?

There are two organs—the liver and the kidneys—that serve to eliminate (metabolize) the majority of medications—and other substances—from the body. Without going into painful detail about how they do this, here are a couple of useful concepts.

You can use the metaphor of a highway when discussing how medications exit the body. If you think about having a certain number of "off ramps," it's easy to see how, at rush hour, these become overwhelmed and the highway backs up until you've got a traffic jam. The majority of drug interactions occur because medications either compete for the same off ramp or influence the number of available off ramps.

In the liver there are systems of enzymes (proteins) that break down medication and other substances. The production of these enzymes can be increased or decreased by many different substances (up regulation and down regulation). Continuing the metaphor we can see how if drug A needs a particular off ramp and drug B has either tied up that off ramp or shut it down, drug A is going to back up in the system.

The number of medications that inhibit or induce enzymes in the liver is staggering. Most physicians and pharmacists now use software to run drug-to-drug interaction profiles when prescribing a new medication. It's always a good idea to ask, "Will this new medication interact with anything I'm already on?"

It's important to remember that not only do prescribed medications cause drug interactions, but so too do over-the-counter drugs, herbal and nutritional supplements, and even some common foods and beverages—grapefruit juice being one of the most frequently cited examples. Cigarette smoking is also associated with increasing the elimination of many antipsychotic medications, in some instances reducing the blood level by half.

What is medication potency?

Potency refers to the relative strength of a medication. It's not to be confused with "efficacy," or how well the medication works. The question of potency most frequently gets raised when people are either starting a new medication or are switching between medications in the same class. For instance, if someone is on the high-potency antipsychotic medication risperidone (Risperdal), he's likely taking a few milligrams a day—on the order of 1–6. If he's being switched to a low-potency antipsychotic such as quetiapine (Seroquel) he could expect to be on a few hundred milligrams. Both drugs are equally efficacious, but their relative potencies are different. In other words, even though the doses look quite different they do the same thing.

Do medications dampen creativity?

One concern many people with bipolar disorder have is that the medication(s) will rob them of their creativity. For some who make their livelihood in the arts, this question extends further to: "Will I lose my authenticity?" or "Will the medication take away the thing that makes me viable as an artist?" Other specific concerns might center on the side effects of specific medications—tremor in a musician or painter could be a bad thing. Tardive dyskinesia (TD), a movement abnormality and potential side effect of antipsychotic medications (discussed in Chapter 6) in a dancer could end a career.

As with many of the questions in this book it comes down to a risk-benefit analysis. The goal is to have a treatment regimen (not just medications) that controls symptoms and decreases or prevents recurrence of mood episodes, without leaving the person feeling drugged-up and inauthentic. What many people who have bipolar disorder come to realize is that the medications, once adjusted to an effective maintenance level, allow them to think clearly enough to be both creative and productive. Patty Duke gives a vivid and very personal description of this phenomenon in her book *A Brilliant Madness*.

Will the medication turn me into a zombie?

High on the list of why people stop taking psychiatric medications is the feeling of being overly sedated. It's also common when trying to rapidly treat a manic episode—especially if the person is also psychotic—to use higher doses of medications, often leaving the person feeling lethargic and slowed down. These side effects (sedation, mental slowing) are not permanent but result from the medications being used and the dosages being given. It's important to clearly communicate these symptoms to your prescriber so that dosages can be adjusted and alternative medications considered if the problem of sedation and sluggishness does not go away.

Chapter 5

MOOD STABILIZERS

What is a mood stabilizer?

Mood stabilizers are medications that decrease the mood swings associated with bipolar disorder. In this chapter we'll discuss lithium and various anticonvulsants being used as mood stabilizers. In the next chapter we'll review antipsychotic medications, which have historically been used to treat mania and psychosis, but currently many of these are being used, or evaluated, as mood stabilizers.

In 1970, lithium became the first medication approved as a mood stabilizer by the FDA. Lamotrigine (Lamictal), more recently has been approved for this use. In this chapter we'll review these, as well as other, "off label," medications currently used as mood stabilizers, such as valproate (Depakote, Depakene), carbamazepine (Tegretol), and oxcarbazepine (Trileptal).

We'll also discuss medications that were thought to have mood-stabilizing properties that subsequent studies have found to be of little, or no, benefit.

What is lithium?

In the 1940s the first effective mood stabilizer—lithium—was identified by Australian researcher John Cade. Early experiments with lithium, a naturally occurring element (a salt), showed it to have nearly miraculous results on a group of individuals with long-standing mania. Some of these people had spent years in mental institutions, and after the initiation of lithium, their symptoms resolved and they were well enough to return home. Yet it wasn't until 1970 that lithium received FDA approval to be used in the treatment of what was then called manic-depression.

Lithium is excreted unchanged (it's an element that does not get broken down) through the kidneys. Its half-life is between twelve and thirty hours depending on age and kidney function.

What are the benefits of taking lithium for bipolar disorder?

Lithium may be the most well-studied medication in psychiatry. It's been shown to be effective in the treatment of manic, mixed and depressed states. It is the only mood stabilizer to date that has been demonstrated to substantially decrease the risk (nearly tenfold) that someone with bipolar disorder will commit suicide.

Lithium has also been shown to significantly decrease the severity and frequency of mood episodes. This becomes an important point when discussing maintenance therapy. Certain medications and treatments may be extremely helpful to get an acute manic or depressed state under control, but may not be required once mood stabilization has been achieved. Lithium is typically continued.

How long does it take for lithium to work?

The benefits of lithium in the treatment of acute mania can start to be seen within ten to fourteen days. The full effect of lithium in decreasing the number and severity of episodes may not be reached for six weeks or even longer. Because of this delay lithium is typically combined with other medications when treating an acute manic episode.

Is bipolar disorder caused by a chemical imbalance of lithium?

It's something of an urban myth that bipolar disorder is 'a chemical imbalance,' caused by too little lithium. And like most urban myths, there's not much truth to it. Researchers have put this question to bed—there is no demonstrable decrease in lithium in the brains of people who have bipolar disorder.

Still, while referring to bipolar disorder as a chemical imbalance may be inaccurate, many people find this concept helpful in either coming to terms with their illness or conceptualizing it.

What are the different types of lithium available?

Lithium is available in both pill and sugar-free liquid forms. There are both generic pills and slow-release name-brand preparations such as Eskalith, Eskalith CR (Controlled Release) and Lithobid.

How does lithium work?

While this has been a hot question in research, the answer is not clear. What is known is that lithium acts on multiple neurotransmitter systems in the brain, most notably glutamate, and seems to affect how nerve cells relay information.

How much lithium would I need to take in order to get the benefits?

Most agree that in order to achieve the desired effects of lithium without heading into a toxic range, the blood levels should be between 0.8 meq/Liter to 1.0 milli equivalent/Liter—Possibly higher (1.2-1.4) when treating someone in an acute manic episode. This range is referred to as the therapeutic window. Below these levels the incidence of relapse goes up, and above these levels people experience worsening side effects.

For some, even the 0.8 meq/liter may leave them with bothersome side effects, and so during periods of stability they, and their prescribers, may try to maintain symptom control at a lower level. Should symptoms begin to worsen, then dosage is increased.

Most people will be maintained on between 900–1200mg of Lithium a day, divided into two doses. The actual dose is individualized and followed by obtaining lithium levels. Occasionally, when treating someone in an acute manic state, the dosage might be increased to a maximum of between 1800–2100mg/day. This is then reduced as the person improves.

What are lithium's side effects?

Before starting lithium, or any medication, it's a good idea to get a tear sheet from your pharmacist (information about the drug written in plain language, often including frequently asked questions and answers). This tear sheet lists many of the side effects and potential adverse reactions of the drug. Lithium has many of these: some will go away in time, others might persist and need to be managed. Still others, such as rare, but serious, kidney damage, may make it necessary to stop lithium altogether.

Common side effects and adverse reactions include (these are all relatively common with the exception of serious kidney damage, which is extremely rare):

- Upset stomach (It's best to take lithium with food to decrease this side effect. This side effect typically goes away in time.)
- Diarrhea
- Increased thirst
- Increased urination (This can progress to a condition called diabetes insipidus (DI)—not to be confused with diabetes mellitus. In DI the ability of the kidneys to reabsorb fluid is diminished, resulting in a markedly increased fluid intake with increased thirst and output with increased urination.)
- Tremor
- Worsening of underlying skin conditions such as psoriasis and acne
- Weight gain
- Swollen feet, ankles, and/or hands
- Decrease in thyroid function (For some this will require taking thyroid replacement hormone.)
- Kidney damage (This includes extremely rare reports of kidney failure.)

What is lithium toxicity?

As beneficial as lithium can be, it is important to be educated about the dangers of having too much in your system, which can develop into lithium toxicity (levels greater than 2.5–3.0 meq/liter). For a brief period in the early part of the twentieth century, lithium salt was actually marketed as a salt substitute for people with heart disease. It was rapidly pulled from the market after several people developed lithium toxicity and died.

So not only is maintaining a lithium level important to ensure that a person is in the therapeutic window—the range in which he'll receive the maximum benefit—but also to make certain his level has not crept too high.

Lithium toxicity presents with a variety of physical symptoms and changes in behavior. While many of these may simply be side effects of lithium, it's important to pay attention to a background side effect that is getting worse, such as a tremor that is much more pronounced combined with an unsteady gait and slurred speech. Symptoms of toxicity can include:

- Upset stomach, especially nausea, vomiting, or diarrhea
- Tremor (or if the person has a tremor to begin with, the tremor gets worse)
- Unsteady gait (The person may feel light-headed, unsure of his footing, and as the toxicity progresses he may appear to stagger like someone who is drunk or "high.")
- Light-headedness
- Slurred speech
- Delirium (This is a mental state in which people may lose track of the day, where they are and what's going on around them. They could appear to be paying attention and then drift (often referred to as a waxing and waning level of consciousness). They may also seem sleepy, confused or giddy.)

Lithium toxicity is a medical emergency that in severe cases can progress to coma and death. If it is suspected, the person should immediately contact his practitioner and seek treatment. If the practitioner is unavailable, the patient should seek treatment in an emergency room. Once there, a lithium level is measured—through a blood test—and the person is monitored closely. Depending on how high the level has gone, interventions may be as simple as 'watch and wait' and recheck the level; in severe cases, putting the patient into intensive care and dialysis in order to remove lithium from the body may be necessary.

There are various reasons why a person might become toxic, including dehydration, a deliberate overdose, or inadvertently taking another medication that can prevent lithium from leaving the body and thereby cause a toxic rise in the level.

To avoid lithium toxicity, it's important to keep hydrated in the warm weather or when ill, and to be aware of—and avoid—different medications that can elevate the lithium level.

A potential risk for people with lithium toxicity is that because its symptoms can be mistaken for other problems, including a manic or mixed episode or acute intoxication with alcohol or other drugs, life-saving treatment may be delayed or withheld all together

If I stop lithium, will I have withdrawal?

There is no withdrawal syndrome with lithium. If lithium has been an effective drug for someone with bipolar disorder, however, stopping it increases the risk for a relapse. Beyond that, there is also this poorly understood phenomenon: After going off lithium, for about 10 to 15 percent of people who go back on it, the drug will no longer be effective.

Also, when stopping lithium, an abrupt discontinuation is not recommended. Instead, the drug is tapered down; this lessens the likelihood that the person will go into a mood episode. Should a mood episode develop while tapering down, it may also provide a person with needed information about the benefits of lithium in her particular situation.

What lab tests need to be checked when someone is taking lithium?

Periodic blood work is a fact of life with lithium—as with many other medications. Prior to starting lithium, it's typical to check the following:

- Electrolytes (sodium, potassium, chloride, bicarbonate)
- Thyroid function tests
- Measures of renal function (blood urea nitrogen/creatinine, aka BUN/CR)
- A complete blood count
- Pregnancy test in women of child-bearing age (Lithium can in a very small number of cases cause birth defects—most notably a cardiac malformation called Ebstein's anomaly—especially during the first-trimester. Women should be warned of this rare but potentially adverse reaction, and if sexually active, birth control is recommended.)

Once started on lithium the following should be checked:

- Lithium levels—This is a blood test that should be performed a few days (usually five on an outpatient basis, but sometimes more frequently on an inpatient) after the person starts taking the medication, and a few days after a change in dosage. The reason that a few days are needed is so that the medication is at a steady state in the body, where what you're taking in on a daily basis is roughly equivalent to the amount of drug being excreted through the kidneys. A lithium level is tested in the morning before taking your dose (a trough level). When on a regular dosage, people typically have their lithium levels checked at least twice a year, more frequently in older people or those experiencing side effects.

- Thyroid function tests—Lithium can damage the thyroid gland and interfere with the production of thyroid hormone. Regular blood tests—twice a year—should be done to monitor this.
- Renal function tests—over time, lithium can cause a decrease in the rate at which the kidneys function to filter waste products from the body. Twice yearly tests of blood urea nitrogen (BUN) and creatinine—measures of kidney health—should be done, more frequently if there is evidence of declining kidney function.

Are there particular medicines that can alter lithium levels?

There are quite a number of commonly prescribed and over-the-counter medications that need to be avoided when taking lithium. Or if they must be taken, extra care must be used in monitoring lithium levels.

Some drugs cause lithium levels to increase, and a person can become toxic on his regular dose of lithium. Some other medications can actually increase the rate at which the kidneys filter the blood and thereby cause a decrease in lithium levels.

The following two tables include many of the more common medications to watch out for. There are more, so it's always a good idea when starting a new medication or over-the-counter pill to ask your pharmacist or prescriber to run a drug-interaction profile.

Figure 13: Medications that can Cause an Increase in Lithium Levels

Generic Name or Category	Trade Names	Comments
non-steroidal anti-inflammatory agents (NSAIDs) ibuprofen, naproxen, indomethacin, oxaprozin, piroxicam, and others	Motrin, Advil, Nuprin, Aleve, Anaprox, Naprosyn, Indocin, Daypro, Feldene, Relafen, and others	■ Be careful with over-the counter cold preparations that may contain ibuprofen or other NSAIDs. When in doubt, ask the pharmacist. ■ Over-the-counter pain medications that do not alter lithium levels include aspirin and acetaminophen (Tylenol)
diuretics (water pills) hydrochlorothiazide (HCTZ), furosemide, triamterene, chlorothiazide, metolazone, bumetanide, sprionolactone, amiloride and other	Hydrodiuril, Lasix, Dyazide, Maxzide, Diuril, Zaroxolyn, Lozol, Bumex, Aldactone, Midamor, and others	Diuretics will sometimes be combined with other anti-hypertensive medications as combination pills.
ACE inhibitor medications for hypertension: lisinispril, benazepril, captopril, fosinopril, enalapril, moexipril, auinapril, ramipril	Zestril, Prinivil, Lotensin, Monopril, Capoten, Vasotec, Univasc, Accupril, Altace, and others	
calcium channel blockers: diltiazam, verapamil	Cardizem, Dilacor, Calan, Isoptin, Verelan, and others	

(Continued on next page)

Figure 13—Continued

Some antibiotics: tetra-cycline, doxycycline		
phenytoin	Dilantin	
metronidazole	Flagyl	
methyldopa	Aldomet	Associated with lithium toxicity even at normal lithium levels.

Figure 14: Medications that can cause a decrease in Lithium Levels

Generic Name or Category	Trade Names	Comments
theophylline	Theo-Dur, Theo-Bid, Theolair, Elixophyllin, Slo-Phyllin and others	
acetazolamide	Diamox	
caffeine	Found in many beverages and chocolate. Also a component in some combination medications.	While caffeine found in coffee, tea, and some sodas can decrease lithium levels, if someone were to suddenly stop his regular caffeine intake, his lithium level could rise.

Are there other drug interactions to watch for when taking lithium?

When combined with lithium, some other medications can put a person at increased risk for a confusional state called neurotoxicity, while still others carry added risk for developing a serotonin syndrome, a potentially life-threatening condition caused by dangerous elevations in the level of serotonin in the brain.

The list of potential interactions is a long one, but the take-home message is that if someone on lithium becomes confused, disoriented, lethargic, or acutely ill either with or without other symptoms of lithium toxicity, the smart thing is to seek emergent help.

What is valproic acid (Depakote, Depakene)?

Valproic acid, or valproate, was originally used as an anticonvulsant (seizure medication) in the treatment of epilepsy. In the 1970s and 1980s a number of studies were conducted that found valproic acid to be effective in treating the mood swings of bipolar disorder. It received FDA approval for the treatment of acute mania in bipolar I disorder in 1995. While it is used extensively for mood stabilization in maintenance therapy (after the mania or mood episode has resolved), it has never received approval for this specific purpose from the FDA.

Valproic acid may be especially useful not only in the treatment of acute mania, but also for treating mixed manic episodes and in rapid cycling bipolar. It is mostly metabolized by the liver and has a half-life of between nine and sixteen hours in adults.

Typical doses for the treatment of bipolar disorder run in the range of 1,000–2,000mg per day. It's usually given in two doses, which can take many forms. They include the generic valproic acid (available in both liquid and capsule form), Depakene (available in both liquid and capsule form), Depakote (available in pill form), Depakote ER (a slow-release once-a-day pill) and Depakote Sprinkles (capsules that can be taken whole or sprinkled into pudding or applesauce).

What side effects and adverse reactions are associated with valproic acid?

Common side effects include headaches, nausea, upset stomach, diarrhea, tiredness and decreased energy, nervousness, depression, dizziness, bruising, weight gain, hair loss, insomnia, blurred vision, muscle aches, tremor, and elevation in liver enzymes.

Rare but serious adverse reactions include liver failure (fatalities have been reported in young children), pancreatitis, electrolyte abnormalities, blood abnormalities, life-threatening rashes (Stevens-Johnson syndrome and toxic epidermal necrolysis), and birth defects. Valproic acid has also been associated with rare cases of severe, and even fatal, pancreatitis.

Valproic acid is also associated with an increased risk of birth defects and women of childbearing age who are sexually active should use birth control when taking this medication.

What lab tests need to be checked when someone is taking valproic acid?

Prior to initiating valproic acid, it's typical to check the following blood tests:

- Liver function tests
- Complete blood count
- Electrolytes (sodium, potassium, chloride, and bicarbonate)
- Pregnancy test in women of childbearing age (Like lithium, valproic acid has been associated with birth defects and should not be taken by a woman who intends to get pregnant. Birth control is a must with sexually active women of childbearing years.)
- Baseline lipid profile including total cholesterol, HDL and LDL cholesterol, and triglycerides

After initiating treatment with valproic acid the following are monitored.

- Valproic acid levels (This should be checked when a steady state has been achieved and after increases or decreases in dosage. When having a valproic acid level checked it's necessary to hold the morning dose, get the blood work done, and then take the prescribed dose.)
- Liver function tests
- Electrolytes
- Complete blood count
- A fasting blood sugar (glucose) especially if there are concerns about weight gain or diabetes

Does valproic acid interact with other drugs?

Yes, and it's a lengthy list. It can, however, be broken down into some broad categories of interactions.

- Combining valproic acid with other sedating medications can lead to excessive drowsiness. Care should be exercised with any painkillers containing opiates (Oxycontin, Percocet/Percodan, and Darvocet/Darvon, to name a few), benzodiazepines (the diazepam (valium) family of medications, which includes lorazepam (Ativan), clonazepam (Klonopin), alprazolam (Xanax), and others), some sedating antidepressants such as trazodone (Desyrel), over-the-counter antihistamines, sedating antipsychotics, alcohol, St. John's Wort, and Valerian root.
- Combining valproic acid with various drugs increases the risk of bleeding. These include non-steroidal anti-inflammatory agents (NSAIDS), aspirin containing compounds, warfarin (Coumadin), willow bark, and valerian.

- Certain drugs, such as erythromycin and clarythromycin.can cause an increase in valproic acid levels. Other drugs can cause a decrease in valproic acid levels, such as lamotrigine and rifampin.
- The combination of valproic acid with lamotrigine may be associated with an increased risk of developing a serious, and potentially life-threatening, skin rash. If used in combination, patient education and close monitoring are recommended.

What is lamotrigine (Lamictal)?

Lamotrigine, another anticonvulsant medication, received FDA approval for the long-term maintenance treatment of bipolar I disorder in 2003; it and lithium are the only two medications that currently have this designation. It has been shown to delay the recurrence of episodes of mood disturbance (mania, hypomania, mixed, and depressed). Where lamotrigine may have the greatest benefit is in the treatment of the depression associated with bipolar disorder.

Lamotrigine is metabolized in the liver and mostly excreted through the urine. Its half-life when taken alone is approximately twenty-five hours. This is greatly influenced when other medications are added that can either increase or decrease its rate of metabolism in the liver.

The average dose in the treatment of bipolar disorder is between 100–200mg/day. Unlike other medications which can be tapered up rapidly, it is recommended that lamotrigine be increased slowly; this has been shown to decrease the incidence of serious skin rashes. The recommended schedule is: 25mg for two weeks, then increase to 50mg for two weeks, then 100mg for a week and then as directed by your physician.

What are the side effects of lamotrigine?

Common side effects include nausea, insomnia, tiredness, back pain, runny nose (rhinitis), mild rash, abdominal pain, dry mouth, constipation, vomiting, cough, and sore throat.

Serious, but very rare, side effects include life-threatening skin rashes (Stevens-Johnson syndrome and toxic epidermal necrolysis). This risk of serious rash is decreased by slowly increasing the medication to its recommended dosage and avoiding combining it with other medications known to cause this reaction, such as valproic acid (Depakote). That said, there are studies that have used lamotrigine in combination with valproic acid for the treatment of bipolar disorder. Also, while much attention has been paid to this rare but serious adverse reaction, it's important to remember that many other medications, including commonly prescribed antibiotics, are far more likely to cause this reaction.

What happens if someone develops a rash on lamotrigine?

Because of the rare—but real—potential for developing a life-threatening rash on this medication, people may have concerns about taking lamotrigine (Lamictal). The incidence of Stevens-Johnson Syndrome (SJS) has been reported at about one in 10,000. SJS is an autoimmune reaction that affects the skin and mucous membranes (mouth, nose, eyes, nose, digestive system, etc.), and it carries a fatality rate as high as 15 percent.

The difficulty for many people on lamotrigine is that in the course of everyday life people get minor rashes and skin conditions—a new detergent, poison ivy, a reaction to something they ate—so it's important to contact your prescriber at the first sign of a rash. She will want to know the extent of the rash, including any blistering on the skin (the central body or trunk in particular) and in the mouth.

Depending on the symptoms you're experiencing, you may be instructed to stop the medication and even to get to an emergency room to be evaluated. If the rash is minor and not consistent with a drug reaction, you may be instructed to do nothing.

What is carbamazepine (Tegretol)?

Carbamazepine (Tegretol) is an anticonvulsant that has been used extensively off label for a number of years as a mood stabilizer. In 2005, the extended-release (ER) form of this medication (Equetro) received FDA approval for the treatment of acute manic and mixed episodes.

While still widely used both alone and in combination with other medications, it is rarely a first-line choice on account of its side effect profile, which includes the risk of a serious bleeding condition in which the body stops producing white blood cells needed to fight infection (agranulocytosis). As a result, blood tests are recommended, especially when starting this medication.

Carbamazepine is metabolized in the liver and has a half life that starts out long (twenty-five to sixty-five hours) but then decreases as it has the unique ability to increase its own metabolism, as well as that of many other drugs. Women taking carbamazepine need to know that it increases the breakdown of oral contraceptives (birth control pills) increasing the risk of an unplanned pregnancy. An alternative means of birth control, or a higher dose oral contraception, is strongly advised.

What is oxcarbazepine (Trileptal)?

Oxcarbazepine, another off label medication frequently used in the treatment of bipolar disorder, has much in common with carbamazepine. Its side effect profile, however, is more favorable, and it is not associated with causing a drop in the white blood cell count (agranulocytosis). This is a medication that is receiving significant attention among researchers and practitioners, largely because of the hope that it has the efficacy of carbamazepine, but with a more tolerable side effect profile.

Oxcarbazepine is metabolized in the liver and has an active metabolite (a breakdown product also believed to have efficacy). Between the parent compound and the metabolite, the half-life is roughly nineteen hours.

As with carbamazepine, the risk of unplanned pregnancy for women on oral contraceptives is increased, and an alternative form of birth control would be recommended.

What is gapapentin (Neurontin)?

This is an anticonvulsant that was being looked at as a mood stabilizer. It was used off label extensively and there was a great deal of anecdotal (single case and small, not rigorously controlled, studies) accounts of its benefit. Subsequent studies of its efficacy as a mood stabilizer have not shown it to have benefit in bipolar disorder. Part of the attraction to this medication was that is has a favorable side effect profile, which if it had been effective would have made this a useful agent.

What is topiramate (Topamax)?

Another anticonvulsant, topiramate, has been used off label, mostly in add-on strategies with other mood stabilizers. As with gabapentin (Neurontin), there was much anecdotal buzz and uncontrolled studies. Recent research has shown that topirimate (Topamax) is not an effective mood stabilizer.

Much of the interest in this medication centered on the finding that some who take topiramate lose a small amount of weight.

What other medications are being assessed as mood stabilizers?

There is a growing trend—and evidence to support—the use of newer antipsychotic medications as mood stabilizers. We'll discuss this in the next chapter. Antipsychotic medications have long been used to help rapidly control the symptoms of acute mania and the psychosis that can be associated with manic, mixed, or depressed episodes. The atypical antipsychotic medications that have received the additional indication in the maintenance treatment of bipolar depression are: quetiapine (Seroquel) and olanzapine (Zyprexa) in a combination pill with fluoxetine (Prozac), marketed under the trade name Symbyax.

Chapter 6

ANTIPSYCHOTIC MEDICATIONS

- What is an antipsychotic medication?
- When are antipsychotic medications used in bipolar disorder?
- How do antipsychotic medications work?
- What are the differences between typical and atypical antipsychotic medications?
- What is tardive dyskinesia?
- What are extrapyramidal side effects or symptoms(EPS)?
- What are anticholinergic symptoms?
- Are some antipsychotics more likely to cause extrapyramidal symptoms and anticholinergic symptoms?
- Which antipsychotics cause the greatest weight gain?
- I've gained thirty pounds while taking an antipsychotic and my self-esteem is sinking. What can I do to stem the weight gain?
- What is the metabolic syndrome?
- Do some antipsychotics work better than others?
- What are long-acting antipsychotic medications and when would someone use one?
- How do I know which antipsychotic is right for me?

What is an antipsychotic medication?

Antipsychotic medications, sometimes referred to as neuroleptics or major tranquilizers, are drugs that lessen and/or eliminate hallucinations, disorganized thinking, and delusions. There are a large number of these medications, divided into two categories, typical and atypical. The term *typical* refers to the older group of medications that first came about with the discovery of chlorpromazine (Thorazine). The *atypicals* are a newer family of antipsychotics that have somewhat different mechanisms of action in the brain and a differing set of side effects. There is currently a great deal of interest and research into the risks and benefits of the various antipsychotic medications. In recent years there has been a trend to prescribe the newer (atypical) antipsychotics almost exclusively. Large-scale studies—and a few lawsuits—are now questioning this practice. So understanding the risks and benefits of the different medications becomes less a question of which one works best, but more a matter of choice, cost, and tolerability of side effects.

When are antipsychotic medications used in bipolar disorder?

Ever since the discovery of Thorazine in the early 1950s, antipsychotics have been used extensively in helping to rapidly control the symptoms of acute mania, whether or not there are psychotic symptoms. Their sedating qualities come on fast, and many can be given either by mouth, through an injection, or intravenously.

It's common practice in emergency rooms and on inpatient psychiatric units when working with a person who is severely agitated, manic, or psychotic, to use a combination of medicines such as haloperidol (Haldol) and a valium-family medication such as lorazepam (Ativan) to rapidly diminish symptoms. This will typically leave the person sedated and calm in a matter of minutes.

Figure 15: Typical Antipsychotics

Compound Name	Trade Name
Chlorpromazine	Thorazine
Haloperidol	Haldol
Trifluoperazine	Stelazine
Fluphenazine	Prolixin
Thiothixene	Navane
Loxapine	Loxitane
Molindone	Moban
Thioridazine	Mellaril (The brand name was discontinued secondary to cardiac concerns, while the generic is still available.)

Figure 16: Atypical Antipsychotics

Compound Name	Trade Name
Clozapine	Clozaril
Risperidone	Risperdal
Aripiprazole	Abilify
Ziprasidone	Geodon
Quetiapine	Seroquel
Olanzapine	Zyprexa

While the tranquilizing effects work fast, the ability of these medications to decrease psychotic symptoms (hallucinations, delusions, and disorganized thinking) occurs over the course of weeks.

Just as antipsychotic medication can be helpful in acute mania, they also play a role in the treatment of acute depression, especially depression accompanied by psychotic symptoms. In recent years, two of the atypical antipsychotics received FDA approval for the use in bipolar depression: quetiapine (Seroquel) and the combination pill Symbyax luoxetine/olanzapine (Prozac/Zyprexa).

How do antipsychotic medications work?

All antipsychotic medications block, or antagonize, the neurotransmitter dopamine in the brain. But this dopamine blockade does not
appear to be the whole story in how these medications work. Other
factors are in play, including the neurotransmitter serotonin, which
many of the newer (atypical) antidepressants also influence.

What are the differences between typical and atyp-
ical antipsychotic medications?

There are a few differences, but as new data emerges, the differences
may eventually turn out to be fewer and less significant between the
two groups. Right now, the major differences include:

- The atypicals act on a number of neurotransmitter systems, not
  just dopamine (this appears to also be true for the older
  medication loxitane (Loxapine)).

- The side effect profiles between the two groups of medications
  shows that typicals are more likely to cause extrapyramidal
  symptoms (symptoms that can mimic Parkinson's disease and
  cause other movement abnormalities).

- The typical antipsychotics are more likely to cause tardive
  dyskinesia—a potentially irreversible movement abnormality.
  The rate of tardive dyskinesia with the newer medications has
  not yet been fully evaluated, but appears to be less.

- The atypicals are more associated with a metabolic syndrome
  that is characterized by weight gain, an increase in abdominal
  girth, elevated cholesterol and lipids, and type II diabetes
  mellitus.

What is tardive dyskinesia?

Tardive dyskinesia (TD) is a potentially irreversible movement abnormality often associated with the use of antipsychotic medications; it can also be caused by other medications, including some used for nausea. TD is characterized by repetitive involuntary movements that are present while a person is awake. Manifestations of TD include lip smacking, tongue thrusting and jaw movements. It can extend to the extremities and the trunk, and in extreme and rare cases can be disfiguring and disabling. For most, however, TD tends to be minor, does not progress, and is mostly confined to the lips, around the mouth and the tongue.

For anyone on an antipsychotic medication, this adverse reaction should be assessed—typically every six months—through the use of a simple evaluation called an AIMS (Abnormal Involuntary Movement Scale). Here the patient sits and goes through a series of instructions while the evaluator assesses and observes them for the presence and/or severity of TD.

The typical antipsychotics are more likely to cause TD, with a risk as high as 5 percent of people per year, and the longer someone is on these medications the greater the risk for developing TD. The atypicals can also cause it, although it's not entirely clear if clozapine does.

There is no known cure for tardive dyskinesia, and it's often worsened in times of stress. Strategies to diminish the onset or severity of TD include using the lowest possible dose and limiting—if possible—the length of time an individual needs to remain on the antipsychotic medication. There are case reports—but no rigorous studies—suggesting that vitamin E in high doses (1600 IU/day) might help diminish TD, especially in those who've not had it long. There are also case reports that the atypical antipsychotic medication clozapine (Clozaril) can decrease TD. In addition, there is active research looking for other treatments to decrease or eliminate TD, including one recent study that found some benefit with a surgical procedure for severe TD (deep brain stimulation).

If someone develops TD and stops taking antipsychotic medication, one of three things can happen. The TD may remain unchanged, it could possibly worsen—a condition called unmasked TD—or it may diminish and even disappear in time.

What are extrapyramidal side effects or symptoms (EPS)?

The term extrapyramidal refers to structures in the brain that are part of the body's motor system. This system is highly susceptible to the effects of medications that inhibit, or antagonize, dopamine, as the antipsychotics do.

Extrapyramidal side effects (EPS) can take many forms, and most are reversible and will go away when the medication is decreased or stopped. The notable exception is tardive dyskinesia. Some EPS can be severe and quite distressing. EPS can also come on suddenly and dramatically, especially in younger people who've never before taken an antipsychotic.

Extrapyramidal side effects (EPS) include:

- Akathisia—an internal feeling of restlessness. This can be quite unpleasant, and make someone who is manic or in a mixed episode feel worse.
- Parkinsonism—Medications that block dopamine can produce symptoms that mimic the neurological disorder Parkinson's disease. Symptoms can include a shuffling gait, tremors/shakes, rigidity in the limbs, and diminished facial expression.
- Torticollis—Muscle spasms of the neck.
- Oculogyric crisis—The muscles that control the movement of the eyes spasm and contract, making the eyes roll up.

- Other dystonias—Spasms of various muscle groups.

For acute dystonic reactions, such as oculogyric crisis and torticollis, a group of medications called anticholinergic agents can rapidly reverse the symptoms. These medications work most quickly when given by injection.

Anticholinergic agents are also used to decrease drug-induced Parkinsonism, and are frequently prescribed in pill form on an ongoing basis for people experiencing EPS while taking antipsychotic medications.

Anticholinergic drugs include:
- Diphenydramine (Benadryl)
- Benztropine (Cogentin)
- Trihexyphenidyl (Artane)

Akathisia (an internal feeling of restlessness caused by some antipsychotics) is often treated with the addition of a beta blocker medication.

What are anticholinergic symptoms?

Many antipsychotic medications, and quite a few others, such as medications used to treat extrapyramidal symptoms and many antidepressants, can cause a cluster of side effects known as anticholinergic symptoms or side effects. So yes, even through you're taking an anticholinergic medication (Artane, Benadryl, Cogentin) to treat side effects of an antipsychotic medication, they carry their own set of annoying, and potentially dangerous, side effects.

These include:
- Dry mouth
- Blurry vision and dry eyes
- Constipation
- Urinary retention

- Sedation
- Confusion and delirium

Anticholinergic side effects are dose dependent and additive—so if you're on multiple medications that can cause these symptoms; it increases the chances of getting them.

The severity of the side effects ranges from mildly annoying constipation and dry eyes to life-threatening emergencies like bowel obstruction, delirium, coma, and death.

Are some antipsychotics more likely to cause extra-pyramidal symptoms and anticholinergic symptoms?

This question can be broken down into some general guidelines.

- All antipsychotics with the possible exception of clozapine can cause tardive dyskinesia (TD). The typical (older) antipsychotics may do this more frequently then the atypical (newer) antipsychotics.
- More potent typical antipsychotics tend to have more extrapyramidal symptoms (EPS). So haloperidol (Haldol), which is very potent, will have more EPS than chlorpromazine (Thorazine).
- Less potent antipsychotics tend to have more anticholinergic side effects and sedation. So thorazine, which is low potency, is highly anticholinergic and highly sedating.

Which antipsychotics cause the greatest weight gain?

The issue of weight gain and antipsychotic medications has become an increasingly important one. It is now clear that certain atypical antipsychotics can cause substantial weight gain (as much as a pound per week). A couple of the newer ones have been able to demonstrate less weight gain, which for many makes them an attractive alternative.

I've gained thirty pounds while taking an antipsychotic and my self-esteem is sinking. What can I do to stem the weight gain?

Diet and exercise continue to be the mainstay of weight loss and weight maintenance programs. Small studies looking at particular strategies for lessening medication-associated weight gain show some benefit in behaviorally based weight loss programs, such as Weight Watchers.

Figure 17: Estimated Weight Gain (Loss) with Atypical Antipsychotic Medications

Antipsychotic	Average weight gain (loss)
Clozapine (Clozaril)	+1 pound/week
Olanzapine (Zyprexa)	+1 pound/week
Quetiapine (Seroquel)	½ pound/week
Risperidone (Risperdal)	½ pound/week
Aripiprazole (Abilify)	+/-
Ziprasidone (Geodon)	+/-

The best strategy when going on a medication associated with weight gain is to try and modify your eating pattern before a weight problem develops. Think about what snack foods will be readily available in the house and eliminate high-fat and high-calorie junk foods and fast foods and pay attention to portion sizes.

Some pharmaceutical companies provide extensive educational materials on healthy diet and nutrition to people on their medications.

Exercise, which we'll touch on later, is critical to maintaining or losing weight and also has been shown to have benefits in combating depression and regulating sleep.

Even with diet and exercise, you may decide that the risks—both to your health and to your self-esteem—associated with the weight gain are too great. Where there are antipsychotic medications less commonly associated with weight gain, a frank discussion with your practitioner and a switch in medication(s) might make sense.

What is the metabolic syndrome?

This term describes a serious cluster of side effects associated with the atypical antipsychotics, clozapine and olanzapine in particular. The metabolic syndrome involves substantial weight gain—mostly in the form of central fat or "belly fat," accompanied by a rise in total cholesterol and triglycerides and a decrease in the "good" cholesterol, HDL. While it's not fully understood what mechanisms in the body are causing this, there is a decrease in the body's ability to handle starch and sugars, through abnormalities in the functioning of insulin, which can result in the onset of diabetes. The negative health consequences of the metabolic syndrome—diabetes, obesity, hypertension, and hypercholesterolemia—can substantially decrease life expectancy. People on atypical medications need to be monitored for the onset of these symptoms.

Increasingly, practitioners should regularly check the following in order to keep tabs on any emerging metabolic syndrome symptoms:
- Weight (basal mass index or BMI)
- Fasting blood glucose
- Lipid profiles, including cholesterol and triglycerides

Do some antipsychotics work better than others?

In terms of decreasing psychotic symptoms and treating acute mania, all of the antipsychotics work well. Clozapine (Clozaril) is the only antipsychotic that has been shown to have a clear clinical edge over the others (this was demonstrated in people with schizophrenia, but has not been specifically proven in bipolar disorder). This is largely why this medication, which requires frequent blood draws due to a potentially fatal side effect in which the body stops producing white blood cells needed to fight infection (agranulocytosis), is allowed on the market. Also, clozapine and lithium are the only two medications to date that have been shown to decrease the rate of suicide. However, clozapine, because of its side effect profile (weight gain, risk of agranulocytosis, sedation, drooling) is rarely used as a first or second line antipsychotic in bipolar disorder. It's more commonly prescribed for people with psychotic symptoms that have not resolved with other medications, such as occurs in some cases of severe schizoaffective disorder and schizophrenia.

What are long-acting antipsychotic medications and when would someone use one?

There are currently three long-acting injectible antipsychotic medications on the market. They are: haloperidol (Haldol Decanoate), perphenazine (Prolixin Decanoate) and risperidone (Risperdal Consta). For people with bipolar disorder, these medications would likely only be used if prone to frequent recurrence of psychosis.

These three long-acting versions can be helpful when working with people who frequently discontinue medications or who would prefer to have fewer pills to take on a daily basis. Studies comparing long-acting medications to the pill form show that people have fewer relapses with psychotic symptoms when on the long-acting version. Prior to starting a long-acting injectible, it's standard practice to use the pill form first to ensure that the person is able to tolerate the medication and doesn't have any adverse reactions. Depending on the medication chosen, the frequency of dosing will be every two to four weeks.

How do I know which antipsychotic is right for me?

A number of factors go into the selection of which antipsychotic might be best to use in acute mania, a mixed episode, or depression with psychosis.

Factors that steer the decision may include:

- Patient choice—Have you been on a medication that agrees with you and has worked in the past?
- Side effect profile—Each of the antipsychotics has a unique side-effect profile. Some, which are very sedating, can be useful when treating someone with insomnia and daytime agitation. Or, if someone is feeling too sedated, the choice might be to use one that is more potent and less sedating.
- Cost—Will you be able to afford this medication? Is it covered on your insurance? Do you even have insurance?
- Drug interactions—Will this negatively interact with your other medications?
- Monitoring concerns—Is this a medication—like clozapine (Clozaril)—that will require close monitoring and frequent blood work? Will this be too impractical?
- Medical concerns—Do you have other medical problems that will make particular medications less, or more, desirable.
- What forms of the medication are available? Is there a long-acting form, a liquid, or an injectible?

Figure 18: Antipsychotic Common Side-Effect Comparison Table

Drug	Sedation*	Weight Gain	TD	EPS Stiffness, tremors, Dystonias*	Constipation urinary retention (Anticholine rgic side effects) *	Metabolic Syndrome	Other
Aripiprazole (Abilify)	0-+	0-+	+	0-+	++	0-+	
Clozapine (Clozaril)	+++-++++	++++	0 (+)	0-+	+++-++++	+++	Requires frequent blood monitoring, for risk of agranulocy-tosis
Olanzapine (Zyprexa)	++	+++-++++	+	+	+-++	+++	Extreme weight gain
Quetiapine (Seroquel)	+++-++++	++	+	+	++	++	Highly sedating, cataract exam-inations recommended
Risperidone (Risperdal)	+-++	++	+	+-+++	++	++	Also available as a long-acting injectible
Ziprasidone (Geodon)	+	0-+	+	+-++	+-++	0-+	Associated with changes on EKGs
Chlorpromazine (Thorazine)	+++-++++	++-+++	++	+	++-++++	0-+	Sedating
Fluphenazine (Prolixin)	++	+-++	++	++	++	0-+	Also available as a long-acting injectible
Haloperidol (Haldol)	+-++	+-++	++	+++-++++	+-++	0-+	Also available as a long-acting injectible
Loxapine (Loxitane)	++-+++	0-+	++	++	+	N/A	An older medication that has prop-erties similar to the atypicals
Molindone (Moban)	++	0-+	++	++	+	N/A	

(Continued on next page)

Figure 18—Continued

Perphenazine (Trilafon)	+-++	++	++	++	+-++	N/A	Important studies underway comparing this older medica- tion with the newer agents
Thiothixene (Navane)	++	0-+	++	+-++++	+-++	N/A	
Thioridazine (Mellaril)	+++- ++++	++-+++	++	+-++++	++-++++	N/A	Associated with dangerous arrhythmias
Trifluoperazine (Stelazine)	++-+++	0-+	++	+-++++	+-++	N/A	

Presence of symptoms 0=not at all, +=minimal or rare, ++=moderate, +++=considerable or common, ++++=severe or frequent, NA=not assessed

*Many side-effects such as sedation, anticholinergic side effects, and EPS have a strong dose-dependant component i.e. the higher the dose the greater the likelihood and magnitude of the side effect.

Chapter 7

ANTIDEPRESSANTS AND OTHER MEDICATIONS

- What is an antidepressant?
- Will taking an antidepressant make me manic?
- Will antidepressants make my bipolar disorder worse?
- Will I need to be on an antidepressant?
- How long does it take an antidepressant to work?
- What are selective serotonin reuptake inhibitors (SSRIs)?
- What are selective serotonin and norepinepherine reuptake inhibitors (SNRIs)?
- What are tricyclic antidepressants (TCAs)?
- What are monoamine oxidase inhibitors (MAOIs)?
- What other antidepressants are there?
- What is a benzodiazepine?
- What are anxiolytics?
- What about herbal and nutritional supplements? Are any of those helpful/harmful in treating bipolar disorder?

What is an antidepressant?

Antidepressants are medications that treat, and lessen, the symptoms of clinical depression. Some, like fluoxetine (Prozac), sertraline (Zoloft), buproprion (Wellbutrin), and venlafaxine (Effexor), are among the most widely prescribed medications in the United States.

The usefulness of antidepressants in bipolar disorder is a complex topic that over the years has gone through various twists and turns, both in clinical practice and in what researchers and experts have had to say. This has gone from the extreme of "never prescribe antidepressants to a person with bipolar disorder" to antidepressants packaged in a combination pill with an antipsychotic—fluoxetine/olanzapine (Symbyax)—specifically for the treatment of bipolar depression.

In this chapter, we'll review many different antidepressants, break them down into their classes, review side effect and safety profiles, and explain current strategies for when they are—and are not—used in the treatment of bipolar disorder.

Will taking an antidepressant make me manic?

Many experts believe that any treatment that is an effective antidepressant can trigger a manic, hypomanic, or mixed episode in a person with bipolar disorder.

This includes non-medication treatments such as electroconvulsive therapy (ECT), and there have even been cases of a triggered mania with trans-cranial magnetic stimulation (TCMS). Some antidepressants—like the tricyclics (TCAs) and monoamine oxidase inhibitors (MAOIs)—carry a high risk for doing this. Others, such as buproprion (Wellbutrin) and the selective serotonin reuptake inhibitors (SSRIs) are less likely to cause a switch into a manic or mixed episode. It's not understood why this occurs, and people will often describe how a particular antidepressant made them "feel wired." If you were to start on an antidepressant and begin to experience insomnia, racing thoughts, agitation, irritability, and other symptoms of a manic or mixed episode, it would be important to seek immediate attention. Most likely the antidepressant will need to be stopped and other medications considered to decrease your symptoms.

Because so many people with bipolar disorder will first be diagnosed with depression and then placed on an antidepressant, a triggered mania or mixed episode may be a sign that the person has an underlying bipolar spectrum disorder. It's also one of the reasons why anyone starting an antidepressant, switching to a new one, or increasing dosages of one, should be carefully monitored.

Will antidepressants make my bipolar disorder worse?

This is a controversial question in which the jury has not yet returned. Part of the concern about the use of antidepressants in bipolar disorder is that it appears, in some individuals, that they can increase the frequency of switching between different mood episodes. A number of studies have raised concerns that the use of antidepressants in bipolar disorder increases the likelihood of developing rapid-cycling bipolar disorder.

While there is little consensus, in those people with bipolar disorder for whom an antidepressant is absolutely necessary, it's important that they be on some kind of mood stabilizing medication at the same time. This strategy has been shown to decrease the rate of antidepressant-associated switching. The addition of a mood stabilizer and/or antipsychotic to an antidepressant can be seen as putting a ceiling, or damper, on how "high" the antidepressant can elevate a person's mood.

Will I need to be on an antidepressant?

The answer is it depends. There are different approaches to treating mood episodes and trying to prevent and diminish relapse. For many people with bipolar disorder, a mood stabilizer such as lithium or lamotrigine will be all that is required. Additional medications such as antipsychotics, sleep aids, and anti-anxiety medications can be used when needed to control specific symptoms. Antidepressants are often reserved for those individuals with bipolar who have severe depressions that aren't responding—or responding enough—to the mood stabilizer.

How long does it take an antidepressant to work?

Antidepressants take an average of three to six weeks before showing a clinical effect in reducing the symptoms of depression. This delay in onset is both a challenge to people with depressions, who want to feel better fast, and it raises interesting—and not fully understood—questions as to how antidepressants work in the brain. In other words, if the answer to depression was as simple as increasing the amount of serotonin and/or norepinephrine, we would expect these compounds to work right away; they don't. Researchers now realize that in response to these medications, the brain cells (neurons) undergo complex changes that occur over a period of weeks and months.

What are selective serotonin reuptake inhibitors (SSRIs)?

This group of medications acts on the brain by causing a relative increase in the neurotransmitter serotonin. The first on the market was flouxetine (Prozac). This was followed by several others. They all work equally well in unipolar depression, but like all antidepressants they can cause a switch from a depressed to a manic/hypomanic or mixed episode in a person with bipolar disorder.

The side effect profiles of the SSRIs are generally favorable, and unlike earlier classes of antidepressants they are much safer in overdose situations. Major complaints include sexual dysfunction in men and women, intense dreams, and irritability.

The SSRIs also have many unique drug-to-drug interactions because of their effects on various liver enzymes. It's important that if you are on other medications—especially ones that have to be kept at a certain level (like blood thinners, anti-seizure medications, some anti-hypertension medications, etc., that levels are monitored closely when starting, stopping, or changing doses of an SSRI.

Figure 19

Compound Name	Trade Name	Typical Dose Range
Citalopram	Celexa	10-60 mg/day
Escitalopram	Lexapro	10-20 mg/day
Fluoxetine	Prozac	10-60 mg/day
Paroxitine	Paxil	10-60 mg/day
Sertraline	Zoloft	50-200 mg/day

What are selective serotonin and norepinepherine reuptake inhibitors (SNRIs)?

As the name implies, SNRIs act to increase the relative amounts of two neurotransmitters in the brain—serotonin and norepinepherine.

Medications in this class include:

Figure 20

Compound Name	Trade Name	Dose Range
Nefazodone	Serzone	Only available as a generic. The name brand was withdrawn from the market by the manufacturer on account of a few reports of liver toxicity including liver failure 300-600mg/day
Venlafaxine	Effexor, Effexor XR	75-375 mg/day
Duloxetine	Cymbalta	40-60mg/day

What are tricyclic antidepressants (TCAs)?

The term *tricyclic* refers to the chemical structure of this family of medications. The TCAs were the first known antidepressants, and their immediate effect on the brain is with the neurotransmitters serotonin and norepinepherine. Some act more strongly on one than on the other and some affect both quite strongly.

The TCAs, which were once widely prescribed, have been largely replaced by the safer SSRIs, SNRIs and other more recent additions to the growing list of available antidepressants. Through their effect on the heart, TCAs can be highly lethal in an overdose—essentially they slow the electrical conduction in the heart—and in high enough doses will cause cardiac arrest.

TCAs also carry a heavy side effect burden that includes weight gain, constipation, blurry vision, sedation, urinary reten-tion, and mental slowing. In bipolar disorder TCAs are well known to trigger manic, hypomanic, and mixed episodes. They are rarely used, but when someone is faced with a severe depres-sion that has not responded to multiple other medications, a TCA might be considered.

Figure 21: Tricylclic Antipressants (TCAs)

Compound Name	Trade Name	Dose Range
Amitriptyline	Elavil	50-300 mg/day
Amoxapine	Ascendin	200-400 mg/day
Clomipramine	Anafranil	150-250 mg/day
Desipramine	Norpramin	100-300 mg/day
Doxepin	Sinequan	150-300 mg/day
Imipramine	Tofranil	150-300 mg/day
Maprotiline	Ludiomil	75 150 mg/day
Notriptyline	Pamelor	50-150 mg/day
Protriptyline	Vivactil	30-60 mg/day

What are monoamine oxidase inhibitors (MAOs)?

This is a highly effective group of antidepressant medications that is rarely prescribed on account of their side effect profile and dietary restrictions. This may change, as in 2006 the FDA approved a patch (transdermal) MAOI version of eldepryl (Emsam).

The MAOIs act by inhibiting enzymes MAOI-A and MAOI-B, which are responsible for the breakdown of epinephrine, norepinephrine, and dopamine.

The major caution with MAOIs is that foods containing a substance called tyramine (a protein subunit) can trigger a potentially fatal rise in blood pressure (hypertensive crisis). There is a long list of foods and medications that need to be avoided when on an MAOI, and it includes aged cheeses, beer and ale, Chianti wine, meat and yeast extracts (Marmite, Bovril, and Vegemite), and certain fruits and vegetables including avocados, pineapples, and eggplants.

Anyone taking an MAOI needs to be closely supervised by her prescriber. It's prudent to wear a wrist bracelet that indicates you're on an MAOI, as not only can tyramine-containing foods cause a hypertensive crisis, so too can many prescription, over-the-counter and illegal drugs. MAOIs must be washed out of the body before switching to another antidepressant (at least two weeks), and they should be discontinued two weeks prior to surgery (obviously not possible in an emergency).

Figure 22: Monoamine Oxidase Inhibitors

Compound Name	Trade Name	Dose Range
Phenelzine	Nardil	45-90mg/day divided into three or four doses
Tranylcypromine	Parnate	30-60mg/day divided in three doses
Selegeline	Eldepryl, Emsam	(6,9 or12mg/24 hour Patch)

As with other antidepressants, MAOIs can trigger a switch from depression to a mixed, manic or hypomanic episode.

What other antidepressants are there?

There are a number of other available antidepressants that don't fit into any of the previously discussed categories. These include widely prescribed medications such as buproprion (Wellbutrin), which is also used in lower doses to help people stop smoking under the brand name Zyban. Mirtazipine (Remeron) is often used for its sedating properties, and trazodone, which was initially approved as an antidepressant, is often used in lower doses as a sleep aid.

What is a benzodiazepine?

Benzodiazepines are used in various anxiety disorders as sleep aids, and they can be helpful in the acute manic and mixed phases of bipolar disorder. Where anxiety symptoms and agitation often accompany bipolar spectrum disorders, these medications are frequently used—clonazepam (Klonopin) in particular. Some also have indications as anti-seizure medications and muscle relaxants. There are many

Figure 23

Compound Name	Trade Name	Dose Range	Comments
Buproprion	Wellbutrin, Wellbutrin XR, Zyban	150-450mg/day	Unique, Effects Dopamine. Also used in smoking cessation. Associated with seizures in higher doses.
Mirtazipine	Remeron	15-45mg given at bedtime	Sedating and associated with weight gain
Trazodone	Desyrel	25-400mg/day	Highly sedating, often used as a sleep aid, men need to be cautioned about serious erectile adverse reaction (priapism)

medications in this family, and perhaps the best known are diazepam (Valium), alprazolam (Xanax), lorazepam (Ativan), and clonazepam (Klonopin). The majority of these medications are metabolized in the liver, with the notable exception of oxazepam (Serax)—a short-acting benzodiazepine largely excreted by the kidneys.

The major side effects of these medications include sedation and mental slowing. They are much safer than older sedatives, such as the barbiturates, in overdoses. If combined with other sedating medications and narcotics (heroin, methadone, oxycodone, etc.), however, they have been associated with death from respiratory depression.

Taken over time, benzodiazepines can cause physical tolerance and dependence quite similar to alcohol dependence. Someone who has been on benzodiazepines for an extended period of time (more than a few weeks) will need to be tapered off them in order to avoid a withdrawal syndrome that could include dangerous elevations in blood pressure, delirium and even seizures.

Benzodiazepines can be abused, and care needs to be taken when a person with bipolar disorder also has problems with substance abuse and dependency. In people who abuse opiates, they should be avoided altogether or used with extreme caution and careful supervision—the combination of benzodiazepines and opiates, such as heroin, methadone, oxycodone (Oxycontin), etc., can be especially lethal.

What are anxiolytics?

Any medication used in the treatment of anxiety can be considered an anxiolytic. Often anxiety symptoms and full-blown anxiety disorders, such as panic disorder, post-traumatic stress disorder, generalized anxiety disorder, and obsessive-compulsive disorder

Figure 24: Commonly Prescribed Benzodiazepines

Compound Name	Trade Name
Alprazolam	Xanax
Chlordiazepoxide	Librium
Clonazepam	Klonopin
Clorazepate	Tranxene
Diazepam	Valium
Flurazepam	Dalmane
Lorazepam	Ativan
Oxazepam	Serax
Quazepam	Doral
Temazepam	Restoril
Triazolam	Halcion

occur along with bipolar disorder, and in those cases it's common to see anxiolytics used. Medications that have anti-anxiety properties include:

- Benzodiazepines
- Antidepressants
- Buspirone (Buspar): This is a medication that binds to specific serotonin receptors in the brain, and is used in a condition called generalized anxiety disorder.
- Hydroxyzine (Vistaril): This is a short-acting antihistamine that can reduce symptoms of anxiety and is often used in an "as needed" or "prn" manner.

What about herbal and nutritional supplements? Are any of those helpful/harmful in treating bipolar disorder?

In psychiatry, as well as in other medical fields, there is an ongoing interest in vitamin- and herb-based remedies. Many practitioners are becoming increasingly well-versed in incorporating non-traditional methods into what is being called complementary and alternative medicines (CAM).

Among the substances receiving ongoing attention in the treatment of bipolar disorder—although no definitive studies have been completed—are the omega-3 fatty acids. Studies looking at these substances have had mixed results—one placebo-controlled study showed benefit, and another did not—further study is required.

Various other compounds that have been looked at for the treatment of mild depression include St. John's Wort (hypericum perforatume), SAMe (S-adenosylmethionine), Rhodiola rosea, and inositol. It's important to remember that any compound that has antidepressant activities can precipitate a mixed or manic episode, and that all substances—natural or man-made—have the potential for drug-to-drug interactions, as well as side effects and adverse reactions.

In general, if you want to explore any of these treatments, it's best to do so in conjunction with a practitioner who is knowledgeable about the research, including specific products, as vitamins, herbs, and nutritional supplements are not under FDA oversight and the standardization (both purity and quantity of a substance) can vary widely between brands.

Chapter 8

OTHER MEDICAL THERAPIES

What is electroconvulsive therapy (ECT)?

Electroconvulsive therapy (ECT) is an important, effective, and potentially life-saving treatment that can be used when someone is in a severely depressed, manic, or mixed episode. While ECT has a somewhat checkered history, largely due to its earlier days when it was not combined with modern anesthesia, it has been extensively studied and shown to be safe and humane. Still, the echoes and stigma of those earlier days and "electroshock" therapy, which could result in bone fractures and broken teeth, persist. When faced with the recommendation of having ECT—especially for the first time—it's quite natural to have a negative, and even fearful, response. Getting up-to-date information will allow you to make an informed choice.

Modern ECT involves using rapid onset anesthesia, which both induces sleep and relaxes the muscles (this prevents injury). After the person is asleep, a measured dose of electricity is delivered through electrodes placed on one or both sides of the head (unipolar vs. bipolar ECT—please note the word bipolar is being used in a different context). The current induces a seizure, which is observed via brain wave activity. (An electroencephalograph (EEG) displays the seizure.) Because muscle relaxants have been used, the body remains still. The seizure lasts for thirty to ninety seconds. The anesthesia wears off and the person wakes up. The entire procedure from start to finish takes about thirty minutes to an hour.

For depressed and manic episodes, several treatments will be required. In the acute phase these are typically given three times a week. Results are often quite dramatic, and the success rate—especially in a psychotic depression—is quite high (80 to 90 percent).

How does ECT work?

The specific mechanism by which ECT exerts its antidepressant and anti-manic benefits is not known. Functional studies looking at the brains of people with depression both before and after ECT show similar results to what is seen when looking at the brains of people with depression before and after treatment with antidepressants.

How do I deal with the stigma attached to ECT?

Few procedures carry the stigma and negative media (*One Flew Over the Cuckoo's Nest,* The *Snake Pit*) that have surrounded ECT. People often feel demoralized when ECT is recommended: "Am I *that* crazy?"

To try and get beyond this negative press it's important to remember that ECT is a medical procedure being used to treat serious and life threatening conditions—most notably depression, severe mania, and catatonic states. This reframe—a medical treatment for medical conditions—is useful especially when dealing with concerns the person considering ECT may have, as well as their family.

Most facilities that perform ECT will have educational materials, which often include a video or DVD that will walk you through the stages of ECT. Some people might also benefit from hearing or reading accounts of others who have had ECT, such as Kitty Dukakis in her recent book with Larry Tye, *Shock: The Healing Power of Electroconvulsive Therapy* (Avery).

When is ECT used in bipolar disorder?

Electroconvulsive therapy has been shown to be highly effective in treating depressed and manic episodes. While some experts argue that because of the strong evidence supporting its efficacy, ECT should be a first-line treatment for psychotic depression (both in bipolar disorder and in unipolar depression) it is usually reserved as a second-line, or third-line treatment, after multiple medication strategies have not worked. Additionally, the availability of ECT varies widely from state to state, and even within states. Strong indications for the use of ECT in bipolar disorder include:

- Severe psychotic depression
- Catatonia
- Severe depression or mania in a pregnant woman (please note the electrical current travels between the electrodes placed on the head and does not make it to the womb and the fetus)

How safe is ECT?

Electroconvulsive therapy (ECT) is a safe procedure that carries the risks associated with receiving general anesthesia. The death rate from ECT is extremely low, at less then two per every one hundred thousand treatments. This risk pales against the substantial risk of death associated with severe depression.

What are the side effects of ECT?

By far the major complaint with ECT is memory loss. Typically people undergoing ECT will lose their memory for events immediately preceding the treatments and for those during the series of ECT treatments. Some people may not remember much—or anything—of the weeks during which they were having multiple treatments. There have been numerous studies reporting that ECT does not cause permanent memory loss. One recent study that looked at people six months after ECT argues against this, demonstrating ongoing problems with memory for things in the past (retrograde amnesia). This supports the experience of many people who have had ECT—often with very good results—who insist they've been left with residual memory difficulties. How the electrodes are placed on the head in ECT (unilateral vs. bilateral placement) show that unilateral may carry less risk of memory loss.

Other common complaints immediately following the treatment include nausea, headache, and muscle aches. These are readily treated with medication, and tend not to be severe. And finally, ECT can trigger a manic episode in someone who is depressed.

What is transcranial magnetic stimulation (TMS)?

TMS or rTMS (repetitive transcranial magnetic stimulation) involves the use of an electromagnet applied to the head—it looks like a helmet—to induce a current in the brain. Unlike electroconvulsive therapy, it does not trigger a seizure—although in high-enough doses it could.

TMS is currently being studied as a treatment for depression, obsessive-compulsive disorder, and migraines. It has also shown some efficacy in decreasing the auditory hallucinations associated with schizophrenia.

There have been case reports that TMS can cause a switch from depression to mania in people with bipolar disorder.

What is vagus nerve stimulation (VNS)?

VNS received FDA approval for the adjunctive (add-on) treatment of resistant depression in 2005; prior to this, its only use was in the treatment of epilepsy. VNS involves the surgical implantation of an electrical device that stimulates the vagus nerve—a complex nerve that originates in the brain, travels down the neck and influences a number of critical functions in the body, including heart rate and sweating to how quickly food passes through our digestive systems.

Implantation of the pocketwatch-sized device in the upper left chest is done under general anesthesia. Once implanted, the device delivers a current at regular intervals. The results of studies looking at VNS were not robust—less than a 30 percent success rate. Still it does offer an option and some hope to people with severe and recurrent depression, where nothing else has worked.

Like other antidepressant treatments, VNS can cause a switch to a manic, mixed, or hypomanic episode. The role of VNS in the treatment of bipolar disorder (especially bipolar depression) has not been well studied.

VNS carries the risks of the surgery and general anesthesia. Other complications that have been reported include damage to the vocal cords and damage to the nerves that control feeling in the lower portion of the face.

How does vagus nerve stimulation work?

While not entirely understood, imaging studies using a positron emission tomography (PET) scanner show changes in blood flow in areas of the brain (the brainstem and limbic system) when VNS is used. These changes are similar to those noted in studies of the effects of antidepressants on the brain. Neurochemical changes observed with VNS involve both serotonin and norepinephrine.

What is light therapy?

Light therapy treatment uses full-spectrum light (like the sun, but not like most light bulbs) in the treatment of seasonal affective disorder. For some people with bipolar disorder, especially those with a strong seasonal component to their mood swings, light therapy may be an effective treatment, or an add-on treatment, to lessen or end a depressive episode.

Special lamps or light boxes are available and the treatment involves daily exposure to a given dose (typically 10,000 lux) of full-spectrum light for a given period of time (between thirty and ninety minutes a day). A lux is a measure of light or illumination, with moonlight equaling 1 lux, an average home between 200–400 lux, and a sunny day between 32,000 and 100,000 lux. Some people find that manipulating the time of day they take their light treatment can also help to regulate sleep. The lamps cost between $150 and $300, and replacement bulbs run around $15.

A common-sense, and cost-effective, approach to light therapy is to get outside on a daily basis and take a walk, or do some other activity, in full sunlight.

Chapter 9

PSYCHOTHERAPIES AND SUPPORTIVE STRATEGIES

- How important is acceptance of the illness?
- What is the recovery model?
- What does the term "evidence-based practices" mean?
- How important is psychotherapy in bipolar disorder?
- Is there a particular psychotherapy that is best for treating bipolar disorder?
- How important is the therapist/patient fit?
- Who is qualified to provide psychotherapy?
- How do I find a good therapist?
- What is psychoeducation?
- What is cognitive-behavioral therapy?
- What is a behavioral chain analysis?
- What is insight-oriented or psychodynamic psychotherapy?
- What is supportive therapy?
- What is interpersonal and social rhythm therapy (IPSRT)?
- What is family focused therapy (FFT)?
- How do I know which type of therapy or treatment is right for me?
- What are assertive community treatment teams (ACTTs)?
- When can case management services be useful?
- How important are self-help or peer-run groups?
- How does someone locate and join a self-help group?

How important is acceptance of the illness?

In bipolar disorder, as well as with many other things in life, until we acknowledge that there is in fact something wrong, there's not much chance of moving forward in an effective way.

Admitting that "I have bipolar disorder" or "My son/daughter/husband/wife has bipolar disorder" is critical if one wants to move forward. Yet for many, coming to a place of acceptance is difficult and, some might argue, impossible. Denial of the illness in both people with bipolar disorder and their families can be hard to overcome. It's what often fuels stopping treatment and entering a revolving door situation of frequent inpatient hospitalizations followed by rapid destabilization once back in the community.

Acceptance of the illness does not mean you have to buy into all of the theory and treatments being offered. As you've noticed in reading this book, there is no perfect treatment for bipolar disorder. What acceptance does is move you out of the quagmire of "This can't be true" and "I can't stand this" or "There's nothing wrong with him/her" to "Okay, I don't like this, but what are my options, how do I move forward?"

It's no coincidence that acceptance of an illness or problem is the first step in many therapeutic programs where change is desired. This includes twelve-step groups, such as AA, and is central to therapeutic techniques such as mindfulness training and cognitive-behavioral therapy.

All of that said, there's another dimension to acceptance of illness, and that is: for many people with bipolar disorder—especially bipolar I—the inability to accept may be more a symptom of the illness (actual brain dysfunction) and less a psychological function, such as denial. As we've discussed earlier, this is anosognosia, and where it exists the notion of acceptance of an illness or disorder will need to be modified in a manner that is meaningful to the individual.

Statements such as "I don't believe I have an illness, but I am able to keep a job and stay out of the hospital when I take these medications," may be the kinds of things that will work.

Finally, insight into the illness and the possibility for acceptance can be influenced by the individual's current mood. Insight is frequently lost or seriously distorted when people are manic, psychotic, or depressed. Yet between mood episodes, insight into the illness can be intact.

What is the recovery model?

The recovery model—or philosophy—has much in common with the harm reduction approach (see Chapter 11). Fueled by dissatisfaction with the status quo and the paternalistic "trust me, I'm a doctor" medical model, the recovery model is about giving control back to the person with the psychiatric disability and/or coexisting substance disorder. In the recovery model, the relationship with doctors, therapists, and paraprofessionals becomes consultative and less authoritarian.

Key principles of the recovery model include:
- It is person centered. This means that it's the person in recovery who sets the goals and the agenda—not the practitioners.
- It is strength-based versus deficit-based. This is quite different from a medical model where the focus is on disease and disability. Here it's looking at what strengths the person brings to the table in working toward his own recovery.
- Peer involvement is critical. Many excellent trainings and courses on the recovery model are run by individuals who have mental illnesses and are themselves in recovery. Numerous agencies around the country now offer recovery-based groups and courses. Some of these are homegrown and some, like the Illness Management and Recovery Program (IMR), which relies heavily

on current research and evidence-based practices and Wellness Recovery Action Planning (WRAP) include well-developed and researched courses with extensive handouts. WRAP materials can be purchased through Mental Health Recovery and WRAP. Their web site is www.mentalhealthrecovery.com

- The IMR materials (resource kits) are available free of charge through SAMHSA's National Mental Health Information Center at:
  - ❑ Substance Abuse and Mental Health Administration (SAMHSA)
    P.O. Box 42557
    Washington, DC 20015   1-800-789-2647
    Monday through Friday,
    8:30 A.M. to 12:00 A.M., EST
    Telecommunication Device for the Deaf (TDD): 866-889-2647
    web page: mentalhealth.samhsa.gov/cmhs/communitysupport/toolkits/illness

Principles of advocacy are encouraged and taught. The person with the mental illness assumes the role of being his own expert. This will extend into useful strategies that might include:

- Self-driven recovery plans
- Drafting of psychiatric advance directives (discussed later in this chapter)
- Learning assertiveness techniques to be direct with providers—and others—in order to get one's needs met. This includes empowering people in the selection of a provider and letting them know it's okay to "interview" a potential doctor or therapist before entering into treatment with them.
- There is an emphasis on hope, and that everyone's process of recovery is highly individual.

- All positive gains are acknowledged.
- People are human and need to be allowed to make mistakes, as this is part of the learning process. Paternalistic strategies to protect the person with mental illness from harm are avoided, and only used when there is a significant risk of imminent danger. Even here, in a recovery model, people may have drafted specific plans (psychiatric advance directives discussed later in this chapter) about their preferences in a behavioral emergency.

As we discuss various therapeutic strategies and techniques, they can all be embedded inside a recovery model. In other words, a person in recovery can use different therapies, medications, resources, and other supports as tools to help them progress. The key distinction is that they are the ones steering their own ship.

What does the term "evidence-based practices" mean?

Evidence-based practices in psychiatry refers to treatment strategies that have been studied and found to be effective in helping people with psychiatric disabilities move forward in recovery. They're sometimes also referred to as "best practices." This is a growing list, but there are a few things to note. First, just because something is found to be effective for some, it may not be helpful for all. Secondly, if a particular therapy is not considered "evidence based" that does not mean it is without benefit, just that it has not been adequately studied and/or received the designation.

Evidence-based practices include:

- Family psychoeducation
- Psychopharmacology (medication management)
- Assertive community treatment teams (ACTT)
- Illness Management and Recovery skills (IMR)

- Supported employment—essentially doing whatever it takes to help someone move forward with her vocational goals. This can include on-the-job coaching and encouraging employment as soon as the individual displays willingness.
- Integrated dual-diagnosis treatment (See Chapter 11)

How important is psychotherapy in bipolar disorder?

Psychotherapy in an ongoing, or as needed, basis is an extremely powerful tool to help people move forward in their lives and their recovery. As it relates to bipolar disorder, there are a number of additional benefits to maintaining a relationship with a therapist or counselor. If someone is recovering from depression, psychotherapy—of varying forms—can speed up recovery. If someone is experiencing early signs of a mood swing or relapse these can be explored in the therapy session and interventions put in place to prevent it from developing further. If someone is struggling with taking his medication, this can become a focus of therapy, and all of the feelings, emotions and beliefs that underlie the complex behaviors involved with taking daily medications can be worked through. Therapy can also help someone deal with the emotional aftermath of a mood episode, especially a manic or mixed one, in which impulsive behaviors may have damaged relationships, personal reputation, employment, or finances, or gotten the person into legal trouble.

Is there a particular psychotherapy that is best for treating bipolar disorder?

To date there are no studies that clearly demonstrate one form of psychotherapy to be superior to another in the treatment of bipolar disorder. Indeed, doing head-to-head studies of psychotherapy in general is quite difficult. Unlike comparing one pill to another or a placebo in a double-blind study, in psychotherapy both people participating in the therapy know what's being provided and received. In this chapter we'll review various therapeutic approaches: cognitive-behavioral, supportive, insight-oriented, family focused therapy (FFT) and interpersonal and social rhythm therapy (IPSRT).

How important is the therapist/patient fit?

As mentioned earlier, the fit between the person with bipolar disorder and his psychiatrist, therapist, and/or other supports is of critical importance. Studies have demonstrated that a positive therapeutic relationship correlates to good clinical outcomes. This just makes sense, because working with people you trust and can confide in and be honest with is the foundation for moving forward in managing any illness.

Who is qualified to provide psychotherapy?

There are a number of different professionals who are trained and licensed to provide psychotherapy. If you have a bipolar spectrum disorder, it's more than likely that the therapist will be different from the psychiatrist or APRN (or some psychologists in the state of New Mexico) prescribing the medications. Therefore, when picking a therapist it will be important that this person has the ability to communicate freely with the prescriber and vice versa.

Medicare identifies specific professions for whom it will reimburse psychotherapy services. These are medical doctors (MDs), doctors of osteopathy (DOs), licensed psychologists (PhDs), licensed clinical social workers (LCSWs), and advanced practice registered nurses (APRNs).

Beyond this, states have the ability to license and provide some oversight of other clinical professionals, such as licensed professional counselors (LPCs) and marriage and family therapists (MFTs).

How do I find a good therapist?

Finding a good therapist can seem daunting, especially if one is in the midst of, or coming out of, a mood episode. As with anything else, referrals and recommendations can be extremely useful. If you already have a prescribing psychiatrist/physician/APRN she will likely have names of therapists she can recommend if she does not provide therapy herself. Many psychiatrists will have formal arrangements with licensed psychologists and social workers, sometimes within the same practice. Many hospital-based or agency-based outpatient clinics will have therapists on staff—this can be convenient and has the added advantage of better communication between members of a treatment team.

Cost and resource will obviously be a factor. Most health plans publish lists of therapists on their provider panels. Still, if at all possible, getting recommendations from family, friends, peers, or professionals you trust will increase the likelihood of finding a good therapist the first time around.

Regardless, it's important to check the therapist's credentials and to pay attention to your own intuition in the first session(s).

- Is this a person you can trust?
- Do you feel that he is listening to what you're saying?
- Is he respectful?
- Does he speak in a manner that makes sense to you?
- Does he know what he's talking about?
- Does he understand bipolar disorder?
- Is he willing to communicate with the rest of your treatment team?
- And, on a very human level, do you like him?

If the answer to any of these questions is "no," it might be best to move on until you find someone that's a better fit.

What is psychoeducation?

This book is a form of psychoeducation, which is the vitally important process of getting the information you need to manage your bipolar disorder, or to understand and support your family member or loved one who has it. There are many excellent sources of information, and they don't have to be dry. There are books, courses, web sites, and organizations that can provide current thinking about all aspects of bipolar disorder. Appendix A includes many sources for information about bipolar disorder and related topics, and in Appendix C I've included chapter-by-chapter sources for much of the information used in this book.

Psychoeducation is also frequently provided in group settings, both on an inpatient and outpatient basis. Some support groups like the National Alliance of Mental Illness (NAMI) also provide psychoeducation courses at no charge, both for people with mental illness and for their families and supports. Another great source of psychoeducation is through local affiliates of Mental Health America (formerly called the National Mental Health Association). Family psychoeducation has been shown to decrease relapse rates and promote recovery in people with mental illness.

What is cognitive-behavioral therapy?

Cognitive-behavioral therapy (CBT) is a well studied and effective treatment for depression, anxiety, and other mental disorders, such as borderline personality disorder. CBT involves the rapid identification of distorted thoughts. We all have these, but in the midst of a mood episode these distortions grow, even to the point of losing the connection to reality. When someone is depressed, everything and everyone can become negative. Thoughts are filled with self-loathing, excessive guilt and catastrophic fears: "I'm never going to get better," "I'm pathetic," and "They'd all be better off without me."

In hypomania and mania the distortions go in the opposite direction: "There's nothing I can't do," "People need to pay attention to me," "I have special gifts and I need to go out and share them with people," "I'm superhuman," and "I'm going to change the world."

In CBT the first step is learning how to identify these rapid thoughts—referred to as automatic thoughts—that can quickly trigger changes in emotion, and subsequently in behavior. A good trick to catch these thoughts is that whenever you notice a change in your emotional state, stop and ask yourself what you were just thinking. With practice, people get quite good at this.

Once the distorted thought is identified, it is then challenged. "Am I really pathetic? Or am I struggling with depression? In fact, I'm working very hard to try and make myself feel better."

CBT has been well-studied and is clearly beneficial for clinical depression. Less is known about its usefulness in hypomania, and it probably has limited utility in mania, where the ability to reason is largely disrupted. As most people with bipolar disorder spend far more time depressed than manic or hypomanic, however, being able to use CBT can be an effective treatment in warding off and decreasing depression and anxiety. CBT can be learned in a relatively short span of time: twelve to fourteen weekly sessions with an experienced therapist. There are also several good self-help books and manuals that can give you the basics—and beyond—of CBT. Because it is a learning-based therapy, the key to success will be regular daily practice. The more you do it, the better you get at it.

What is a behavioral chain analysis?

With CBT and related therapies it's helpful to learn how to map out changes in your mood and to identify problem behaviors, so that you can understand the sequence that caused the painful emotional state or worrisome behavior. One technique for this is chain analysis. It's not hard to do, and with practice you can do it quickly in your head.

Step one: Identify the painful emotion, problem behavior or thought.

Step two: Identify what prompted that thought, emotion or behavior. This is sometimes referred to as the "prompting event." It can be an actual event, or a thought.

Step three: Identify what thoughts and emotional changes occurred between the prompting event and the problem behavior. Take your time and come up with everything you can think of. Think of these like links in a chain.

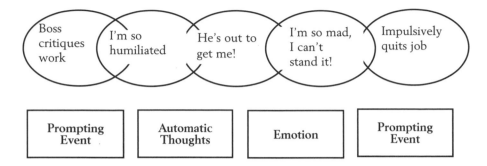

Prompting Event	Automatic Thoughts	Emotion	Prompting Event

Step four: This is where you challenge and test automatic thoughts, and break and rework the chain. Is your boss really out to get you? What are the ramifications of impulsively quitting your job? Was there some validity to the content of the critique? Are you perceiving it in a more-negative manner than was intended? What are your alternatives to quitting?

What is insight-oriented or psychodynamic psychotherapy?

This is a form of therapy that has its roots in psychoanalytic theory. Unlike psychoanalysis, in which the patient meets with the psychoanalyst multiple times a week for a number of years, psychodynamic psychotherapy usually occurs once a week. The therapist in psychodynamic therapy is also more active than the traditional psychoanalyst who sat behind the patient on the couch. This is a talking therapy, where past history and current motivations and actions are discussed and examined.

The relationship between the person and the therapist also becomes grist for the mill. How the person in therapy feels about the therapist (transference) and how the therapist feels about their patient (counter-transference) become useful tools for looking at relationships outside of the therapy.

Unlike cognitive-behavioral therapy that has a here-and-now approach, often with an emphasis on problem solving and behavior-modifying strategies, psychodynamic psychotherapy effects change through bringing unconscious desires and motivations into the light where they can be examined, interpreted, and challenged, if necessary.

While not studied extensively in bipolar disorder—it does have quite a good track record with unipolar depression—it is widely used as an adjunctive treatment, and is what most people think of when seeing a psychologist or other therapist.

What is supportive therapy?

Supportive therapy is a pragmatic approach in which the therapist helps the person she's working with negotiate crises and achieve symptom relief. As with CBT, the focus is on the present and on problem solving through whatever the most pressing issues might be. While a supportive therapy may well incorporate CBT techniques to help someone learn new ways of dealing with a situation or to alter problem behaviors, it takes a more medical approach. Symptoms are viewed as manifestations of the underlying illness. Tracking symptoms, and symptom reduction, is the focus of the therapy.

Supportive therapy incorporates psychoeducation, medications, social interventions (help with housing, family sessions, couples sessions), and behavioral strategies in the pursuit of symptom reduction.

What is interpersonal and social rhythm therapy (IPSRT)?

Interpersonal and social rhythm therapy (IPSRT), developed by Ellen Frank, PhD, and colleagues, takes a two-pronged approach that seeks to manage mood symptoms and resolve interpersonal problems.

IPSRT helps the person regulate and stabilize his daily routines, including his sleep patterns. It teaches the individual about bipolar disorder and works toward diminishing interpersonal conflicts in his life, i.e., marital problems, issues of social isolation when depressed, excessive—and possibly problematic—socialization when manic, and so on. The clinician and the person with bipolar disorder work to regulate both the daily schedule and to examine and diminish interpersonal conflicts. Heightened insight into the relationship between mood episodes and disruptions in both relationships and routine are sought and examined. Attention is paid to the individual's sense of loss for the "healthy self," i.e., the life he might have had were it not for the disruptions caused by his bipolar disorder.

Studies on IPSRT in which medication was also part of the treatment have been shown to increase and stabilize daily routines and to delay the time of a relapse. One study combined IPSRT with family focused therapy (FFT), which appears to be a useful strategy in delaying relapse. Both IPSRT and FFT have published manuals (see Appendix C) that outline the course of therapy.

What is family focused therapy (FFT)?

As the name implies, family focused therapy (FFT) involves bringing the person's family into therapy to work on enhancing communication between family members, diminishing conflict, and improving problem-solving skills.

FFT is an outpatient treatment that is used in combination with medication. It's conducted in twenty-one session spread out over nine months, and the therapy is broken up into specific modules that include: an initial assessment, psychoeducation, communication enhancement, and problem solving.

Studies of FFT have found it to be useful in diminishing rates of relapse and improving rates of adherence to medication regimens. Additionally, families that had been through this therapy were found to have enhanced problem-solving skills and were better able to communicate with one another.

Family focused therapy (FFT), along with IPSRT and CBT, are currently being studied as adjunctive treatment (in addition to medications) in a large multi-center study, the Systematic Treatment Enhancement Program for Bipolar Disorder (STEP-BD) funded by the National Institute of Mental Health. FFT is described in full in the book *Bipolar Disorder: A Family-Focused Treatment Approach* by David J. Miklowitz and Michael J Goldstein.

How do I know which type of therapy or treatment is right for me?

The selection of one type of therapy or treatment over another will have everything to do with personal preference, availability, need, and in some instances, financial ability—what will your insurance cover and what can you afford?

While we've gone through specific types of therapy, it's important to know that many therapists take an eclectic approach in which they combine strategies found in cognitive-behavioral therapy, insight-oriented therapy, motivational therapies (discussed in Chapter 10), supportive psychotherapy, and other techniques. This allows a great degree of flexibility in helping people work through various issues as they arise.

For most people it comes down to finding a good fit and developing a sense of what works for you. A good rule of thumb in evaluating all types of therapy is to ask yourself, "Am I making progress? Are the areas of my life that weren't going well now moving in a positive direction?"

What are assertive community treatment teams (ACTTs)?

ACT teams are multidisciplinary teams (made up of psychiatrists, nurses, social workers, case managers, substance abuse specialists, housing and employment specialists, etc.) that provide wrap-around services in the community for people with severe and persistent mental illnesses. Their goals are to help people stay out of the hospital and to help people build or rebuild lives that are as normal and meaningful as possible. They have been shown to decrease hospitalization rates and are considered one of the evidence-based practices in psychiatry.

For people with bipolar disorder who are having multiple hospitalizations combined with severe social problems, such as homelessness, lack of insurance, inability to pay for medications, and unemployment, an ACT team can be an incredibly powerful support to help get back on track. Services provided by a traditional ACT team include everything from medication management to assisting with housing, insurance, vocational and educational rehabilitation, follow-up with medical care, substance abuse services, and twenty-four-hour crisis service availability. Contacts with an ACT team are frequent, in some instances multiple times a day, especially if supervised medication is one of the services being provided.

ACT teams are not available everywhere and not all of them provide the entire array of services. To see if ACT teams are available in your area, contact your regional community mental health center or mental health authority. (See the state-by-state chart of mental health departments in Appendix B.) The admissions process for ACT teams varies; in some states a self-initiated referral may be acceptable, but more frequently the referral is started by a physician, social worker, or other behavioral health professional. ACT teams are often part of a state's "safety net" for people with severe and persistent psychiatric disabilities. As such, ability to pay may not be included in the equation, and in fact a lack of financial resources may be required.

When can case management services be useful?

Case management, whether as part of an ACT team or as a separate service, can provide a number of important functions, ranging from linkage/connections to other providers to help with finance, housing, shopping, and medications. Case management services typically have a rehabilitative focus with written goals and objectives that the service, and its client, is actively working toward.

Case management services are available through various state and private nonprofit agencies, as well as through some in-home nursing services. Funding for case management varies and may be covered by Medicaid, some insurances, and through some state-funded assistance programs.

How important are self-help and peer-run support groups?

Self-help groups have a long track record of helping people move forward in various aspects of their lives. The twelve-step groups such as Alcoholics Anonymous, AlAnon, etc., are good examples of this. For people with bipolar disorder and their families and friends, getting together with other people who are dealing with many of the same issues you are accomplishes a number of important things:

- Sharing of information
- Networking about available resources in your community
- Receiving emotional support and validation
- Having a safe environment in which you can freely disclose your diagnosis and chat with others about medications, treatments, and anything else that others who do not have bipolar disorder wouldn't understand.
- Maintaining and generating hope by seeing other people at various stages of recovery

The importance of peer-run groups can't be stressed enough. For many people with bipolar disorder, it is the development of a peer-support system that may do far more than any trained psychiatrist or therapist. At times, it's difficult to say exactly why these groups are so important, but more than anything else they keep hope alive. So that someone who has just been through a serious mood episode and is wondering, "Will I ever get my life back" or "Will I ever be able to work again" will have some other person in that room who can say with authority, "Of course you will. I did."

How does someone locate and join a self-help group?

There are both national and local organizations and agencies that will offer support groups and self-help for people with bipolar disorder and their families. Some groups will be specific to bipolar disorder; others will be more inclusive of people with a variety of mental illnesses. Increasingly, the internet has also become a source on online chat rooms and virtual support groups for people with bipolar disorder and their families and loved ones.

The Depression and Bipolar Support Alliance (DBSA) boasts over one thousand support groups nationwide. To locate a group, visit their website at www.dbsalliance.org or contact them at: (800) 826 -3632.

Local groups can also be found through Mental Health America (Formerly the National Mental Health Association. www.nmha.org

The National Alliance on Mental Illness www.nami.org has chapters and groups in all fifty states, Puerto Rico, and the District of Columbia. They have also established chapters on many college campuses. They maintain a list of contacts on their website and they have a toll free information number 1-800-950-NAMI (6264).

In addition to these national organizations many communities—especially urban ones—will have additional peer and family support groups through club houses for people with mental health issues. Many mental health clinics, community hospitals, and religious organizations will also sponsor groups. If your community supports an information line (211), they will likely have information on existing groups, meeting times, locations and contacts.

Chapter 10

RELAPSE PREVENTION STRATEGIES

- What are relapse prevention strategies?
- What are the warning signs for relapse?
- What should be done when warning signs develop?
- What can be done for disturbed sleep?
- How important is managing stress in bipolar disorder?
- What can be done to decrease stress and feelings of being overwhelmed?
- What can be done to limit the damage caused by impulsive behaviors?

What are relapse prevention strategies?

This is a broad approach toward decreasing, and hopefully preventing, recurrences of mood episodes. It's looking at what is known about the science and art of treating bipolar disorder, and adding in what you know about yourself to be true. A relapse prevention plan will likely include:

- Strong relationships and supports; people who will be there for you—and vice versa
    - ❏ Family, friends, coworkers, significant other
    - ❏ Support groups
    - ❏ Faith-based support (church, synagogue, mosque)
- A maintenance regimen of medication(s) that is low on side effects and easily tolerated so it can be taken on a consistent basis
- A good understanding of warning signs of relapse, and strategies to address each one
- A healthy lifestyle that allows for adequate sleep, exercise, nutrition, and down time
- Regulation of daily activities—having a general schedule and sticking to it
- Avoiding alcohol and mind-altering substances (both prescribed and illegal)
- Effective stress management techniques, including learning how to say "no" when asked to do more tasks or projects than is healthy for you, and how to ask for what you want
- Treatment provider(s) who are competent and whom you can trust to take your concerns seriously, and who will be available should you experience side effects, warning signs of a relapse, or a full-blown mood episode

What are the warning signs for relapse?

As with many other conditions, mood swings in bipolar disorder often present with early warning signs. Learning to recognize yours—or your loved one's—can alert you to seek early intervention and hopefully prevent the full-blown episode from developing.

The key here is that everyone is different, although there are some common signs to watch for, including:

- Decreased need for sleep or any changes in sleep pattern (A decrease in sleep might be a warning sign for a manic episode, and increased sleep could be the first sign of a blossoming depression.)
- Changes in appetite
- Increased irritability
- Changes in activity level—either increased or decreased
- Impulsive behavior—increased spending, sexual activity, or gambling (Many with bipolar disorder will also describe impulsively saying things they shouldn't—like telling your boss he's stupid, or your wife that she's fat—as they become hypomanic.)
- Increased spending, especially on things that are too extravagant for your budget
- An increase in alcohol or drug consumption
- Shifting enthusiasms—suddenly deciding to switch jobs, or becoming completely absorbed in some new scheme or project
- Feelings of being overwhelmed or stressed out
- Fear of relapse
- Unfamiliar experiences and situations, especially those that may disrupt your normal daily rhythms

As discussed in Chapter 2, getting a handle on or identifying warning signs of a relapse can be helped through the use of detailed life charts or mood charts, i.e., mapping out the mood swings over the course of your life and making notations of what was going on (various stresses), how you were feeling, sleeping, eating, etc. More importantly, knowing your warning signs can help you make the interventions necessary to prevent a full-blown episode from developing, often through the use of relapse prevention strategies.

What should be done when warning signs develop?

It's a good idea to have predetermined strategies for each warning sign. For some, writing down relapse prevention strategies can be useful, because when a mood episode is brewing it may become more difficult to think clearly.

It's important to communicate any warning signs to your psychiatrist/therapist/treatment team/family/spouse, because the interventions may include changes in medication, an extra visit, therapy sessions, or other recommendations. Similarly if you're involved in a

Figure 25: Mood Chart with Warning Signs

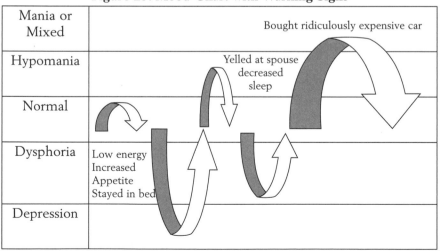

peer support group—and again this is highly recommended—contact with a group member may provide added strategies to rapidly address concerns and symptoms. The following questions in this chapter provide common warning signs of relapse and strategies that can help.

What can be done for disturbed sleep?

Most bipolar experts, including people with bipolar disorder, agree on the importance of maintaining a good sleep-wake cycle. Diminished sleep is often the first sign of an approaching mood episode—typically manic, mixed, or hypomanic. For others, an increased amount of time in bed can be a symptom of an approaching depression. Strategies to improve sleep include:

- An increase in strenuous morning exercise
- Elimination of all non-sleep behaviors from the bed; i.e., don't read, eat, or watch TV in bed, just sleep there
- Avoidance of alcohol, because while alcohol may put you to sleep—or pass out—the quality of sleep is poor, and the overall amount of sleep is diminished
- Avoidance of caffeine—especially after noon; if you think you're shifting to a mania, cut it out all together. If you're on lithium, be aware that this may increase your lithium level.
- Arrangement with your provider to have a sleeping medication when needed
- Establishment of a regular bedtime and wake time
- Making sure your bedroom and bed are comfortable, free from noise, at the right temperature, etc. Some people who are highly sensitive to noise and light find ear plugs and sleep masks to be helpful.
- If you're lying in bed and are unable to sleep for more than half an hour, get out of bed, do something relaxing—watch TV,

listen to music, have a glass of warm milk—and only return to bed when you think you'll be able to fall asleep.

How important is managing stress in bipolar disorder?

Many people with bipolar disorder can trace their first mood episodes back to specific major life stresses, such as loss of a loved one, extensive use of drugs and alcohol while in college, the rigors of military basic training, a breakup with a significant other, etc. Although it's common for the first few mood episodes of bipolar disorder to correlate with specific stresses, this becomes less true over the course of the illness, where mood episodes may occur in the absence of an identifiable stress.

While the literature on the cause-and-effect relationship between bipolar disorder and stress is inconsistent, the experience of most people with bipolar disorder is that indeed their symptoms are worsened in times of greater stress, and that learning to manage day to day stress is a crucial part of any recovery plan.

Another point to make is that stress is neither good nor bad; it's simply a situation or change in routine or environment that somehow disrupts our sense of balance or equilibrium. For example, losing a job could certainly be considered a stress, but so too could be getting a promotion with an increase in salary and responsibilities.

So as we go on to talk about managing stress, it's helpful to stop and think about some of the more common things that can create stress.

- Changes in daily routines—sometimes referred to as "social rhythms"
  - ❏ Inconsistent bedtime and wakening time
    - ■ Work schedules that have rotating shifts

■ A newborn infant with nighttime feedings
❑ Poor diet
   ■ Missing meals
   ■ Extreme diets
   ■ Eating on the run
❑ Drugs and alcohol
❑ Lack of exercise or inadequate amounts of exercise
❑ Lack of regularly scheduled enjoyable activities throughout the course of the day
   ■ Down time
   ■ Reading
   ■ Hobbies
   ■ Inadequate time with friends and family

- Work related-stress
  - ❑ A supervisor with whom you do not get along
  - ❑ Coworkers with whom you do not get along
  - ❑ Employment that is not enjoyable
  - ❑ A work schedule that has either too many or too few hours
  - ❑ Inconsistent work schedules
- Finance-related stress
  - ❑ Debt and fear of debt
  - ❑ Overdue bills
  - ❑ Lack of savings and a rainy day account
- Health concerns
  - ❑ Active medical problems
  - ❑ Worry and concerns regarding diagnoses, medications, and treatments
- Lack of supports
  - ❑ Being socially alone
  - ❑ Lack of friends, family, peer supports, etc.

What can be done to decrease stress and feelings of beings overwhelmed?

Learning to manage stress is important for everyone, and doubly important for people with bipolar disorder. This stands to reason because when feeling good, many people with bipolar disorder can get a lot done, and may find themselves taking on more and more tasks and responsibilities. But should a depression start to develop, all of those daily activities may suddenly feel burdensome and overwhelming.

If possible, it's best to develop, build, and practice your relapse prevention strategies or plan when you're feeling well. The reason is that the more you practice when feeling calm, good, and relaxed the more likely you'll be able to call up and use your skills effectively when things are going less well. Sitting down to play the piano at Carnegie Hall without having ever taken lessons is not a good idea. More than ever, the adage "practice makes perfect" is crucial in the development of relapse prevention strategies that work.

Here is a short list of techniques, mostly cognitive and/or behavioral approaches, that can help. There are many others, as well.

- Identify specific sources of stress—work, home, finance, etc., and map out specific strategies for diminishing the problem. One helpful cognitive technique is to decide what is in your control in the situation and what isn't. As they say in twelve-step groups, "change what you can change and learn to accept and let go of those things not in your control."
  - ❑ For example, if you're working a job that requires you to do rotating shifts, or if you can't stand your supervisor, weigh the pros and cons of staying versus leaving. If the cons come out on top, take active steps to find a less stressful job.

❑ If you know that when manic or hypomanic you can drain your bank account, take real steps to limit your access to credits cards, ATM machines, and online shopping

- Learn how to say "no" when asked to take on additional chores, responsibilities, and tasks. For some people with bipolar disorder, who may run on the hyper side, people around you may be used to you being a ball of energy that gets a ton accomplished. At times this is fine, but when you're feeling stressed, it's important to know how to put the brakes on. To completely misquote Nancy Reagan, when asked to take on a new task or responsibility, "just say no."
- Learn how to effectively ask for what you want, whether it's a day off, an urgent visit with your therapist/psychiatrist, or some favor that might lessen your overall sense of feeling burdened. For people with bipolar disorder who are also parents and/or caregivers, this might be getting someone else to look after the kids or Mom/Dad. This could be just for a bit, or it might involve asking for ongoing assistance and on a regular basis.
- Carve out regular times, at least three to four times a week, for exercise. There is good evidence that demonstrates the positive benefits of moderate to strenuous exercise in combating depression, fatigue, and anxiety. Join a gym, buy a treadmill or elliptical machine, go for daily walks, play tennis, swim, you decide . . . just do it.
- Try yoga, meditation, and mindfulness techniques. On the flip side of strenuous exercise is an equally robust body of evidence that shows the positive benefits of these non-medication methods for decreasing symptoms of depression, anxiety, and stress and promoting an overall sense of health and well-being. If you're someone who needs others around, sign up for a yoga, meditation, or mindfulness class. If you prefer to exercise alone,

buy a couple of tapes or a book on mindfulness such as *Full Catastrophe Living* by Jon Kabat-Zinn or *The Miracle of Mindfulness* by Thich Nhat Hanh. The important thing is to set aside the time for this and do it daily. All of these techniques work, but they must be practiced.

What can be done to limit the damage caused by impulsive behaviors?

Impulsive behaviors, such as out-of-control spending, reckless sexual behavior, and serious missteps at home and at work while hypomanic or manic, can destroy credit, create financial ruin, leave one with a host of sexually transmitted diseases (hepatitis, syphilis, gonorrhea, HIV/AIDS, herpes, etc.), destroy relationships, and ruin careers. People who've gone through one or more manic or hypomanic episodes can typically tell you what their risk behaviors will be; it's often a triad of alcohol/drugs, sex, and spending.

Clearly alcohol and drugs greatly increase the ability to act impulsively. So at the first sign of increased consumption, it's going to be vitally important to get into, or back into, substance abuse treatment. If you've been an AA member in the past and that's fallen by the wayside, start getting to regular meetings. Be honest with your treatment team/therapist and family/spouse about your consumption. This way they'll be able to help you track whether things are calming down or accelerating. If the former, well done! If the latter, it will be important to step up the treatment possibly with either an inpatient or outpatient dual-diagnosis program (see Chapter 10).

Increased and out-of-character sexual behavior is common in mania and hypomania. With drugs and alcohol often clouding the picture, it's easy for people to make serious mistakes in the heat of the moment. Clearly, 'just saying no' may not work, and so, while not foolproof by any means, knowing and sticking to safe-sex practices can be a life saver—latex condoms are a must, and if you use personal lubricant with them, it should be water based. If the manner of sexual activity can be contained to things that are less likely to transmit potentially fatal diseases (such as oral sex versus vaginal or anal) that will also diminish the overall level of risk. Additionally, birth control is strongly advised for women, not just for this reason, but also to protect against early exposure of a fetus to potentially damaging medications.

For spending problems, which can drain bank accounts and max out credit cards, having a good predetermined plan can save someone from years of digging out of a financial mess. With the easy ability to spend fast and furious over the Internet, figuring out a way to prevent that behavior will also need to be addressed. Some people with bipolar disorder who don't want to eliminate their love of shopping have found that limiting their access to credit cards and ATM machines and taking a predetermined amount of cash to flea markets, garage sales, and thrift shops keeps shopping satisfying and fun without leaving them with guilt and debt.

Additionally, if someone does go into a serious mood episode, handling the day-to-day finances can create an additional stress, so thinking through whom you'd like to pay the bills, the mortgage, etc., for you makes good sense. (Getting this in writing can be especially useful.) Strategies that might help include:

- Have low limits on credit cards or no credit cards
- Don't have an ATM card or have someone else take responsibility for it at the first sign of becoming hypomanic
- Arrange direct deposit of paychecks; never get paid in cash
- Give someone the legal authority to pay your bills if you are hospitalized. Additionally, having direct payment of regular monthly bills can ensure that the car payment, electric, phone, and rent and/or mortgage are handled.

Chapter 11

BIPOLAR DISORDER AND SUBSTANCE ABUSE AND CHEMICAL DEPENDENCY

- How common is substance abuse and chemical dependency in people with bipolar disorder?
- What's the difference between substance abuse and substance dependence?
- What is meant by self-medication?
- What is dual diagnosis (DD) treatment?
- What is motivational interviewing and how is it used in dual diagnosis treatment?
- What is the harm reduction model?
- What is the abstinence model?
- What are twelve-step groups?
- How do I locate a twelve-step group that's right for me?
- How serious is withdrawal from drugs and/or alcohol?
- When should I seek an inpatient detoxification program?
- Where do I go to find an inpatient detoxification program?
- When is an inpatient rehabilitation program needed?
- How do I find a program that provides dual diagnosis treatment?
- Does insurance, including Medicare and Medicaid, cover the cost of detoxification and rehabilitation programs?
- What medications are used in the treatment of alcohol abuse and dependence?
- What medications are used to treat alcohol and/or benzodiazepine withdrawal?
- What medications are used in the treatment of opiate abuse and dependence?
- What other medications are used in the treatment of chemical dependencies?

How common is substance abuse and chemical dependency in people with bipolar disorder?

It's estimated that between 50 and 60 percent of people with bipolar disorder will at some point have problems with alcohol and/or drugs. Some studies put this number as high as 75 percent.

While the whys for this connection between bipolar disorder and chemical dependency are not completely understood, there are a number of theories that hold pieces of the puzzle.

First, we go back to genetics. Just as bipolar disorder runs in families, so too can alcohol and substance dependence.

For others, being drawn to alcohol and drugs can be viewed as part of the pleasure-seeking symptom that is often a part of mania and hypomania, just like sex, gambling, and reckless spending.

Finally, there is the very real issue of self-medication, which we'll discuss later in this chapter.

What's the difference between substance abuse and substance dependence?

The simplest way to think about these diagnoses is that substance abuse is the less severe of the two. Both involve the repeated use of mind-altering/mood-altering substances in a manner that causes disruption and harm to a person's life. As abuse progresses to dependence, additional symptoms of tolerance (needing to take more of something to achieve the same "high") and physical and psychological dependence occur. Additionally, as more areas of a person's life become negatively impacted by use (loss of job, loss of important relationships, and legal problems such as receiving a Driving under the Influence Citation DUI/DWI), the diagnosis will shift from abuse to dependence.

Substances of abuse and dependence include alcohol, some over-the-counter drugs, nicotine, and many prescription medications, as well as illegal substances. Some consider all use of illegal drugs as meeting the criteria for substance abuse, as it places the individual at risk for being arrested.

What is meant by self-medication?

Self-medication describes the process in which people with bipolar disorder and other conditions use alcohol and drugs in an attempt to reduce their symptoms. Because bipolar disorder is a mood disorder, it makes intuitive sense that people will turn to mood-altering drugs to try and make themselves feel better.

Common strategies that people with bipolar disorder try include the use of alcohol and sedatives to get to sleep at night, especially when in a hypomanic, manic, or mixed state. Stimulants and cocaine are often sought to try and break a crushing depression. Unfortunately, these strategies that might give some momentary relief tend to worsen things over time. While alcohol might cause someone who is manic to eventually pass out, the sleep will be broken and not restful. (Alcohol diminishes deep sleep and dream (REM) sleep and once awake the person may have even more difficulty falling back to sleep.) The person who uses cocaine or amphetamines to achieve some temporary relief from depression will eventually crash, having depleted important neurotransmitters in the brain, and become even more depressed and possibly paranoid, psychotic, and suicidal.

Other substances frequently used by people with bipolar disorder include marijuana and opiates, such as prescription painkillers, methadone, and heroin. Opiates appear to be especially prevalent in people with bipolar disorder who have histories of significant traumas (physical, sexual, or emotional). The notion of self-medication with these individuals is often described as, "wanting to deaden the pain."

Figure 26: Comparison between Symptoms of Substance Abuse and
Dependence

Symptom	Substance Abuse	Substance Dependence
Duration of at least one year	Yes	Yes
Use interferes with some major aspect(s) of a person's life (job, school, family, friends)	Yes	Yes
Substance use places individual in at-risk situations (driving under the influence, getting into high-risk sexual situations, etc.)	Yes	Yes
Legal problems related to substance use (DUI, breach of peace)	Yes	Yes
Continued use despite relationship problems caused as a result of the substance use (fights with significant other/family, loss of friends)	Yes	Yes
Tolerance has developed	No	Yes
Unsuccessful attempts to cut down or quit	No	Yes
Withdrawal syndrome can occur when the substance is stopped.	No	Yes or no

What is dual diagnosis (DD) treatment?

This model, sometimes referred to as the Drake model for Dartmouth researcher Bob Drake, MD, takes the stance that both the substance abuse/dependence and psychiatric illness need to be treated at the same time and in an integrated fashion. While this makes intuitive sense, it does represent a turnaround in treatment practice. Up until very recently—and there are still many proponents of this approach—it was believed that you had to get one under control before you could start to work on the other issue.

In the dual diagnosis model, the approach to treatment is person-centered and incorporates the concepts of stages of change theory. That is, when someone is trying to change a behavior, they go through typical stages that include:

- Pre-contemplation: "I don't have a problem."
- Contemplation: "This could be a problem."
- Planning: "What can I do about this?"
- Action: "I'm changing my behavior to make the problem go away, or at least be less."
- Consolidation of gains, sometimes referred to as relapse prevention
- Termination—the problem is no longer an issue

In the DD model, having an appreciation for where someone is, related to wanting to change a behavior, guides treatment. It's an attempt to match the person with interventions that are more likely to help. A good example of this might be someone who is currently manic and abusing cocaine and alcohol. They might not think there's any problem whatsoever (a precontemplation stage of change), thus for this person, interventions might include hospitalization, medication, and possibly detoxification. Three months later, this same person might be in a stable mood but struggling with cocaine cravings and occasional relapses with alcohol, despite trying to be abstinent (an action stage of change). Interventions at this point might include an outpatient substance abuse program and twelve-step self-help groups such as Alcoholics Anonymous (AA), Narcotics Anonymous (NA) and/or Cocaine Anonymous (CA).

DD treatment relies heavily on a therapeutic technique called motivational interviewing or motivational enhancement that keys in to the person's stage of change and helps her move forward.

What is motivational interviewing and how is it used in dual diagnosis treatment?

The motivational interviewing technique is an approach to therapy that supports people making positive changes in behaviors that are causing them problems. It's quite different from strategies in which a therapist or other professional would reprimand or even scold someone for continuing to do things that could be harmful: "If you don't stop drinking, you're going to be dead, Mr. Jones." When working with a loved one who is engaged in high-risk behaviors, a motivational approach can help diffuse a lot of the anger and struggle around the behavior. One way to think of this is that we are much more likely to change our behavior if we really want to do so (high motivation). We're less likely to change if someone is telling us we have to. Key components of motivational interviewing include:

- Empathy—letting the person know that you understand their struggle, pain, concerns, etc. This should never appear fake; you need to show genuine concern and understanding.
- Reflective listening—As the person talks, you mirror back to them what they've said, and continue to do so until there's absolute clarity. This form of interviewing involves many questions: "You said you drink to help you get to sleep at night, is that right?" "As I heard it, you like the numbing effects of

painkillers, but don't like the way you have to hide taking them from your wife, is that correct?"

- Heightening internal struggle around a problem behavior— This involves stepping away from directives and nagging, such as: "You must take your medications!" or "Just say no to drugs!" to helping the person find his own reasons for making needed changes. This could include making lists of pros and cons around the problem behavior. In one column could be the euphoric feeling someone gets from an opiate like heroin, and on the other side could be the negative consequences (legal, financial, health marital, etc.) that have come from using.
- Supporting all positive change—Here it's crucial to be a bit of a cheerleader. Every gain needs to be acknowledged. "Well done." "That must have been hard." "I'm so proud of you."
- Avoiding struggle and debate/rolling with resistance—Again, in motivational interviewing you're not telling the person what to do. If someone is talking about how much they like cocaine and how they're not ready to stop, you need to avoid jumping in with statements like, "Don't you know it's going to kill you?" and "Can't you see how it's destroying your life?" Instead, stay the course with empathy, reflective listening, and increasing the internal struggle. A motivational interviewing stance might be, "You just told me how much you love the high of crack, and earlier you were saying how you hated the feeling of crashing after a three-day run, where the last time you ended up in the emergency room saying you wanted to kill yourself. How do you put those two things together?"
- Having no stated agenda—This may be the most difficult part of using a motivational strategy. Of course you want your loved

one, or in the case of a therapist, your patient/client, to stop engaging in the behavior that is causing them so much harm. It's important to try and keep this to yourself and work with the goals that the person has stated. If the issue is drinking and she's saying she's not ready for abstinence, that's where you start. If the behavior is that she stops her medications every time she leaves the hospital and is saying she doesn't want/need to take them, that's where you begin. .

While motivational interviewing is incorporated into the dual diagnosis model, it can be used with good effect in working with people who want, or need, to change a variety of behaviors. It's also being used with good effect in working with people who have serious mental illnesses and lack insight (anosognosia) into their illness.

What is the harm reduction model?

The harm reduction philosophy or model takes the pragmatic stance that people have always engaged in risky behaviors, such as taking drugs and alcohol or refusing necessary treatment, and will probably always continue to do so. Here, the strategy is one of decreasing risk, while acknowledging that one can never fully eliminate it—after all, we're all going to die someday. Some often-cited examples of harm reduction strategies include methadone or buprenorphine programs for people who are dependant on opiates. With these programs, the risks of transmitting deadly viruses such as HIV and hepatitis are significantly diminished as is the risk for accidental overdose with heroin. Seatbelt laws and safety seats for children are also harm reduction strategies, as they increase the chances of surviving an automobile accident. In bipolar disorder, in which substance abuse and issues around taking medications and following treatment recommendations may be problematic, a harm-reduction approach is useful in assessing the overall risk and trying to diminish it.

Key components of a harm reduction approach include:

- Meeting the person where they're at. If you, your loved one, family member, or patient is unwilling to take medication and actively abusing drugs and alcohol, this is where you need to start.
- Radical acceptance and honesty. This goes along with the previous bullet point. It basically means that whatever the reality of a particular situation is, it must be acknowledged before any change can occur. Wishing things were different, or denying what's actually happening, doesn't allow for progress.
- Empathy. For the person with the harmful behavior, this means cutting yourself some slack and not beating yourself up over the issue. If you had a relapse with drugs or alcohol, it's being able to pick yourself up and say, "Today is a new day, and I'm not going to use today." For loved ones and professionals it's about showing your genuine care and concern.
- Being nonjudgmental. This includes respecting the individual's personal beliefs and choices.
- Supporting all positive change. "You cut down; that's tremendous!" "You've decided that the lithium helps you focus better; that's great!"
- Weighing the pros and cons. This is where a person might actually sit down and do an accounting of everything they like and dislike about the behavior in question.

Figure 27

Pros of drinking alcohol	Cons of drinking alcohol
Helps me get to sleep at night	Leaves me hung over in the morning if I drink too much.
Makes me comfortable in social situations	Makes me do embarrassing things that I feel bad about afterwards
Lets me relax after a long day at work	Has made me gain weight
Fills hours where I'd otherwise be bored.	I'm worried about the long term health effects.
	My partner doesn't like my drinking and it strains the relationship
	I spend too much money on alcohol that I could use for other things
	I got a DUI

What is the abstinence model?

Abstinence involves the total elimination of a particular substance, such as alcohol, opiates, or nicotine. As it relates to stage of change theory, someone needs to be in an action stage of change or beyond for an abstinence-based approach to work. If someone does not yet believe he has a problem with drugs or alcohol, he is unlikely to embrace abstinence as a goal.

Examples of abstinence-based programs include Alcoholics, Narcotics, and Cocaine Anonymous (AA, NA, and CA), as well as the cognitively based Rational Recovery (RR) and SMART Recovery. Also, many rehabilitation centers insist on total abstinence in order for a person to be enrolled and to continue in programs. For many people, this is the best way to go. There are limitations to abstinence-based programs, especially when you take into account that many people with substance abuse and dependence issues will have multiple relapses and may not be at a point where abstinence is their goal, even if they acknowledge there is a problem with drugs and/or alcohol.

What are twelve-step groups?

The twelve-step groups began with Alcoholics Anonymous (AA), and the approach has been adopted by many self-help groups (Narcotics Anonymous, Al-Anon, Cocaine Anonymous, Overeaters Anonymous, etc.) and some professionally run ones that are incorporated in treatment programs. In a typical twelve-step group, individuals come together with a shared goal; in the case of AA or NA, the goal is to be clean and sober.

The twelve-step approach involves admitting that there is a problem and giving over one's will to a "higher power," however a person chooses to define that. Groups typically meet on a weekly basis, and some people may choose to attend multiple groups in the course of a week—this can be an especially effective technique early on in someone's recovery from an addiction. Groups take a number of different formats, from a general sharing of experience to a single speaker to a discussion of a particular topic, such as one of the twelve steps, or a particular reading in the group's literature.

Shared experience, fellowship and peer support are key components of twelve-step groups. In addition, people are encouraged to obtain a sponsor—an individual with a significant period of sobriety (usually many years)—to act as a sort of coach or mentor. This relationship can be crucial during periods of high craving, when a phone call to one's sponsor, and maybe meeting for a cup of coffee, may stave off a relapse.

The advantages of twelve-step groups can't be overstressed. They are available in virtually all communities, they're free, and they have a track record of success in helping people achieve and maintain sobriety.

How do I locate a twelve-step group that's right for me?

Depending on the addiction(s) involved, people will typically select twelve-step groups that speak to their particular issue(s). In the case of multiple chemical dependencies, most individuals will use Alcoholics Anonymous (AA) and Narcotics Anonymous (NA). There's no hard and fast rule, but you'll want to find groups in which you feel relatively comfortable. In many areas, especially urban or more populated communities, there will be groups geared toward professionals; women's and men's groups; and groups geared for gay, lesbian, and transgender individuals.

Alcoholics Anonymous groups can be located through their web site: www.alcoholics-anonymous.org .

Narcotics Anonymous groups can be located through their web site: www.na.org

How serious is withdrawal from drugs and/or alcohol?

Withdrawal states run the gamut from uncomfortable to life-threatening. Substances of dependence that carry the highest risk for a dangerous—even deadly—withdrawal syndrome include alcohol and sedatives such as the benzodiazepines (diazepam (Valium), alprazolam (Xanax), oxazepam (Serax), clonazepam (Klonopin) and others). The most severe withdrawal from alcohol and/or benzodiazepines can result in a condition call delirium tremens (DTs). Here, a person's blood pressure and pulse rise dangerously, and she becomes shaky, confused, and delirious—often with hallucinations and disorientation. She is at risk for withdrawal seizures, which can result in aspiration, pneumonia, coma, and death. Medical attention, including a supervised detoxification treatment, may be necessary for a person with alcohol and/or benzodiazepine dependence.

Other withdrawal states include:

- Opiate withdrawal: extremely uncomfortable but not life-threatening. A person will feel physically ill: "dope sick" or "jonesing." Symptoms include nausea and vomiting, diarrhea, cramping, runny nose, goose flesh, diffuse muscle aches, yawning, anxiety, agitation, depression, irritability, and intense craving. It is due to this withdrawal state that opiate dependence (heroin, prescription pain killers, methadone, etc.) can be so difficult to break. People addicted to opiates are thrown into a vicious cycle of constantly needing to find drugs in order to not feel horribly sick.
- Cocaine withdrawal: includes intense depression—even to the point of being suicidal—and exhaustion immediately after heavy usage (crashing). Physical changes are minor, but craving for the drug becomes intense. The craving waxes and wanes over time, and it is common for the craving to be high weeks and even months after last use. This experience of crashing can occur in all types of cocaine use but is especially severe for individuals using smoked (crack) and injected cocaine.
- Cannabis (marijuana, hashish)—feeling down and craving are the major symptoms.
- Nicotine—sadness, anxiety, irritability, and craving.

When should I seek an inpatient detoxification program?

Inpatient detoxification admissions are typically brief—on the order of a few days—and may or may not be followed by a longer inpatient period of rehabilitation. Medically supervised inpatient detoxification would be needed for somebody with severe alcohol or sedative-hypnotic (benzodiazepine, barbiturate) dependence, especially if he has a history of withdrawal seizures, significant changes in blood pressure or pulse, or delirium tremens (DTs). These are also the major conditions for which insurance companies are likely to reimburse.

Opiate detoxification, often with the use of buprenorphine (Suboxone, Subutex) or methadone, may also be done in an inpatient setting, as well as on an outpatient basis.

While the physiological withdrawal from cocaine, including crack, is not life-threatening, many individuals seek an inpatient admission as a means to break the cycle of a severe addiction.

Where do I go to find an inpatient detoxification program?

Finding detoxification programs for drugs and/or alcohol can be done in a number of ways. In areas that have crisis centers or a 211 Infoline, this is a good place to start. If you have commercial insurance, there will likely be facilities that are covered under your plan. If you don't have these in writing, you'll need to call your insurer to see which programs are "in network." Some programs will accept Medicare and Medicaid; others will not. Most states will also have a facility or facilities for people with minimal or no insurance coverage. Crisis centers should be aware of these, and state agencies that oversee mental health and addiction services will have more information about their particular facilities and eligibility requirements (See Appendix B).

When is an inpatient rehabilitation program needed?

Inpatient rehabilitation stays for drugs and alcohol are an option for people who have been unable to achieve their substance use goals on an outpatient basis. Rehab programs typically run from a couple of weeks to several months. The average stay is roughly thirty days. There are even therapeutic communities where a person can stay for a more extended period (a year or more) to increase her chances of maintaining sobriety while reintegrating into the world at large.

For people with bipolar disorder and others with both mental health and substance abuse issues, it's important to select a program that provides dual diagnosis treatment.

How do I find a program that provides dual diagnosis treatment?

Finding a program that accepts individuals who are dually diagnosed and, more importantly, is able to meet their needs, can be a challenge. Additionally, questions about payment need to be addressed up front. Resources that can be helpful when hunting down a program include:

- Infoline. While not available everywhere, this 211 service can be helpful in locating a variety of mental health and substance abuse treatment options.
- The Substance Abuse and Mental Health Services Administration (SAMHSA). This government organization maintains a treatment finder on their website. Basic information about programs in your area—such as what insurance is accepted—is included. http://findtreatment.samhsa.gov
- Crisis centers.
- State and community mental health and substance abuse agencies. (See Appendix B)
- Health plans. Most insurers will maintain lists of programs that are "in network" or are covered. Be aware, though, that these lists are not always kept current, and they might not explicitly state which programs are able to work with people who have both substance and mental health issues. In general, it's best to call the program and ask if they are geared toward people who have both bipolar disorder and substance abuse/dependence issues.

Does insurance, including Medicare and Medicaid, cover the cost of detoxification and rehabilitation programs?

Most insurers, including Medicare and Medicaid, will cover a medically necessary detoxification admission—primarily for alcohol and sedative-hypnotics (benzodiazepines, barbiturates). Some will also cover brief inpatient detoxification admission for opiates. There are few inpatient detoxification programs for cocaine, as the withdrawal is not typically medically hazardous. Most insurers will also not reimburse for inpatient cocaine detoxification treatment.

As for longer inpatient rehabilitation stays, there is a tremendous range of what each private insurance plan will cover. Additionally, many private rehabilitation centers insist on payment up front, although they will assist in helping people submit necessary paperwork to their insurance company.

What medications are used in the treatment of alcohol abuse and dependence?

Medications commonly used for the treatment of alcohol abuse and dependence include:

- Acamprosate (Campral). This is a medication used to decrease craving in people with alcohol dependence and abuse. It can be continued even in the event of a relapse, and is typically taken three times a day. It is begun after the person has stopped drinking.
- Disulfiram (Antabuse). This is a medication for people who are highly motivated to maintain total sobriety. If someone drinks while taking Antabuse, she will become violently ill. It should not be given to people with significant heart conditions. It works by preventing the breakdown of an important metabolite of alcohol. As this substance—acetaldehyde—builds up a

person will become increasingly sick. There are a number of medications with which disulfiram interacts, and it's recommended that people on this medication wear a Medical Alert bracelet.

- Naltrexone (Revia, Vivitrol). This is used to diminish craving and alcohol consumption in people with alcohol dependence. It comes in both pill form (Revia) and a long-acting (once every four weeks) injectible form (Vivitrol).

What medications are used to treat alcohol and/or benzodiazepine withdrawal?

Alcohol or sedative-hypnotic detoxification is most-frequently managed through the use of the same class of medication the person is addicted to. People who are alcohol dependent know that if they start to get the shakes in the morning, a drink or two calms that down. It's the same general principle that guides a medical detoxification. By following vital signs (heart rate, blood pressure, temperature) and other signs and symptoms of withdrawal (tremors, anxiety, agitation, etc) the individual is dosed with a medication—most frequently a benzodiazepine—and then this medication is tapered down over the course of a few days to a few weeks. The choice of benzodiazepine varies from facility to facility and many hospitals and clinics will have specific protocols for when and how to dose. Commonly used drugs include oxazepam (Serax), lorazepam (Ativan), clonazepam (Klonopin), chlordiazepoxide (Librium), and diazepam (Valium).

In addition to the use of benzodiazepines, it's common to treat elevations in blood pressure with antihypertensive medications. Because poor nutrition and specific nutrient deficiencies are associated with more severe withdrawals, multivitamins, thiamine, and folate are part of a standard withdrawal protocol.

While most detoxification programs/facilities are inpatient, less severe cases of alcohol and benzodiazepine withdrawal can be medically managed on an outpatient basis, typically in a partial hospital program (PHP) or intensive outpatient program (IOP). (See Chapter 3 for more information)

What medications are used in the treatment of opiate abuse and dependence?

Opiates, which include heroin, methadone, and many prescription painkillers such as oxycodone (Oxycontin, Percodan, Percocet), propoxyphene (Darvon, Darvocet), and codeine, are substances that create a powerful physiologic dependency that can be difficult, and for some near-impossible, to overcome. The treatment of opiate dependency breaks down into three general approaches:

- Detoxification with opiates
- Detoxification without opiates
- Maintenance therapy with the use of opiates

Medications used for both opiate detoxification and maintenance treatment include:

- Buprenorphine/Naloxone (Suboxone). This combination medication, which can only be prescribed by physicians who have obtained additional training and have received approval by the Drug Enforcement Agency (DEA), is an office-based alternative to methadone maintenance. This pill is taken under the tongue (sublingually) and produces less euphoria while blocking symptoms of opiate withdrawal. Because the buprenorphine component blocks opiate receptors in the brain, if someone tries to use additional opiates on top of this medication, he will not obtain an additional "high." The naloxone (Narcan) component has no effect when taken under the tongue. However, should someone attempt to inject the combination pill, the naloxone kicks in and will push the person into opiate withdrawal. At present, authorized physicians can only prescribe Suboxone for up to one hundred patients (only thirty if they've been prescribing it for less than a year). The clear advantage to this treatment is that an individual, once stabilized on maintenance therapy, does not need to attend a daily clinic, but can have a prescription with regular follow up appointments. One major limitation to this treatment is that individuals on higher doses of opiates (greater than 40–60mg/day of methadone or its equivalent) will experience withdrawal symptoms, and may not be suitable. An excellent source of information on Suboxone is available through the government's Substance Abuse and Mental Health Service Administration (SAMSHA) web page: www.buprenorphine.SAMSHA.gov or by calling 1-866-287-2728.

- Buprenorphine (Subutex). As with buprenorphine/naloxone, buprenorphine provides relief from symptoms of withdrawal and can be used both for detoxification and maintenance treatment. It does not have the naloxone component, and just as with the combination pill Suboxone, can only be prescribed by physicians with specific DEA approval. It is also taken under the tongue. Because it is not combined with the naloxone, there is greater risk for this medication to be abused.
- Methadone (Methadose). Available only in FDA-approved treatment programs. These programs are heavily monitored and daily attendance for dosing is initially required. Individuals who are in these programs for extended periods and who are fully adherent to the rules may eventually take home some of their doses. Methadone programs will include mandatory treatment groups and frequent urine toxicology screens.

What other medications are used in the treatment of chemical dependencies?

Depending on the substance, there are a number of on label (FDA-approved) and off label strategies currently being used, with varying success rates.

- For nicotine dependence (cigarettes in particular), which has a high relapse rate, available medications include nicotine replacement (gum, patches) and medications to try and decrease craving, such as buproprion (Zyban, Wellbutrin) and varenicline (Chantix).

- For the treatment of cocaine dependence and craving, there are currently no FDA-approved medications. However, a number of off label approaches are being studied. Medications that may have some benefit include: topiramate (Topamax), modafinil (Provigil), disulfiram (Antabuse), amantadine (Symmetrel), Baclofen (currently being studied), buproprion (Wellbutrin), and other antidepressants.

Chapter 12

OTHER COMMON COEXISTING PSYCHIATRIC DISORDERS AND TREATMENT STRATEGIES

- How often do anxiety disorders co-occur with bipolar disorder?
- What are panic attacks?
- What is panic disorder?
- What is generalized anxiety disorder (GAD)?
- What is a phobia?
- What is social phobia?
- What is obsessive-compulsive disorder (OCD)?
- What is post-traumatic stress disorder (PTSD)?
- What medications can be used to treat an anxiety disorder in a person with bipolar disorder?
- What therapeutic strategies can help diminish symptoms of co-occurring anxiety disorders?
- How often does borderline personality disorder co-occur with bipolar disorder?
- Is there a connection between borderline personality disorder and bipolar disorder?
- What treatment options are there for people with co-occurring borderline personality disorder?
- How often does attention-deficit hyperactivity disorder (ADHD) co-occur with bipolar disorder?
- What treatment considerations need to be taken into account with co-occurring attention-deficit hyperactivity disorder (ADHD) and bipolar disorder?

How often do anxiety disorders co-occur with bipolar disorder?

Anxiety disorders cover a range of conditions in which the major symptoms are nervousness, intense fear, being easily startled, having panic attacks, avoiding feared situations, and, for some, having intrusive thoughts and compulsive behaviors. The severity of the anxiety disorders can range from mildly annoying to so severe that a person becomes a prisoner to paralyzing fears, no longer leaving the home and sometimes trapped in compulsive rituals for most hours of the day.

Anxiety disorders commonly co-occur with bipolar disorder. Multiple studies have found that over 50 percent of people with bipolar disorder will meet criteria for one anxiety disorder and over 30 percent will have multiple disorders. Panic disorder is the most frequently co-occurring, at around 20 percent, followed by generalized anxiety disorder (GAD), social phobia, obsessive-compulsive disorder, and post-traumatic stress disorder (PTSD).

The presence of anxiety disorders is associated with higher rates of suicide, substance abuse, social impairment, and diminished quality of life. Targeting symptoms of co-occurring anxiety, through therapeutic and pharmacological strategies, is both important and challenging.

What are panic attacks?

A significant number of people with bipolar disorder will also experience panic attacks. These can occur in a number of the anxiety disorders and involve the rapid development of severe anxiety. The symptoms of panic attacks can be broken down along three lines: physical, emotional, and cognitive (thoughts). Physical symptoms may include palpitations, increased pulse rate, shortness of breath, tingling in the fingers and toes, light-headedness, and nausea. Emotional symptoms include intense and overwhelming fear and anxiety. The cognitive symptoms include thoughts of impending doom, that something terrible is about to happen, that the person is about to lose control, or that they are having a catastrophic medical event—such as a heart attack—and are going to die. It's common for people with panic attacks, thinking that something is medically wrong, to seek treatment in an emergency room.

The onset of symptoms occurs over a few minutes, and unless the attack is re-triggered, lasts from ten to fifteen minutes.

Panic attacks can be brought on by specific feared events, such as going outside the home, having to get up and speak in public, or having to cross a bridge. They can also occur without a specific cue, and it's often this fear, of not knowing when an attack is coming, that can lead someone to develop a fear of leaving the house, also referred to as agoraphobia.

In terms of diagnoses, under the current DSM-IV system, panic attacks can occur in a number of disorders, including panic disorder with and without agoraphobia, obsessive-compulsive disorder, post-traumatic stress disorder, and various phobias.

What is panic disorder?

Panic disorder is a condition in which someone experiences multiple panic attacks in the course of a week. In some cases this progresses to multiple attacks on a daily basis. Panic disorder can occur with a related condition called agoraphobia (fear of leaving the home). Some people with panic disorder can become so immobilized by anxiety and fear of having attacks in a public place that they will stop leaving the home entirely. The diagnosis of panic disorder will be used if the person does not also meet criteria for one of the other anxiety disorders, such OCD or PTSD. If a person has bipolar disorder and also meets the criteria for panic disorder she will be given both diagnoses.

What is generalized anxiety disorder (GAD)?

This condition is characterized by diffuse and constant worry and anxiety. It's often accompanied with vague physical complaints, frequent headaches, neck, back and muscle aches and an unsettled stomach. It is common in the general public and can co-occur with bipolar disorder.

What is a phobia?

Phobias, which can occur with bipolar disorder, are intense fears that are out of proportion to a given situation. When faced with the feared situation (public speaking, heights, leaving the house, needles, spiders, snakes, etc.) the person's anxiety rapidly spikes and can escalate into a panic attack.

What is social phobia?

Social phobia centers on an intense fear of being in public places and social situations, such as cafeterias, classrooms, parties, etc. People with social phobia may have specific areas that are more problematic for them, such as public speaking, in which they become frightened that they will embarrass or otherwise humiliate themselves. Unlike the general pre-performance anxiety that is normal—and probably healthy—people with social phobia can become paralyzed by their fears and turn their worst nightmare—public humiliation—into a reality. People with social phobia may experience panic attacks triggered by specific situations, or triggered by even thinking about, or anticipating, these same social settings.

What is obsessive-compulsive disorder (OCD)?

OCD involves intrusive and repetitive thoughts (obsessions) typically accompanied by behaviors such as checking and counting that need to be performed, often many times (compulsions) in order to get the anxiety and uneasiness to diminish. Typical obsessive themes/thoughts can center on cleanliness, fear of contamination, and an intense need for order, where everything must be arranged just so. Compulsive behaviors include frequent hand washing/bathing/showering, counting, and arranging. When the compulsive behavior is interrupted, anxiety spikes. Panic attacks and depression are common in OCD. The severity of OCD can range from minimal daily symptoms, such as checking the stove a few times to ensure that it's off, to a point where most hours of the waking day are spent in an unending cycle of obsessive thoughts and compulsive behaviors.

As with the other anxiety disorders, OCD can co-occur with bipolar disorder, and if criteria are present for both, the two diagnoses are used.

What is post-traumatic stress disorder (PTSD)?

PTSD affects individuals who have either directly experienced traumatic events—rape, combat, assaults, child abuse—or have witnessed them, and subsequently go on to manifest a number of symptoms. Elevated rates of PTSD exist in people with bipolar disorder, with women being at a higher risk then men.

The trauma may have been a single event or a series of things that occurred over a span of time, such as frequently happens with children in abusive households, prisoners of war, soldiers, and civilians in times of war.

So too do many people with bipolar disorder have experiences as a result of their illness that can be traumatizing, such as involuntary hospitalization on a locked ward, relapse, or being restrained by police, ambulance, or hospital personnel when in an agitated and manic state.

The onset of PTSD symptoms can occur immediately after the event or can be activated at some time in the future. Symptoms of PTSD can include generalized anxiety, depression, irritability, panic attacks, suicidal thought and behavior, hyper vigilance, an exaggerated startle response, insomnia, intense nightmares, and flashbacks of the traumatic event. Individuals with PTSD may also develop avoidant symptoms for things, people, etc. they relate to the traumatic event(s). Some people with PTSD describe symptoms of becoming emotionally numb and feeling as though they are not really present.

Treatment for people with both bipolar disorder and PTSD will likely involve both medication(s) and therapies targeted for symptoms of both conditions. Cognitive-behavioral therapy (see Chapter 9), which is considered a first-line treatment for PTSD, may be especially useful, although it has not been specifically studied in individuals with both PTSD and bipolar disorder.

What medications can treat an anxiety disorder in a person with bipolar disorder?

When anxiety symptoms, or full-fledged disorders, co-exist with bipolar disorder, there are a number of pharmacological and non-medication approaches that can be tried.

The challenge in bipolar disorder is that the mainstay of drug treatment for OCD and panic disorder is antidepressants—often in higher doses than one usually uses in depression. The difficulty is that this may trigger a manic or mixed episode. If someone is already struggling with symptoms of anxiety and/or panic attacks, this is moving things in the wrong direction.

There's tremendous variability here, and what people will often say is that while antidepressant A made them "go crazy," antidepressant B seemed to help and didn't cause those same feelings.

If antidepressants are used to target panic and OCD, the first line treatment will be with an SSRI. Of all the antidepressants these are also the ones that seem to be associated with a lower rate of triggering manic, hypomanic, and mixed episodes—especially when combined with a mood stabilizer.

Another group of medications that has a role in the treatment of anxiety disorders are the benzodiazepines (clonazepam (Klonopin), lorazepam (Ativan), etc.—see Chapter 4). The downside here is that when used on an ongoing basis these are habit forming and can be difficult to manage in someone with a history of substance abuse. That said, the near-immediate relief people receive from these agents can't be discounted.

Buspirone (Buspar) has an FDA indication for the treatment of generalized anxiety disorder—although clinical response with this medication is not robust.

Finally, many medications are being evaluated in an off label way for their usefulness in the anxiety disorders. Included in this group are mood stabilizers and the atypical antipsychotics, which are already widely prescribed in bipolar disorder.

What therapeutic strategies can help diminish symptoms of co-occurring anxiety disorders?

In Chapter 9 we looked at various therapeutic strategies to enhance the treatment of bipolar disorder. For people who have co-occurring anxiety problems many of the same techniques, with some adaptation, have been shown to be quite effective. The best studied is cognitive-behavioral therapy (CBT), which helps people learn to identify distorted thoughts, challenge them, and change them. With practice, this becomes an extremely helpful technique that gives people a greater sense of control. While CBT focuses on the present—the here and now—over time, and with practice, CBT can help people work backwards in their lives to where they can examine how their thought distortions may have come to exist.

For someone with panic attacks CBT might involve identifying the triggering thoughts for the panic attack. For example: "If I have to get up to speak I'm going to die." Then the person would quickly challenge, "Are you really going to die? You've gotten up to speak before and you're still breathing." And finally they would reframe the thought: "While public speaking clearly makes you anxious, some of that is normal nerves. You know the material you're supposed to present and if you just focus on that it's going to be fine."

Alternatively, if someone is already in the midst of a panic attack, CBT can help get her through and make it less severe. Here, the catastrophic thoughts that typically accompany the panic attack are identified, challenged, and reframed. "Oh my God, I'm having a heart attack! I need to go to the emergency room." The challenge and reframe might be, "No, you've had a full cardiac workup from the twelve other times you went to the emergency room; this is a panic attack and if you can get yourself to calm down the adrenalin rushing through your system will get broken down by your body in just a few minutes. Then the palpitations will stop." You could even add in additional behavioral techniques such as distraction or a grounding exercise—"Why don't you watch TV (listen to music, bake something, go for a walk, play with the cat, do some house cleaning, try to feel your feet on the floor)?" to further diminish the severity of the attack.

With obsessive-compulsive disorder and with phobias, an often-used technique is something called graded exposure and reciprocal inhibition (response prevention). This is typically done with a therapist over a series of weekly sessions and it involves identifying the feared thing/event and gently and consistently confronting it. At first this might involve just thinking about the thing (germs, spiders, heights, public speaking, or the need to count things or check the stove repeatedly) and eventually introducing the real thing. After the person confronts his fear, he is then instructed in techniques to either lower his anxiety or just sit with the anxiety, and in the case of OCD, not engage in compulsive behavior (hand-washing, counting, checking rituals, etc). In time the fear diminishes and the anxiety is reduced. In order for this technique to work, practice on a daily basis is important.

A related technique that no one seems to like but which is mentioned throughout the literature is a process called flooding. Here, instead of gradually introducing the fear, one is made to come face to face with it, and to sit with the anxiety that is generated. The similar principle applies; over time the reality that the person is in fact not being hurt by the thing she's afraid of diminishes the anxiety. This can be traumatic, however, and while the literature may support its efficacy, getting people to come back for a second session can be difficult.

How often does borderline personality disorder co-occur with bipolar disorder?

Bipolar disorder and borderline personality disorder—a condition characterized by extreme emotional instability (see question on personality disorders in Chapter 2)—probably co-occur in around 10 percent of individuals with bipolar disorder. As the bipolar spectrum has been expanded, this number has become hard to pin down, because the symptoms of rapid cycling bipolar, cyclothymia, and borderline personality disorder can look similar, as they all include rapid and often dramatic changes in mood states.

Is there a connection between borderline personality disorder and bipolar disorder?

Not surprisingly, this has been a hot question among researchers and others, as both borderline personality disorder and bipolar disorder are characterized by extreme shifts in mood. In the case of borderline personality disorder, the shifts happen rapidly, and often in response to real or perceived insults, rejection/abandonment, and frustrations. This is somewhat different from the experience of switching in bipolar disorder, in which there is more of a kindling phenomenon in which symptoms build over a period of time, and may include substantial disturbances in sleep, changes in energy, changes in behavior and thought, and so forth.

The discussion around a connection between the two conditions is further fueled by the expanding theory of a bipolar spectrum. Looking at the variants of bipolar II and rapid and ultra-rapid cycling, it makes sense that people would look at the mercurial mood changes and unstable emotions of borderline personality disorder and wonder if the two conditions might exist along a single spectrum or have some other connection. What is emerging is that for individuals with both conditions it appears that both environmental and genetic factors are at play. Many people with borderline personality disorder, which affects a greater number of women then men, have experienced significant trauma in their lives. The clinical picture of a person with both bipolar disorder and borderline personality disorder is of someone who is bouncing from crisis to crisis. Every element of his life—social, occupational, financial—is in chaos, and the person's subjective experience of the world is like a sort of living hell.

What treatment options are there for people with co-occurring borderline personality disorder?

While there are many treatment models for borderline personality disorder, the best studied treatment is a highly intensive form of cognitive-behavioral therapy (CBT) called dialectical behavior therapy (DBT). Developed by Marsha Linehan, PhD, this therapy, which has as its stated goal "getting a life worth living," has five key components:

- Weekly individual therapy that is structured around a hierarchy of symptoms in the following order:
  - ❑ Suicidal and parasuicidal (self injurious behavior such as cutting and burning) behaviors
  - ❑ Therapy-interfering behaviors (such as frequent cancellations of appointments on the part of both the patient and the therapist)
  - ❑ Quality-of-life-interfering behaviors (such as reckless spending, drugs and alcohol, eating disorder behaviors, sexual promiscuity, etc.).
- Weekly skills training groups, which are typically two and a half hours long, focus on teaching participants a broad range of cognitive and behavioral techniques to manage and regulate their emotions, to improve their interpersonal effectiveness (relationships), to stay present and mindful, and to make it through various crises without making the situation worse.
- Therapists who do DBT meet weekly in a consultation group to ensure that they are sticking to the model and to provide "therapy for the therapist."

- In the DBT model, phone consultation to the client means that the person can call her therapist for coaching. Hours must be agreed upon, as maintaining a positive and real relationship with the therapist is critically important.
- Accessory services as needed, typically including psychopharmacology (medications) and whatever organizational interventions might need to be made to maintain the structure and intensity of the therapy.

DBT has been studied extensively in individuals with borderline personality disorder, and there are case series to report its benefit in people with bipolar disorder who have co-occurring borderline personality disorder; other studies are ongoing.

How often does attention-deficit hyperactivity disorder (ADHD) co-occur with bipolar disorder?

In recent years it's been determined that ADHD does not always end with childhood and adolescence, but that many adults continue to exhibit symptoms. In childhood, ADHD is the most common co-occurring psychiatric disorder with bipolar disorder (60 percent or more of pre-pubertal children with bipolar disorder have ADHD, as well as greater than 30 percent of adolescents with bipolar disorder).

In adults, it's estimated that roughly 10 percent of people with bipolar disorder will have co-occurring ADHD.

What treatment considerations need to be taken into account with co-occurring attention-deficit hyperactivity disorder (ADHD) and bipolar disorder?

Adults with both bipolar disorder and ADHD are more likely to have had an early onset. There is a high percentage of substance abuse in this group, and being able to clearly identify mood states is difficult.

Pharmacological regimens can become complicated and there are few controlled studies in this complex group to guide the practitioner.

Chapter 13

AGE, GENDER, AND CULTURAL ISSUES

- What kind of symptoms will a child with bipolar disorder have?
- How do you differentiate between bipolar disorder and attention deficit hyperactivity disorder?
- How can you tell the difference between bipolar disorder and Asperger's disorder or other developmental disorders, such as autism?
- Who can make the diagnosis of bipolar disorder in children and adolescents?
- How important is family input in getting a diagnosis of bipolar disorder in a child?
- How do you minimize disruptions in education when your child has bipolar disorder?
- What planning can be done for a young adult with bipolar disorder going off to college?
- What can you do if you, or your child, develops bipolar disorder while at college?
- When should my son/daughter return to college?
- What happens if someone develops bipolar disorder in the military?
- What happens if someone is discharged from the military because of bipolar disorder?
- Are there gender differences in the manifestations of bipolar disorder?
- What is known about a woman's menstrual cycle and her bipolar symptoms?
- What does a woman need to know about birth control if she has bipolar disorder and is on medication?
- I have bipolar; should I get pregnant?
- Can a woman with bipolar disorder take medications when she is pregnant?
- How does someone manage medications for bipolar disorder while pregnant?
- If I decide to go off medications prior to conceiving, how should I do this and when should I start them again?
- Are there connections between post-partum depression, post-partum psychosis, and bipolar disorder?
- Can women with bipolar disorder breast-feed if they are taking medication?
- Are there special considerations for people who are gay, lesbian, bisexual, or transgender who have bipolar disorder?
- Does bipolar disorder improve or get worse as someone ages?
- Can people over the age of sixty develop bipolar disorder for the first time?
- Is the treatment of bipolar disorder different in older people?
- Is there a cultural bias in the diagnosis and treatment of bipolar disorder?
- Should someone find a practitioner of his own cultural/racial group?
- What other cultural factors might impact the treatment of bipolar disorder?

What kind of symptoms will a child with bipolar disorder have?

Children and adolescents will have symptoms that are somewhat different from the adult forms of bipolar disorder. Mood swings, such as mania and depression, will typically not meet the DSM-IV duration criteria (days to weeks). More typically, mood symptoms are intense and rapid, often lasting minutes to hours, with several occurring over the course of the day.

Other symptoms of mania, mixed, depressed, and hypomanic states seen in the adult forms of bipolar disorder will be present, but need to be evaluated in terms of the child or adolescent's developmental stage—that is, some symptoms look different in the childhood forms of bipolar disorder. Symptoms include:

- Irritability—This can manifest as intense rages and tantrums, often triggered by seemingly trivial frustrations.
- Grandiosity—This might take the form of out-of-proportion role play: the difference between throwing on a cape and saying "I'm Superman" and running around the back yard vs. throwing on a cape, saying "I'm Superman," and jumping off a two-story roof with the belief that you can actually fly.
- Euphoria—an over-the-top feeling of well being
- Diminished sleep, but not feeling tired
- Rapid, or pressured, speech
- Racing thoughts
- Distractibility
- Increase in goal-directed activities—Staying up all night and writing a book, or deciding to put on a play and then running around the neighborhood to collect money for tickets, while simultaneously bullying playmates into long rehearsals.
- Excessive involvement in pleasurable or risky activities—This can even include sexually provocative behavior in very young

children. A prepubertal boy asking women—often strangers—for kisses, or wanting to feel their breasts. Older children and teens may become sexually promiscuous.

- Psychotic symptoms—These must be differentiated from the normal make-believe of childhood. It's more than having an imaginary friend, and can assume bizarre proportions, including hearing voices and seeing visions.
- Suicidal thinking and behaviors

One insightful literary description of bipolar disorder in children can be found in the early chapters of Danielle Steele's excellent biography of her son who had bipolar disorder, *His Bright Light: The Story of Nick Traina.*

How can you tell the difference between bipolar disorder and attention deficit hyperactivity disorder?

As seen in the previous question, many of the symptoms of bipolar disorder will overlap with those of attention deficit hyperactivity disorder (ADHD), most notably the irritability, impulsivity, and distractibility. The major symptoms used to try and differentiate childhood bipolar disorder from ADHD are the presence of multiple distinct mood episodes (depression, mania, hypomania, and mixed), psychosis, grandiosity (inflated sense of self esteem), diminished sleep, and an increase in goal-directed activities. Bottom line—making the distinction between ADHD and bipolar disorder is difficult, but sometimes the diagnosis becomes clearer as the child gets older. This could be the case in an eight-year-old who is hyper and has difficulty paying attention but by age eleven has progressed to having distinct and extreme changes in mood. In other cases, a good response to particular medications (such as stimulants frequently used in ADHD or a mood stabilizer) may steer the diagnosis. And for some, there may be enough evidence that both diagnoses are appropriate.

How can you tell the difference between bipolar disorder and Asperger's disorder or other developmental disorders, such as autism?

There is overlap between the symptoms of bipolar disorder and those seen in Asperger's (sometimes referred to as autism without retardation) and autism. In all of these disorders, irritability, oppositional behavior, rages, and tantrums can be present. With bipolar disorder, however, the predominant problem is with moods and mood swings, which are excessive. In Asperger's and autism the core deficits are in the ability to socially interact with others—this is not the case with bipolar disorder.

Who can make the diagnosis of bipolar disorder in children and adolescents?

Making an accurate diagnosis of bipolar disorder in a child or teen is difficult, but can be important so that disruptions to development are kept to a minimum. Often parents have the clear sense that something is wrong with their child, but are not able to find a professional who can give them the answers and the direction they need. One recommendation is to locate a board-certified child and adolescent psychiatrist, or a licensed child psychologist, particularly one with expertise in the diagnosis and treatment of bipolar disorder.

Child and adolescent psychiatrists are physicians (MDs or DOs) who've attended four years of medical school and three years of additional general medical and psychiatric training (internship and residency), followed by two years of a fellowship in child and adolescent psychiatry. To become board-certified they must pass rigorous tests in both adult and child-and-adolescent psychiatry.

Admittedly, finding a board-certified child and adolescent psychiatrist can be a challenge. In addition to your insurance company's provider list, sources of referral might include:

- The American Academy of Child and Adolescent Psychiatry (AACAP). Their website includes a lot of useful information for parents, as well as a "Child and Adolescent Psychiatrist Finder." www.aacap.org
- An evaluation clinic at a medical school that has a child-and-adolescent psychiatry training program. A list of programs (over one hundred nationwide) is available via the following link to the AACAP website: www.acgme.org/adspublic/. The advantage to this approach is that your child will receive an extensive evaluation that will be overseen by one—or more—of the medical school's faculty members. The down side is that some clinics only offer evaluation, while others will provide both evaluation and ongoing treatment. The ones that provide only evaluation, however, will typically assist with referrals.
- The Child and Adolescent Bipolar Foundation. This web-based not-for-profit parent-to-parent organization run by parents of children diagnosed with bipolar disorder includes, as a public service, a state-by-state search engine for child and adolescent specialists. Their web site is: www.bpkids.org

How important is family input in getting a diagnosis of bipolar disorder in a child?

Evaluating a child for bipolar disorder may occur over multiple sessions. Family involvement is critical and all additional information from school, medical doctors, etc. will assist in arriving at the appropriate diagnosis. The professional(s) doing the workup will need to know how the child is doing in all spheres of his life. Are problems occurring only in the home, or are the mood swings, tantrums, etc. happening in all arenas? The more information you're able to provide, including reports cards, prior evaluations, and psychological testing that may have been done in the school, the greater the chances of getting an accurate diagnosis in a timely fashion.

How do you minimize disruptions in education when your child has bipolar disorder?

Depending on the severity of symptoms a child experiences, he or she may require a variety of accommodations and/or interventions in the school setting, as well as in the home. Funding and eligibility for various services may depend on whether or not a child is in special education and covered under the Individuals with Disabilities Education Act (IDEA), although the majority of schools will make some level of mental health services available to all students.

Interventions to minimize educational disruption might include:

- Mental health services delivered within the school setting (school psychologist, counselor, social workers, nurses, aides)
- School-funded services, in which the school system hires professional staff to provide mental health services
- Administration of medication by the school nurse
- Tutors
- Integrated educational plans that include recommendations from outside behavioral health providers, parents, and the child, as well as from within the school
- Classroom accommodations with tailored assignments, activities, etc.

What planning can be done for a young adult with bipolar disorder going off to college?

Going away to college represents an important transition for many adolescents. It's a time of increased freedom and responsibility. For some, it will be their first prolonged stay away from home. The challenges faced by all students can be even more daunting for someone with bipolar disorder—easy access to drugs and alcohol, all-night cram sessions, sexual experimentation, academic rigor and competition, etc. This is then complicated with issues of whether or not to disclose their bipolar disorder to friends, classmates, or professors. In places where most freshmen are placed in communal dormitory living situations, someone who is on medication will need to decide how to explain—or not explain—their daily drug regimen.

In recent years, colleges and universities around the country have experienced an increase in the number of students who are being admitted having already been diagnosed with serious mental illnesses. Some common-sense planning can go a long way toward increasing the individual's chances for academic and social success while at college.

- Make contact with the college's counseling service to see what they provide for the students. If their resources are adequate, go ahead and make certain that an intake appointment is scheduled for early in the academic year. It will be helpful to have releases of information already signed so that the person's existing psychiatrist/therapist can communicate freely with the new provider.
- If the university/college counseling center is not a good fit, get referrals and locate a provider in the area. While for some staying with a trusted therapist back home is an option they might want to use, it's important to also have a local contact in case of emergency.
- For those who find support groups to be helpful, many universities and colleges have NAMI and/or Active Minds

chapters (a student-run organization that provides advocacy and education) on campus.

- Talk to the student affairs office and their disability coordinator to assist with accommodations if needed.

What can you do if you, or your child, develops bipolar disorder while at college?

Because bipolar disorder so often first manifests in the late teens and twenties, it's common for a first major mood episode to occur while at college. Many have speculated that the added stresses and freedoms of college—easy access to drugs and alcohol, late hours, changes in diet, academic demands, etc.—may precipitate a first episode in a vulnerable person.

As with any first episode, it can be a scary and confusing time. Depending on the nature of the episode—depressed, manic, or mixed—the interventions will vary. Ultimately, what's needed is quick access to treatment; an accurate diagnosis, and a strategy that can help get the person feeling better and stable.

There are a few broad issues to be addressed here. For parents, if their child is now eighteen or older, the rules have changed. This can be frustrating and scary when you're listening on the phone to your son or daughter, who is clearly manic, refusing treatment and enraged that you even mentioned there is something wrong with them.

Necessary strategies may include contacting the university's counseling or mental health clinic. If you're concerned that things have reached an emergent level—your son or daughter is manic, suicidal, or psychotic—you'll need to contact the emergency services (typically 911) in the town or city where your child is in school. It's at this point that many parents will pack a bag, book a flight, or get in their car to see first-hand what is happening with their adult child, and to be there for him.

If hospitalization seems likely—or necessary—it's a good idea to have someone advocate for your son or daughter. Attempt to have your child sign releases for all providers, but even if they don't or won't, you are able to talk with various doctors and counselors without written permission, if you have information to give them. They, being bound by the rules of confidentiality, cannot divulge information. This can be a frustrating form of communication, but at least you are able to give you child's treators important information. Maintaining contact with the treatment team also lets them know that you are concerned and involved. As your child's condition improves, he or she will be more likely to sign a release and you will be able to communicate in more of a give-and-take fashion.

Emotions of all involved will be running high, and it's easy to give in to catastrophic thinking: "My son will never finish college," "He's going to lose his scholarship," "He's going to kill himself." People with bipolar disorder and their parents will experience a mixture of strong emotions: loss, anger, and fear. Denial of the illness is frequently seen, not just with the person who has bipolar disorder, but with her parents as well: "This can't be happening," "It's just the drugs she was doing," etc. These responses are natural and normal and it's critically important to get beyond them—especially the denial.

When should my son/daughter return to college?

There is no doubt that success in higher education goes along with future success in many areas of life. Studies have shown that people with mental illnesses who have also received higher education do better than those who haven't. So once the emergency has passed, it's time to take a sober and realistic look at what is reasonable for the next few months. This will depend on the individual's preferences, how he's doing emotionally and physically, and what can be negotiated with the school. If someone is in the middle of the semester, it's important to work with the counseling or mental health clinic to make whatever arrangements are necessary to avoid failing grades, and to either have courses changed to incompletes, which can be completed at a later time, or to withdraw altogether. Typically this involves working with a dean.

One of the biggest decisions is whether to remain at school or to return home for a period of time and recuperate. This too can be negotiated with the dean, often with input from the university's counseling or mental health clinic.

It's important to remember that there's no one right answer here and that a person's educational goals are to be taken seriously. An individual who went off to a large high-powered university and had a first episode might decide that the intensity, constant stimulation, and stress were too much. It might be that transferring to a smaller college or program could be a better fit. Someone else may decide that at least for the time, it's better to stay home with the parents and attend a local community college. There's also a lot to be said for easing back into the academic cycle. If someone is still dealing with residual symptoms of depression, a full course-load may be too much, but one or two classes could provide added daily structure, purpose, and meaning.

The truth is that people with bipolar disorder can and do succeed in higher eduction; depending on the person's skills, abilities, and desires, there is no limit.

What happens if someone develops bipolar disorder in the military?

Just as going away to college coincides with a high-risk, high-stress period for developing bipolar disorder, so too is enlisting in the military in the late teens and early twenties a recipe for a susceptible individual to have their first episode. The stresses of: boot camp, sleep deprivation, communal living, new surroundings, possibly leaving home for the first time, and the traumatic nature of combat duty are significant. One study looking at first diagnoses of major mental illnesses in enlisted personnel found that over 1,600 servicemen and women were hospitalized with a new diagnosis of bipolar disorder over a five-year period.

If someone becomes psychotic or manic once enlisted, the armed services have guidelines as to how to work with that individual. Typically, if serious symptoms appear early after enlistment and before deployment, it's likely that the individual will be separated from military service. This is especially true if there is evidence that this was a pre-existing condition. If the individual has been deployed, and/or has been in the armed services for a longer period, significant efforts are made to work with the person and to provide necessary treatment—a medical discharge is not a foregone conclusion. The regulations state that the service member should receive the maximum benefit of treatment, and only be separated if he is unable to return to an acceptable level of functioning. In the end, it's whether or not someone can do the job, versus any particular diagnosis, that determines fitness for duty. Behavioral services provided by the military can include medication management, individual cognitive therapy, post-traumatic stress disorder groups, substance abuse groups/programs, marriage counseling, and groups that address issues of anger management.

The Department of Defense recently published a guidance memorandum that explains the armed forces' response to the deployment of individuals with psychiatric conditions. The stated goal is one of restoration, but if an individual's condition does not respond to treatment within one year, or is not anticipated to respond, then the person would be referred to a medical evaluation board for a possible medical discharge.

Individuals on particular medications (antipsychotics, lithium, and other mood stabilizers and benzodiazepines) may be disqualified from certain branch-specific jobs, such as flight pilot. The memo lists other issues around medications, such as special storage, the need for blood work to monitor levels, and recently started psychiatric medications, that might preclude an individual from being deployed or limit the positions in which she could be deployed.

The memorandum specifically states that during deployment, "Personnel diagnosed with psychotic or bipolar spectrum disorders will be recommended for return to their home station." And that "Psychotic and Bipolar Disorders are considered disqualifying for deployment."

This memo, dated November 7, 2006, can be read in its entirety at: http://www.ha.osd.mil/policies. Of note, the memorandum is not laying out a black-and-white policy—these are guidelines—and there is significant leeway for interpretation. So if someone with bipolar disorder wishes to remain in the military, his symptoms are under control, and he is able to fulfill the requirements of his job, his treating psychiatrist and superior officer may determine that a discharge is not warranted.

What happens if someone is discharged from the military because of bipolar disorder?

If someone is referred to the Medical Board for discharge, and it appears that she did develop her first episode of bipolar disorder while enlisted, the individual may be eligible for a variety of benefits, including medical care through the Veteran's Administration. If it is determined that the psychiatric disability, or some portion of it, was a result of active duty, ongoing monetary compensation will be determined by the Medical Board (referred to as Percent of Service-Connected Disability). Additionally the individual will likely be eligible for free healthcare—including psychiatric services and medications—through the Veteran's Administration. Information on compensation and benefits can be obtained through the Veteran's Administration (800-827-1000, www.vba.va.gov).

Are there gender differences in the manifestations of bipolar disorder?

While bipolar disorder affects men and women equally, there are gender differences.

- Women are more likely to develop the rapid cycling form of bipolar disorder.
- Women are more likely than men to have bipolar II vs. bipolar I.
- Women have a higher percentage of depressed and mixed episodes than manias. This has been shown in two separate studies.
- Women with bipolar disorder are at very high risk for relapse (roughly 80 percent)—or a first mood episode toward the end of pregnancy and in the period after giving birth (post-partum depression, mania, or psychosis).

- Mood symptoms in women may be influenced by the menstrual cycle and other hormonal life events, such as menarche (the first period) and menopause (cessation of periods).

What is known about a woman's menstrual cycle and her bipolar symptoms?

Some women with bipolar disorder, especially type II and rapid cycling, report mood variations that correlate with their menstrual cycles. Common symptoms include depression and irritability in the premenstrual and menstrual period followed by an elevation in mood once the period is over. Premenstrual symptoms run the range of irritability and low mood to all-out depressed and mixed states.

What does a woman need to know about birth control if she has bipolar disorder and is on medication?

It is advisable that women taking medications practice birth control to avoid the risks of unplanned pregnancy and potential harm to the fetus through early exposure to medications. A slightly increased risk of serious malformations has been reported with lithium (Ebstein's anomaly, a cardiac malformation) and especially with the anticonvulsants valproate (Depakote) and carbamazepine (Tegretol) (neural tube defects in the developing nervous system, including spina bifida and facial abnormalities).

Additionally, the choice of birth control will need to be influenced by the medications being used. The anticonvulsants carbamazepine (Tegretol), oxcarbazepine (Trileptal), and topirimate (Topamax) all increase the breakdown of oral contraceptives (birth control pills), rendering them less effective or ineffective. Women on these medications should use an alternative form of birth control, such as an intrauterine device (IUD) or higher doses of combined oral contraceptives, such as the older ones.

I have bipolar; should I get pregnant?

This may seem like a horrible question, but it's one that many women with bipolar disorder face. Should I get pregnant? What are the risks? And what can I do to manage them?

A woman's decision to have a child or children is highly personal. In general, giving birth is not without risk for both the mother and the child. With improvements in public health, nutrition, sanitation, and modern obstetrical techniques, these risks have diminished markedly in the past century. Infant and maternal mortality rates are low, and many of the concerns women used to face are minimal. That said, women with bipolar disorder who wish to get pregnant are taking on a variety of risks, both to their own health and to that of their unborn child. If the decision is to go ahead and get pregnant, finding strategies to diminish these added risks—such as the high risk of a mood episode toward the end of pregnancy and the post-partum period, the risk of exposing the fetus to various medications, etc.—is important.

Can a woman with bipolar disorder take medications when she is pregnant?

Yes, and for many it will be essential, both for her health and for that of the infant. But as we'll discuss in the following questions, the medications selected and approaches to medication need to be modified prior to conceiving (if at all possible) and especially during the first trimester when the developing fetus is the most vulnerable.

How does someone manage medications for bipolar disorder while pregnant?

Helping a woman with bipolar disorder manage her symptoms and medications through pregnancy involves highly individualized care. Key issues that need to be addressed explicitly include:

- The particular woman's history of bipolar disorder, especially the frequency with which she has had previous mood episodes. If she has gone years between episodes, coming off medications in order to get pregnant and through the first trimester—or longer—may be the way to go.

- The woman's reproductive history, age and general medical history. Is this someone who may not get pregnant for a period of time and/or will require the additional assistance of a fertility specialist? If the decision is to come off medications, the increased time to conceive will also increase the overall risk of having a mood episode.

- Understanding potential risks to the developing fetus of different medications. In general, the risks are greatest in the first trimester when the major organ systems are developing. Certain medications, such as the anticonvulsants valproic acid (Depakote) and carbamazepine (Tegretol), are typically avoided. Likewise, multiple medications increase the overall risk to the fetus. It's also important to understand that even though medications may increase the risk of certain birth defects, there's always an underlying risk for these same events even off of medication. In other words, it's not always the medication that causes a problem.

- Understanding potential risks to the health of both the mother and the unborn child should a major mood episode develop in the course of the pregnancy.

- Understanding the risk for developing a mood episode toward the end of pregnancy and the period after (post-partum), and the potential dangers this represents to both the mother and child.
- Encouraging overall good prenatal care and health. This includes eliminating all alcohol, drugs, and tobacco; regular visits and screenings with the obstetrician/obstetrical clinic; attendance at birthing classes; good nutrition; pre-natal vitamins; etc.

For women with bipolar disorder who want to have children and minimize the risks to both their own health and that of their baby, planning is critical and should start before conception. It is important that you, your spouse, your psychiatrist, your obstetrician, and other major supports are working together as a team.

If I decide to go off medications prior to conceiving, how should I do this and when should I start them again?

Where some women will opt to discontinue medications before conceiving and during the first trimester—or longer—frequent visits to your prescribing practitioner will make sense. Abrupt discontinuation of mood-stabilizing medication should also be avoided; it's better to taper off.

Once off of mood-stabilizing medication, the risk of relapse increases. Some women may not be able to take the risk of stopping medication, or will begin to experience symptoms as they taper down. Here, careful planning and selection of medications less associated with birth defects makes sense. Strategies to minimize risk will include using as few agents as possible, and using medications—often ones that have been around longer, such as the typical antipsychotics—where the relative risks to the fetus are minimal and known.

As roughly half of all pregnancies are unplanned, many women with bipolar disorder will conceive while on medication. The same general planning and discussions of relative risk needs to occur. The difference here is that the fetus has already been exposed to various medications during the first trimester. Goals around treatment will be to maintain the mother's health and minimize potential risks to the unborn child. The use of ultrasound and possibly amniocentesis (examination of cells from the fluid surrounding the fetus), may help detect serious birth defects early in the pregnancy.

As a woman approaches her delivery date—and immediately after delivery—if she has been off medication this may be the time to restart a mood stabilizer and/or antipsychotic, to decrease the risk of a serious post-partum mood episode. The best studied medication for this is lithium, which has been shown to decrease the relapse rate from 50 percent to lower than 10 percent.

Are there connections between post-partum depression, post-partum psychosis, and bipolar disorder?

There is a strong correlation between bipolar disorder and post-partum mood disorders, including post-partum psychosis and depression. For women who have never been diagnosed with bipolar disorder, a significant mood episode following a pregnancy may be the first indication of an underlying bipolar disorder.

Additionally, women who already carry a diagnosis of bipolar disorder are at high risk for experiencing a serious mood episode after they give birth (seven-fold higher than for non-bipolar women). Symptoms of a mood episode may present quite rapidly toward the end of the pregnancy and in the days and weeks after delivery.

Can women with bipolar disorder breast feed if they are taking medication?

Most medications, including lithium, the anticonvulsants, and the antipsychotics, will make their way into breast milk. The level to which each medication is found in the breast milk varies.

If a woman taking medication intends to breast feed, depending on her specific medications, additional monitoring of both mother and baby will be required. The type of monitoring will relate directly to the medications, i.e., if a woman on lithium is breast feeding it will be important to monitor lithium levels and other blood work in the infant, and to educate the parents about warning signs of toxicity in their child.

Because maintaining healthy sleep cycles is so important in bipolar disorder, getting up to breast feed every two to three hours may be too disruptive and will make a woman more susceptible to a mood episode. The use of a breast pump and a spouse—or someone else—to handle nighttime feedings will make sense.

Are there special considerations for people who are gay, lesbian, bisexual, or transgender who have bipolar disorder?

In thinking about treatment options for people with bipolar disorder who are also gay, lesbian, bisexual, or transgender (GLBT), an issue that frequently arises has to do with disclosure around sexual identity and preference. The ease and comfort with which people are able to "come out" to family, friends, and treatment providers varies greatly and is influenced by the setting. Many in the GLBT community have met with repeated prejudice and stigma. Some have experienced the loss of important relationships (parents disowning them, excommunication from certain religious organizations, severed friendships, job discrimination, etc.) as a result of disclosing their sexual identity.

If someone is experiencing a serious mood episode, the issue of disclosure in an unfamiliar setting with strangers—an inpatient unit, partial hospital program, group, etc.—can add an additional stress, as well as a barrier to treatment.

The issue of disclosure is a highly personal one, and requires the development of a safe and trusting relationship with the person's practitioner (psychiatrist/therapist/counselor) and treatment team (if we're talking an inpatient unit, PHP, IOP, etc). Sometimes this relationship is found, but other times prejudice and discrimination are apparent in the treatment setting.

Inclusion of significant others, family, and supportive friends in psychoeducation groups, therapy sessions, etc. needs to occur in the same manner as it does for non-GLBT individuals.

To feel comfortable, some may specifically seek out practitioners who specialize in working with GLBT people, or who themselves are out. Additionally, some self-help groups, such as AA, will have meetings specifically targeted to the GLBT communities.

Does bipolar disorder improve or get worse as someone ages?

There's tremendous variability in how bipolar disorder changes/progresses through the years. Finding studies that can give definitive answers is difficult, because most research focuses on people with recurrent mood episodes, and those who have had few episodes are harder to track. In general, we can break this question down into three groups of people. Those who get better, those who get worse, and those who stay about the same.

First, there are some with bipolar who have had long periods between episodes. Or perhaps they only had episodes in their twenties or thirties. Often these are people whose mood episodes were clearly related to specific stressors such as drugs, child birth, etc. Many of these people will continue to have significant symptom-free periods, minor episodes, or no further mood episodes at all.

For others, the course is more challenging, and progression to the rapid cycling variant of bipolar disorder is common in later life. There are a number of hypotheses as to why this is. For example, is it just the natural course of things, or is it the product of antidepressant-induced acceleration, or diminishing sensitivity to mood stabilizers, or the additive effects of co-morbid medical conditions? The answer is not known.

Finally, there is a third group that continues to have mood episodes, but they do not progress in frequency. In this group we find a large number of people with bipolar disorder who have effectively learned strategies to diminish both the frequency and severity of their episodes.

Can people over the age of sixty develop bipolar disorder for the first time?

Yes, although when a careful history is taken, it becomes evident that most of these people have had bouts of depression earlier in their lives. Regardless, a first episode of mania in an older person should trigger a complete medical workup, paying particular attention to any subtle signs of memory loss or dementia. While it is possible to have a first manic episode of bipolar disorder after sixty-five, the chances that there is a medical cause for the mood episode are great. As reviewed in Chapter 2, many medications and medical conditions (everything from steroids to a thyroid abnormality to strokes) can mimic a manic episode.

Is the treatment of bipolar disorder different in older people?

Perhaps the single most important principle in working with older people has to do with the use of medications and normal—and pathological—changes that occur as we age. The adage "start low, go slow" as it relates to medications can't be overstressed. As people get older, their kidneys clear medications less rapidly, and lower doses may be required. People will also have a greater number of other medical conditions for which they'll likely be on a variety of medications. The risk of adverse and potentially life-threatening drug reactions and interactions goes up tremendously, and having good communication between different doctors is crucial. Anytime medications are changed it's important to be vigilant for the emergence of problems. Even something as seemingly trivial as eye drops can be problematic—say, using b-blocker eye drops for glaucoma. When combined with certain antidepressants that inhibit their breakdown in the liver, such as fluoxetine (Prozac), the drops can slow the heart to dangerous levels (heart block), which if not addressed immediately can lead to heart attack and death.

Medications that have narrow safety windows, such as lithium, the blood thinner warfarin (Coumadin), digitalis (Digoxin, Lanoxin), and various anticonvulsants need increased monitoring in older individuals. Levels of these medications are easily influenced by the addition, subtraction, or change in the dosage of other drugs.

It's also important to keep and carry an accurate and up to date list of your medications, including over-the-counter ones.

Another issue in working with older people is that they are more prone to the sedating effects of medications, placing them at risk for falls, broken hips, and falling asleep behind the wheel of a car. Cognitive impairment is often worsened with medications such as lithium, valproic acid (Depakote), the benzodiazepines (Ativan, Xanax, Valium etc.), and sedating antipsychotic medications.

Finally, for older people on lithium there is often concern about its effects on the kidneys. It's well known that lithium can damage the kidneys; this is then combined with the normal decline in kidney/renal function that is seen as people age. Someone who has been stable on lithium for many years may be faced with tough decisions about whether or not to remain on this medication in the face of declining kidney function. The answer for a particular person will be based on a number of factors—the severity of the kidney damage, the rate of progression of the damage, whether or not another mood stabilizer will work for her, personal preference, and recommendations from her practitioner(s).

Is there a cultural bias in the diagnosis and treatment of bipolar disorder?

As discussed, making an accurate diagnosis of bipolar disorder continues to be a challenge, with the most-often-missed diagnosis being unipolar depression. An added finding is that there are cultural biases as well, and that more African Americans and Hispanics with bipolar disorder will be misdiagnosed as having schizophrenia, which often carries a worse prognosis.

Also, studies have shown that in the United States, long-acting injectible antipsychotic medications are prescribed more frequently to people of color.

Should someone find a practitioner of his own cultural/racial group?

This is a frequently asked question, and for many people it comes from a natural desire to feel comfortable and connected to whoever will be their behavioral health practitioner(s). For others, for whom

English is not their first language, it could be about overcoming language barriers and not wanting to work with someone who needs a translator.

There's no right or wrong answer here, but looking at one's desire for a doctor/therapist with a similar cultural and/or racial background may get to deeper issues. Ask yourself,

"Why is this important to me?" and see what answers emerge. Members of any given minority group may have little in common with one another, just as individuals from different races and cultures may be closer than expected.

There's also the practical question of whether or not there are good practitioners of the cultural/racial group you belong to in your community. If there are, and you think that working with such a person will be helpful to your recovery—and it's well known that a good fit is important—by all means go ahead.

What other cultural factors might impact the treatment of bipolar disorder?

Cultural beliefs about mental illness can significantly impact how an individual—and his family—views bipolar disorder. In some Asian cultures, the stigma of mental illness is quite severe, and having a mental illness can be viewed as shameful (loss of face). Certain religious groups will have strong beliefs against the taking of medications (Christian Scientists) or against having blood drawn routinely (Jehovah's Witnesses). Still others, like the Church of Scientology, view the entire mental health field as a conspiracy.

Bottom line is that a person's cultural identity (including religion and spirituality), level of acculturation/assimilation, and family beliefs and norms must be factored into the overall picture.

On a physiologic basis, specific ethnic groups are more likely to metabolize (break down) medications at different rates. This has to do with specific enzymes found in the liver.

Finally, much as we'd like to believe that racial prejudice and discrimination are things of the past, they are not. Additionally, where practitioners in various settings may have their own fears and prejudices (even on a subconscious level) toward different groups, it becomes important for friends and family to take an active role when their loved one is manic, hypomanic, or psychotic—essentially any state in which the behavior the person is exhibiting is scary, threatening, or out of control. This becomes especially true in situations where police, emergency personnel, and emergency rooms are involved.

One of the decisions made in the setting of out-of-control behavior is whether or not this is something medical/psychiatric or something criminal. A family member or friend who can clearly state to a police officer or paramedic that, "This is my son/daughter/ husband/friend; he has bipolar disorder and is off his medications and needs to go to an emergency room for evaluation," may prevent an unwarranted, stigmatizing, and potentially harmful, trip to jail. Once in the emergency room, it will be important to stay around and ensure that providers know you are there, you are concerned, and you are available. Make certain that the social worker or crisis worker assigned to your loved one's case has a way to contact you, and if at all possible see if a release of information can be signed so that you can receive information about what decisions are being made. If that's not possible, you can still provide vital information (past psychiatric history, prior functioning, current medications, use of alcohol and drugs, etc.) to the professionals who will help ensure the appropriate care is provided.

Chapter 14

LIVING WITH BIPOLAR DISORDER

- Why is there still stigma associated with bipolar disorder?
- How do I cope with things like hospitalization and involuntary treatment?
- How do I advocate for the treatment I want, especially if I need treatment when I go into a mood episode and can't provide information on my preferences?
- What are psychiatric/behavioral health advance directives?
- When should I disclose my bipolar disorder in the workplace?
- Is bipolar disorder covered under the Americans with Disabilities Act?
- What advocacy groups exist for people with bipolar disorder?
- How do I talk about my bipolar disorder with someone I'm dating?
- How can I limit the impact bipolar disorder has on my relationship with my spouse?
- How can I limit the impact my bipolar disorder has on my kids?
- Are there advantages to having bipolar disorder?
- Is there a connection between creativity and bipolar disorder?
- What famous people have acknowledged they have bipolar disorder?

Why is there still stigma associated with bipolar disorder?

Despite the vast number of Americans who will have at least one major mental illness over the course of their lifetime (roughly 50 percent by the time we include substance abuse disorder, dementias such as Alzheimer's, mood disorders, anxiety disorders, schizophrenia, eating disorders, etc), we continue to struggle with a societal prejudice against and fear of mental illness. Media representations of mental illness typically focus on scary, out-of-control people who do bad things, further worsening the perception of mental illness. On the plus side, in recent years we've seen more high-profile individuals willing to talk about their own struggles with mental illness and substance abuse. As mental illness is demystified and given a human face, stigma decreases.

Connected to stigma is the issue of disclosure. Many people with bipolar disorder and other mental illnesses are frightened of disclosing their conditions, often with good reason: fear of discrimination, losing a job, not getting a promotion, etc. This presents something of a dilemma, because without putting the face of your family member, neighbor, you, or your boss on bipolar disorder, it continues to be something unknown and scary.

With the rise of the consumer movement and with the advocacy and education work of groups like the National Alliance on Mental Illness (NAMI), the Bazelon Institute, Mental Health America, and others, the stigma of having a mental disability or illness is slowly lessening, although there's still a long way to go.

How do I cope with things like hospitalization and involuntary treatment?

Hospitalization on a psychiatric ward can, for many people, be extremely traumatizing. This can be compounded by being admitted on an involuntary basis. In addition to the feelings of fear, helplessness, and powerlessness this can cause, many people with bipolar talk about the emotional pain of being treated as a child and of being talked down to by family and professionals.

Ways to regain a sense of control can include:

- Being clear with friends and family about what your preferences are should you have a relapse and require inpatient hospitalization
- Completing psychiatric advance directives (See below)
- Insist on being treated as an adult
- Familiarizing yourself with the hospital's "Patient Rights and Responsibilities." This is a piece of paper given to all patients at the point of admission. It clearly spells out what your legal rights are while you are in the hospital.
- Asking for clarification if something is not clear to you. This can include unfamiliar medications as well as concerns you might have about your treatment.

How do I advocate for the treatment I want, especially if I need treatment when I go into a mood episode and can't provide information on my preferences?

Because bipolar disorder is characterized by recurrent mood episodes, it's a good idea to have done some planning should a severe mood episode develop. If you have preferences for facilities, treators, and medications that you know do—or do not—work for you, it's important to communicate this to whoever you view as your primary support. This could be your spouse/significant other, members of your treatment team, a close friend, parents, etc. Increasingly, there is a movement to be even more explicit with the creation of psychiatric or behavioral advance directives.

What are psychiatric/behavioral health advance directives?

Advance directives are documents that give instructions to health-care providers and others about your preferences should you become incapacitated. They've been used in general medicine for some time and can be legally binding documents that cover topics such as what kinds of life support you might want and who you would want to make medical decisions for you in the event you couldn't make your own.

This approach has more recently taken root in psychiatry, and allows for people to prepare legal documents stating what their wishes are for healthcare should they have a severe mood episode and be hospitalized. These documents can cover everything from preferences for medications, hospitals, physicians, and electroconvulsive therapy to whom you would want to be contacted should you require involuntary hospitalization, and many other options. A psychiatric advance directive can also specify a person to be your appointed decision maker, or "Agent for Mental Health Care."

At present it's not known how psychiatric advance directives will hold up in a court of law should they not be followed, especially in emergency situations. Even so, psychiatric advance directives give clear guidance to providers about an individual's preferences for treatment. They help the individual maintain a sense of dignity and control in situations, such as involuntary hospitalization, where personal freedoms can be drastically and precipitously curtailed.

Free forms that cover an array of psychiatric advance directives are available online and by mail from the Judge David L. Bazelon Center for Mental Health Law, 1101 15th Street, NW, Suite 1212,

Washington, DC 20005. Phone: 202-467-5730; fax: 202-223-0409. Email: webmaster@bazelon.org.Website: http://www.bazelon.org

When should I disclose my bipolar disorder in the workplace?

The answer about disclosure in the workplace is a personal one. Your decision to disclose to some—or all—of your colleagues will be based on several factors:

- Will disclosure increase or decrease your perceived level of stress at work?
- Will disclosure enhance your effectiveness at your job? For instance, someone working in the mental health profession who discloses her own bipolar disorder could achieve an added credibility when working with colleagues and people with mental illnesses.
- Is there a particular reason why disclosure—perhaps to your immediate supervisor—is necessary? Following a manic episode there may be behavioral events that occurred in the workplace that need to be addressed. In some circumstances, but not all, disclosure might help reframe what happened in a less negative manner.
- Is disclosure necessary in order to obtain accommodation(s) on the job under the Americans with Disabilities Act (ADA)?

Is bipolar disorder covered under the Americans with Disabilities Act?

Yes, bipolar disorder and other mental disabilities are explicitly covered under the Americans with Disabilities ACT (ADA). This legislation, which was signed into law in 1990, has multiple parts that have as their overarching goal the integration of people with disabilities into all aspects of the American mainstream.

In the workplace the ADA provides some degree of protection for people with disabilities. The ADA prohibits discrimination in the workplace—including the hiring process—based on a disability.

If an individual can prove that he has a disability that is covered under the ADA, employers may be required to make reasonable accommodations in the workplace. These could include flex work schedules, a job coach, and possibly a change in position altogether.

What advocacy groups exist for people with bipolar disorder?

Major advocacy groups for people with bipolar disorder and other mental disabilities include (complete contact information is in Appendix A):

- Protection and Advocacy for Individuals with Mental Illness (PAIMI). This is a federally funded program begun in 1986. Each state has a funded office of Protection and Advocacy. PAIMI's purposes are:
  - ❏ To protect and advocate for the rights of people with mental illness
  - ❏ To investigate reports of abuse and neglect of people with mental illness
- The Judge David L Bazelon Center for Mental Health Law
- The National Alliance on Mental Illness (NAMI)
- Mental Health America (MHA)

How do I talk about my bipolar disorder with someone I'm dating?

The questions of how and when to talk about your bipolar disorder with a romantic partner are complex. There is no one right answer, and personal preference, style, and comfort with the other person, as well as with disclosure, will guide the time and place when you discuss your bipolar disorder. For some, it makes sense to hold off until it appears there is a connection and that this is a relationship that could develop into something long-term. Fears and concerns over how the other person will handle the information are normal.

One practical way to enter into the discussion is by using terms that most people will be familiar with: "I've had issues with depression and mood swings and am currently in recovery with this."

Depending on the other person's response, you'll get a feel for his or her ability and desire to want to know more. This may be the time to introduce the actual diagnosis: "I have bipolar disorder, and it's manageable." It's common for people to have misconceptions about bipolar—some can be quite extreme—and by getting things into the open you can address these.

There is of course the risk that the person you're interested in is just not able—for whatever reasons—to handle the information. If that's the case, the consolation may be that it's better to find out now than down the line when you need him for support and he's not there.

As the relationship progresses and your partner expresses a willingness to become a part of your life, you might want to consider including him in a session, or more, with your practitioner(s). This further decreases the mystery around your bipolar and can enhance the bond that you share.

How can I limit the impact bipolar disorder has on my relationship with my spouse?

While it's difficult to get consistent data, people with bipolar disorder do have a higher divorce rate than the general population. Considering that more than 50 percent of all marriages end in divorce, we can see how maintaining long-term relationships in general is challenging, and for people with bipolar disorder there will be added considerations.

Some important points to remember are:

- Let your spouse/significant other know that it's okay for her to talk about your bipolar disorder, and that if she believes you're having symptoms it's safe for her to say that. For many couples this becomes an effective early warning system that a mood episode is starting to brew.
- While your spouse/significant other is not your therapist, including her in occasional visits with your practitioner(s) can be useful. This will offer her the chance to ask questions and get answers.
- Avoid making important decisions about your spouse or significant other while in the midst of a mood episode.
  - ❏ When depressed, people often overstate the burden they believe they are.
    - ■ "You'd be better off without me."
    - ■ "I'm holding you back. You can do better."
  - ❏ When manic or hypomanic, increased self-importance and grandiosity and heightened sex drive may have the person with bipolar disorder look toward what he considers a more exciting partner.
    - ■ "You're too dull . . . no fun . . . a bore."
- If you did something to hurt your spouse emotionally while in the midst of a mood episode, it's important to say, "I'm sorry."

This can be a challenge, as you want to take responsibility for your behavior but also acknowledge that some element of it came as a result of your mood state.

- Consider couples counseling, either in an ongoing way or when needed, to get through the rough spots. This will be different than having your spouse come to meet with you and your regular therapist. In couples work it's best to have a therapist who isn't going to take sides.
  - ❏ It's also important to remember that the problems occurring in a relationship may have little or nothing to do with your bipolar.
  - ❏ Control issues (especially around taking medication and following treatment recommendations) are a frequent source of conflict in relationships. Being able to air these in therapy and come up with compromises that you and your spouse are comfortable with can be very helpful.

How can I limit the impact my bipolar disorder has on my kids?

The most important thing you can do is to keep yourself as healthy as possible. This approach may sound a bit jarring, as culturally we're encouraged to sacrifice for our children. But where there is such a strong connection between stress, disturbed daily rhythms, and mood episodes, it's important to manage your stress and pay attention to routines, especially your sleep-wake cycle.

Create contingency plans, i.e., specific plans to have in place should you have a serious mood episode. Having designated family members (spouse, grand-parents, siblings) who are willing and ready to step in can decrease the disruption.

It's important that your children know they are not responsible for your mood episodes. Young children can easily feel that they've done something wrong or bad if their parent is depressed, unhappy, or irritable. Letting them know in clear language that, "Daddy is sad right now, it's not your fault, he loves you very much and he's going to feel better," will help relieve unnecessary worry and guilt.

Providing age-appropriate education to your kids will help them understand what's going on. Let them ask questions, and reassure them that the moods will pass.

As your children get older, their concerns will change. They'll wonder about their own risk for developing bipolar disorder and may want to know their chances for passing it on to their own children. As questions arise, help them find the answers they need.

Just as couples counseling can be a useful addition to treatment, so too can some family sessions help get all the unstated fears and questions on the table. Once out in the open, the specific issues can be addressed in a safe setting. Support groups can also be important sources of information and shared experience.

Finally, as your children become adults they may want to talk about their experiences—often painful ones—of growing up with a parent with bipolar. It's important to listen without getting defensive, because at the end of the day, letting them know it's okay to talk about these things will strengthen the relationship.

Are there advantages to having bipolar disorder?

Yes, there can be advantages to having bipolar disorder. These advantages, however, often come at a cost. For those people with bipolar disorder who are able to keep their mood swings in check, or for those few who are able to maintain a highly energized state, having bipolar creates the opportunity to be remarkably productive and creative. The benefits of bipolar disorder are mostly connected to being just a bit hypomanic, or experiencing the "highs" of cyclothymia that never quite meet criteria for a hypomanic,

manic, or mixed state. This makes a great deal of sense for a number of reasons.

- On a cognitive level, when people are hypomanic their belief in their own ability to succeed and do what they set out to do is quite high. The negative self-talk and pessimism of depression is nowhere to be found. There's a confidence that helps people accomplish their tasks with an unswerving belief in their own abilities. "I can get that book written in four weeks, no problem!" "Cater a party for three hundred, sure, why not?" "Run for president? Okay." Many people who've gone far in the fields of politics, the arts, business, law, medicine, etc. have likely had, or have, bipolar disorder.

- In a slightly hypomanic state, there can be an ease with the creative process—writing, drawing, composing, decorating, etc. This may be in part due to the enhanced sense of one's own abilities. The critical mind, which can create a total buzzkill to creativity, is quiet, allowing imagination to flourish.

- When hypomanic, people often enjoy the sense of increased energy, of thoughts moving quickly and smoothly from topic to topic.

On the depressed side too, the world of arts and letters is filled with the creative, and often heartbreaking, output of artists able to tap into their darker hours and give voice. Much of the strongest prose comes when people boldly venture into the heart of their greatest pain.

Is there a connection between creativity and bipolar disorder?

The truth is there is a connection between creativity of all sorts and bipolar disorder. An important point to make, however, is that not every person with bipolar disorder will have the poetic grandeur of Lord Byron, the musical talent of Robert Schumann, the artistic eye of Vincent van Gogh, or the political brilliance of Winston Churchill.

The list of famous artists, composers, writers, painters, dancers, etc believed to have bipolar disorder is a long one—too long to say that this connection between creativity and bipolar is just due to chance. A wonderful book on this topic is Kay Redfield Jamison's *Touched with Fire: Manic-Depressive Illness and the Artistic Temperament.*

What famous people have acknowledged they have bipolar disorder?

Over the past couple of decades a number of celebrities have publicly disclosed their own struggles with bipolar disorder. Perhaps the first to do so was Patty Duke with her excellent and moving biography, *Call Me Anna* (1987). Others to publicly acknowledge their bipolar disorder include Ned Beatty, Dick Cavett, Carrie Fisher, Linda Hamilton, Mariette Hartley, Red Sox baseball player Jimmy Piersall, bipolar disorder expert Kay Redfield Jamison, PhD, and television host Jane Pauley.

Chapter 15

SURVIVAL TIPS FOR FAMILY AND FRIENDS

- How can family members manage the caregiver stress associated with bipolar disorder?
- Are there support groups for family members?
- Are there courses that friends and family can take to learn about the illness?
- How do you balance the needs of a child with bipolar disorder against the needs of the rest of the family?
- My adult child has bipolar disorder and frequently asks me for money. Should I give him financial support?
- Should I manage my adult child's medications?
- What kinds of things can a spouse/significant other do to maintain his or her own sanity?
- How do you care for someone who is depressed?
- How do you talk to someone who is manic?
- How do you get someone to take medications when he doesn't think he has a problem?
- What do you do when someone says she's thinking of committing suicide?
- What do you do when someone says he's thinking of hurting someone?

How can family members manage the caregiver stress associated with bipolar disorder?

The stress associated with having a family member or loved one with bipolar disorder can be severe. When someone is in a manic state, she can say and do terrible things. When depressed she might lay around the house for months on end, not helping out with the chores, barely able to even turn on the television set. While it's easy to say, "she's not doing any of these thing deliberately, it's her illness," the reality of living with or caring for a person with bipolar disorder can be difficult. Learning to take care of yourself and not just the patient is not easy, and can involve some painful decisions, such as telling an adult child who refuses to take medication and is engaging in dangerous behaviors that they are no longer able to stay in your house.

This chapter will go though various resources and approaches designed to give you the information you need. That said, here are a few basics

- You are not alone. Millions of families each year are going through similar situations.
- Knowledge is power. The more you know about bipolar disorder and the treatments and resources available—especially those in your state and local area—the better equipped you'll be to handle the different situations as they arise.
- Trust your instincts. If you start feeling overwhelmed, or that a particular situation is out of control, you're probably right. If someone is saying something that is frightening you, and you're not certain as to whether it warrants calling 911, go ahead and call anyway. They're the trained experts, let them evaluate the situation.
- No one has all the answers. What works for one family in a given situation may just be wrong for you and yours. If your five

senses are telling you that a particular strategy or approach is working, trust your gut.

Are there support groups for family members?

Yes. NAMI, the largest advocacy group for people with mental illnesses and their families, has over 1200 affiliates in all fifty states, as well as Puerto Rico and DC (http://www.nami.org/). They offer excellent and state-of-the-art courses, some tailored for families and others geared toward consumers of mental health services. They can also assist in tracking down area mental health providers and they offer an Information Helpline, 1-800-950-NAMI (6264), Monday through Friday, 10 am to 6 pm, Eastern Time. To find a group near you, either call or visit their website.

In addition to the facilitated support offered by NAMI, there are other local grassroots support groups. Also, some inpatient and outpatient programs offer family psychoeducation and support groups as a part of their overall treatment.

Are there courses that family and friends can take to learn about the illness?

NAMI offers a series of courses that can be helpful. In particular the Family to Family twelve-week course is outstanding, and to date has graduated over one hundred thousand family members. It's free, and the instructors are well trained—often bringing in area experts as various topics are covered. The information provided in the Family to Family course is kept up to date, and the focus is on getting people the practical information they need about everything from medications to handling a crisis to finding providers in the community. Information on where and when these courses are held is available through the NAMI website, www.nami.org.

How do you balance the needs of a child with bipolar disorder against the needs of the rest of the family?

This answer is based on a number of factors. How old is the child with bipolar disorder, and how old are the other children? How symptomatic is the child with bipolar? And what other special needs do the other children have?

In younger families, managing the intense mood swings and tantrums of a child with bipolar disorder can turn into a full-time job for both parents (assuming we're even talking about a two-parent household). Frequent visits to doctors and therapists and regular meetings with teachers can shift much of the focus from other children.

For children who have severe mood episodes as well as significant management and behavior problems, finding a therapeutic after-school program can free up three or more afternoons a week. Some insurance companies will reimburse for these, especially if the child has had prior inpatient hospitalizations. If a school system, through their evaluation of the child, believes a therapeutic program is needed, it's possible that they will pick up the tab.

Enlisting the regular aid of another adult, either a family member, friend, or paid assistant, can also diminish the overall parenting burden. In some instances a grandparent who has a good emotional connection with the child with bipolar disorder may be able to provide regular respite through overnight, or weekend, away visits.

Finally, in some states, and in extreme circumstances, state agencies may be able to provide parenting assistance through programs offered through the agency that oversees children (in some states this will be Department of Children and Families, in others it will fall under Health and Human Services, Public Health, Mental Health, etc.)

My adult child has bipolar disorder and frequently asks me for money. Should I give him financial support?

Because the onset of bipolar disorder so frequently occurs in the late teens and twenties, it's common for parents to find themselves with a child who was leaving the nest, or had left the nest, who is now dealing with a serious mood episode. Their son or daughter's ability to pay the rent and maintain a household may be seriously impaired. If your finances are such that you can step in and help out, it can seriously diminish the overall level of stress the person with bipolar disorder is facing.

A common and complex question then needs to get answered: Do you help support your child in his own place, or would it be better if he returned home for a while? The answer will depend on several factors, including finances, how well you and your child get along, the physical layout of your home, and how he is functioning overall.

In general, you may want to overestimate the amount of time your child will need financial support. Some will bounce back fast, others will have a slower and more-protracted return, and for some—who have frequent and serious mood episodes with little or no periods that are symptom-free—longer-range planning will be needed.

If the decision is for your adult child to return home, it will be important to remember that he is in fact no longer a child. Whatever can be done to arrange the home so that his independence, autonomy, and dignity are maintained is recommended. Approaches that might be more supportive include in-law suites, basement, over-the-garage or attic apartments, or a room with its own bath and outer door. Clearly not everyone has such set-ups, but whatever can be done to make the space suitable for an adult will be a help.

Should I manage my adult child's medications?

This is an important question that can cause a great deal of friction between the person with bipolar disorder and her family. Heated arguments can arise over the daily question of, "Did you take your medication?" Followed by the rebuttal, "I'm not a child! I can manage my own medication!"

The negotiation around managing medications can be a sensitive one, and it's one that will evolve over time. In other words, if someone has no difficulty with her medications, takes them regularly and is not in a depressed or suicidal state, she should manage her own medication. On the other end of things, we could have a person who frequently stops her psychiatric medications, quickly falls into a mood episode, and/or has periods of suicidality that might include thoughts—or a history—of taking overdoses with her medications. This person will need assistance and some safeguards with the medication. Then we have everything in the middle.

Finding the balance between supporting autonomy and independence and trying to prevent your adult child from having mood episodes is tricky. A few suggestions that could help include:

- Avoid using medication as a punishment or in a coercive way, i.e., "If you don't take your medication you'll have to go to the hospital."
- If someone has a history of overdose, try to limit the amount of medication in his possession at any given time. Weekly, or even daily, pill boxes can be helpful.
- If your adult child is eligible for either in-home (visiting nurse) services or receives case-management or ACTT services (see Chapter 9) these are often able to provide medication management in the home. This would be prescribed by the psychiatrist/APRN and helps take the family out of the discussion altogether.

- Try a motivational approach toward talking about medication (See Chapter 11). Avoid debate, listen, empathize, and help the person find her own reasons for why taking the medication makes sense.

What kinds of things can a spouse/significant other do to maintain his or her own sanity?

If you are married to someone, or have a significant other with bipolar disorder, probably the most important thing you can do is educate yourself about the illness. Living with a person with bipolar disorder will at times be hard. In a manic or mixed state, people can say and do very hurtful things. When someone is profoundly depressed—a condition that can drag on for months and even a year or more—the strain on the relationship becomes profound.

Just as managing stress and paying attention to daily routines are important for people with bipolar disorder; these are also helpful approaches for the spouse/significant other. Some specific areas to pay attention to include:

- Develop a strong support system (religious, friends, family, NAMI or other support group). This will help nurture hope and compassion. It can be incredibly powerful to talk with someone else who has been through a similar experience and hear them say, "You're going to get through this. I know, because I did."
- Maintain a healthy sleep pattern
- Regular exercise
- A healthy diet
- Use humor. Sometimes a good joke in the midst of a bad situation can give a sense of control to what otherwise feels out of control.
- Know what your limits are. Realize that it's okay if you can't be everything all the time for your spouse/significant other.

- Avoid becoming your spouse/significant other's therapist or doctor. If he's becoming symptomatic, direct him toward his practitioner(s). Make sure you always have permission to communicate with his treatment team.

How do you care for someone who is depressed?

The depression associated with bipolar disorder can be severe and disabling. The burden on family and friends is often intense. At times it will be difficult to remember that the person who's depressed is ill. The behaviors of depression can put great strain on relationships and families: "She just lies in bed all day." "He doesn't help out with any of the chores." "If only he'd snap out of it." "I feel bad too sometimes, but I still get up and go to work."

Without intending to, it's quite easy to add to the person's sense of failure, hopelessness, and being a burden to those around her. Things that can help get you through are:

- Understand as much as you can about the illness.
- Try to be a part of the treatment team. Be able to communicate with the person's therapist/psychiatrist/case manager. This will involve keeping releases of information up to date.
- Try to validate and support the feelings of your family member or loved one.
- Avoid blaming them for the way they feel. Don't say things like: "Maybe now you'll stay on your medications!" "See what happens when you drink?" "I said you were taking on too many projects."
- Push, but don't nag. Try suggestions like: "Here, let's go for a walk, and get some sunlight."
- Let him know he is loved and that you care about him.
- Join a support group, and gain strength from others who've been through similar experiences.

How do you talk to someone who is manic?

Your ability to communicate with somebody who is manic and possibly psychotic as well greatly depends on their present state. If somebody is manic and grandiose, you will have to struggle to get a word in, often having to talk over her. It's important to keep anger out of your voice, and if the person has a sense of humor—and many people who are manic can have wicked senses of humor—a light tone and smile may work: "Excuse me, can I please speak?"

People who are psychotic will often want to know that you believe them—after all, they are really hearing that voice, or are firmly convinced that the FBI has hundreds of invisible agents following them. It's a fine line between validating the reality of the person's experience and not wanting to feed into the psychotic experience. If the person has become fixed on a particular delusional theme, you might be able to get them off of it by distracting her or changing the subject. When people are manic, distraction can work quite well: "Let's go see what mom is up to?" "What are the chances of the Red Sox winning the pennant this year?"

With delusions—fixed false beliefs—it's a bit trickier and more often than not you have to sidestep and not directly confront or challenge the delusion, especially if someone is in an irritable mixed or manic state. It's a good idea to keep your voice pitched low and to try not to let your emotions take over: The calmer the better.

As relationships get stronger, people will be more willing to allow you to gently confront their psychotic beliefs.

How do you get someone to take medications when he doesn't think he has a problem?

This is one of the most-asked questions of practitioners working with people who have serious mental illnesses. It's a complex question because the answer(s) depend on the various reasons the person isn't taking his medication. Is it side effects or a total lack of insight into his illness? The former can probably be managed by adjusting dosage, frequency, etc, but the latter—lack of insight—is harder, because, why on earth would you take medication if you didn't have an illness?

This lack of insight into illness (anosognosia) often creates incredible conflict and strain within families. In bipolar disorder the issue of insight can vary based on the phase—such as a manic or mixed episode—or it may persist at all times, even when the person is in a stable mood. The struggle for families can be one where they watch the person relapse, get put on medications in the hospital, come out, stop the meds and . . . around and around we go. This is sometimes called the revolving-door phenomenon.

The best approach to helping someone with anosognosia find his own reasons for taking the medications may be put forward in the book *I Am Not Sick I Don't Need Help* by Xavier Amador, PhD, in which he suggests that through using and modifying techniques of motivational interviewing (reflective listening, empathy, avoiding debate, avoiding pushing your own agenda, working as equals), one can diffuse the struggle around medications and treatment. An important point that we see with people who have both anosognosia and take their medications consistently is that they may never believe they have an illness, but they have found their own reasons why taking medication on a regular basis is important and even meaningful: "I can hold a job when I'm on my meds," "I don't get hauled off to the hospital," "I don't do crazy stuff," "Without them I couldn't stay with my wife and kids."

Other approaches, although more heavy-handed and restrictive, might include the use of mandatory outpatient treatment, sometimes referred to as assisted outpatient treatment, although this is not available in every state.

Finally, for some people with various active legal issues (driving under the influence, breach of peace, probation, etc.), a judge may mandate outpatient treatment as a condition of release, probation, or parole. Having this very real consequence—doing jail time—hanging over someone's head may motivate her to take medications and to participate in treatment. The trick here is to think beyond the court order, probation, or parole, because once they're over it's common for people to drop out of treatment.

What do you do when someone says she's thinking of committing suicide?

There is no doubt that people with bipolar disorder are at high risk for committing suicide. If a family member or friend voices suicidal thoughts, plan, or intent, this is an emergency that requires attention. Likewise, if someone is engaged in behaviors that indicate a plan to end his life, such as giving away valued possessions, saying goodbye to people, writing suicide notes, or assembling the means to kill himself, help is needed ASAP. What you don't want to do is minimize the seriousness of what the person is saying or doing. Most people who kill themselves will have told at least one other person what they intended to do in the weeks preceding.

You'll want to have a well-thought-out emergency plan. This could be as basic as having needed phone numbers at hand, and can extend to making sure you're able to communicate with your loved one's therapist and/or psychiatrist.

- Have the number for your local crisis center, many of whom are able to do outreaches into the person's home. Crisis centers are often affiliated with local hospitals or community mental health centers (CMHCs) or mental health authorities (MHAs).

- Know how to activate the emergency response system in your area. For most of us this involves dialing 911. Always remember to stay on the line until instructed to hang up.
- Contact the National Suicide Prevention Lifeline. This is a federally funded network of crisis centers located across the country. Tel: 800-273-TALK, or for the hearing impaired TTY: 800-799-4889

Once the immediate crisis has passed, it's important to decrease easy access to lethal substances and weapons. Impulsivity, one of the hallmarks of bipolar disorder, especially in the manic, hypomanic, and mixed episodes, predisposes a person to act without thinking things through. An urge to self-harm can come on quite quickly, and if lethal means are in easy reach the result can be catastrophic. Here are some things you can do diminish risk:

- Because over 50 percent of completed suicides involve firearms, ensure that there are no guns in the home.
- Keep potentially lethal means of overdose locked up.
- Someone in a severe mood episode should not operate a motor vehicle or heavy equipment.

What do you do when someone says he's thinking of hurting someone?

As with suicidal thinking and behavior, expressions or actions indicating that someone intends to do physical harm to another person represents an emergency. It's important not to minimize or discount aggressive threats or overt actions: "He doesn't mean it." "She wouldn't hurt a fly."

Part of the difficulty for family and friends is that when he's manic or in a mixed episode the person we know is very different. His ability to control his behavior can be severely impaired, even more so if he's actively using drugs or alcohol. It's a bitter lesson to learn that the time to act is before somebody gets hurt. Those at the greatest risk for being harmed by a person in a mixed or manic state are those closest to him, such as family—parents and spouses in particular—and friends.

Chapter 16

FINDING RESOURCES: THE PATCHWORK QUILT OF BEHAVIORAL HEALTHCARE IN AMERICA

- ■ What will insurance cover?
- ■ Will insurance cover additional resources to help out at home?
- ■ What happens when a person with bipolar disorder does not have commercial insurance?
- ■ What state agencies provide services for people with bipolar disorder?
- ■ How does someone become eligible for Medicare?
- ■ How does someone become eligible for Medicaid?
- ■ What is Supplemental Security Income (SSI)?
- ■ How does someone become eligible for state assistance?
- ■ Are there special assistance programs to help pay for medication?

What will insurance cover?

This varies widely from policy to policy. The mental health or behavioral health components of a person's insurance coverage may or may not be covered by the same company that handles other medical issues. In many policies specific limits are set on the number of inpatient psychiatric days a person can have over the course of a year, or even over the course of a lifetime. Each insurance plan also specifies which practitioners and even facilities that they will reimburse.

In an attempt to create some equality, a law was passed in 1996, the Mental Health Parity Act. This law created a set of rules for group health plans whereby coverage for mental health could not be less than that for other medical conditions. In reality, this legislation is filled with loopholes—it does not apply to health plans with less than fifty-one employees, it does not state that a health plan even has to offer a mental health benefit (some do not), and it does not apply to federal and state programs such as Medicare and Medicaid. So you can never assume that just because you have health insurance it will cover mental health services.

The question of what is and what is not covered can become complicated and frustrating. Most hospitals, clinics, and private practitioners go through a pre-certification or pre-approval process, before starting services. They should let you know if you're covered or not. Additionally, most health plans publish annual descriptions of their benefits that include lists of "in network," or approved providers.

Will insurance cover additional resources to help out at home?

As we've seen, there is a wide range of what health plans cover. It's important to check your policy, and if necessary call for clarification.

You may want to document all phone calls to your insurer that include the name of the representative you spoke to. If possible, when clarification is obtained, ask to have a written copy mailed, faxed, or emailed.

Additionally, even with state and federally funded healthcare plans such as Medicare, Medicaid, and state assistance, there is great variability at the state level and even within states of what services can be accessed and reimbursed.

One thing to remember is that most insurance plans—including Medicare and Medicaid—require all services to be under a physician's order. So if in-home services are needed, a doctor will have to consider them "medically necessary" and write for them.

Many in-home health agencies will have behavioral health specialists—typically nurses. Some of the kinds of services they can provide include assistance with medication management (up to multiple visits a day), psychoeducation, and some minimal counseling.

Another important consideration is that all in-home services need to meet criteria for "medical necessity," a term that is defined in different ways by different insurers. For Medicare, "medical necessity" requires that there be specific achievable goals. Using in-home services to maintain the status quo will not cut it in most instances for Medicare. Medicare also requires that a person meet their definition of "homebound" in order to qualify for in-home services. This may not hold true for Medicaid, but the rules vary from state to state.

What happens when a person with bipolar disorder does not have commercial insurance?

In emergency situations it's important to get help. Emergency rooms and crisis centers will typically see people regardless of the ability to pay. This doesn't mean that you won't get billed after the fact, though.

If you, or a family member, are admitted to a hospital or require emergency services, you will be billed. It's critically important to contact the hospital/emergency room social worker or patient accounts manager to identify your financial situation up front. This may not only save you unnecessary stress down the line—such as being referred to a collection agency—but it can also get the ball rolling with referrals to appropriate programs that can help out with the assistance you'll need.

What state agencies provide services for people with bipolar disorder?

Each state has a funded mental health agency or department that provides something of a safety net for people with mental illnesses. Often these agencies will define "target populations," that is, the people they've decided meet eligibility for state-funded services. Eligibility is typically based on severity and duration of illness combined with lower economic status.

See Appendix B for a state-by-state listing of mental health agencies. They are all structured differently. This was made abundantly clear in a recent NAMI report entitled "Grading the States 2006: A Report on America's Health Care System for Serious Mental Illness." In many states these agencies are broken up by regions or districts into community mental health agencies/centers or authorities.

How does someone become eligible for Medicare?

Medicare is a federally funded healthcare benefit for people over the age of sixty-five who have worked for more than ten years for a Medicare-covered employer, and it's also for many younger individuals with disabilities.

For younger individuals with disabilities, including mental disabilities, eligibility for Medicare is tied to Social Security Disability

Insurance (SSDI). That is, you must first be deemed eligible and receive SSDI before becoming eligible for the Medicare benefit. To be considered eligible for SSDI, the individual must be considered disabled (at least for twelve months, or the disability must be expected to last at least twelve months) and have worked at a job long enough, and recently enough, and have paid payroll (FICA) taxes.

- Information on SSDI eligibility and starter kits are available through the Department of Social Services (DSS): www.socialsecurity.gov/; toll free 800-772-1213; TTY 1-800-325-0778.
- Information on Medicare eligibility is available from the Centers for Medicare and Medicaid Services (CMS): www.cms.hhs.gov/; toll free 877-267-2323; TTY 866-226-1819.

How does someone become eligible for Medicaid?

Medicaid is a program that provides health insurance to low-income families and others who fall below state-designated financial guidelines. This typically includes children of low-income families, older low-income Americans—especially those requiring nursing home level of care—and people with disabilities, including psychiatric disabilities, that fall below a certain income level.

Unlike Medicare, which is fully funded by the federal government, Medicaid's funding is split between each state and the federal government. The oversight of Medicaid is managed at the state level, and each state is able to set its guidelines for who is eligible and what services will be covered under the benefit. In most states Medicaid covers a broad array of services, which include inpatient and outpatient care, medication assistance, home health care services, laboratory tests, vaccines, and long-term nursing home care.

Medicaid goes by different names in different states, which makes this a bit confusing. To find out more information about Medicaid in your state, contact your state Department of Social Services, Welfare, Social Security, or Office of Health Plans.

What is Supplemental Security Income (SSI)?

Supplemental Security Income (SSI)—not to be confused with Social Security Disability Income (SSDI)—is a federally funded assistance program for low-income older people, people who are blind, and people with disabilities, including mental disabilities.

Eligibility requirements are based on being a United States citizen and falling below a certain income and financial asset level ($2,000 for an individual and $3,000 for a couple).

To meet the disability requirement for SSI, the disability must:

- Result in the inability to engage in any substantial gainful activity; and be expected to result in death; or
- Have lasted, or can be expected to last, for a continuous period of not less than twelve months
  (www.ssa.gov/notices/supplemental-security-income/text-eligibility-ussi.htm)

How does someone become eligible for state assistance?

Many states offer additional assistance to people who receive Supplemental Security Income (SSI). The following link to the Social Security web site provides a state-by-state overview of what each state does and does not provide, as well as the eligibility requirements:

www.ssa.gov/policy/docs/progdesc/ssi_st_asst/2002/index.html

Are there special assistance programs to help pay for medication?

In addition to programs we've already reviewed—Medicaid, Medicare, etc.—there are other avenues by which people who can't afford needed medication may be able to receive it at either a discounted rate or free.

Some states have medication assistance programs for people who fall bellow a certain income and means level. Examples include ConnPACE in Connecticut and Prescription Advantage in Massachusetts. Many states will offer medication assistance programs, but only for those sixty-five and older. There are a number of websites that can direct you to what is available in your state. Additionally, contacting your state's department of social service, welfare, or health (they all have different names in different states) can get you the information you need.

In addition to state-run programs, pharmaceutical companies— especially with medications that are still on patent—will offer medication-assistance programs. In order to qualify, most companies require that a simple application be completed and that the medications are given under a physician's (or other licensed prescriber's) written order.

Web sites that provide information, eligibility criteria, etc. on free or discounted medications including downloadable applications are:
- Needymeds.com—Run by a non-profit organization, Needymeds, Inc., out of Massachusetts
- Rxassist.org—Operated by a non-profit organization, Volunteers in Healthcare, which comes out of Brown University
- Ppark.org—Partnership for Prescription Assistance; 1-888-4PPA-NOW (477-2669)
- NAMI.org—National Alliance on Mental Illness. On the NAMI web site is a page with links to all of the major pharmaceutical

companies that produce and market psychiatric medication: www.nami.org/Content/ContentGroups/Helpline1/Prescription_Drug_Patient_Assistance_Programs.htm

Appendix A RESOURCES AND READINGS

First-Person and Family Accounts of Bipolar Disorder:

Clifford Whittingham Beers, *A Mind that Found Itself, An Autobiography*, Kessinger Publishing (current paperback version) originally published in 1908
Patty Duke, Call Me Anna
Kay Redfield Jamison, PhD, *An Unquiet Mind*, 1995. Alfred A. Knopf (a division of Random House)
Jane Pauley, *Skywriting: A Life out of the Blue*. 2004. Random House,
Danielle Steel, *His Bright Light, The Story of Nick Traina*, 1998 Dell Publishing (A Division of Random House)

Organizations, Resources and Supports for Families and People with Bipolar Disorder:

Active Minds on Campus
A student-run advocacy group with chapters on many college and university campuses
1875 Connecticut Ave, NW Suite 418
Washington, DC 20009
(202) 719-1177
Website: www.activemindsoncampus.org

American Academy of Child and Adolescent Psychiatry
This is a membership organization of Child-and-Adolescent Psychiatrists and other interested physicians. The website has a wealth of information for families, including a free physician-finder to locate local child and adolescent practitioners.
3615 Wisconsin Avenue, N.W.
Washington, DC 20016-3007
Phone: 202.966.7300
Fax: 202.966.2891
Toll-free: 800-333-7636
Website: www.aacap.org

American Association of Suicidology (AAS)
5221 Wisconsin Avenue, NW
Washington, DC 20015
Local: (202) 237-8255
Toll-free: (800) 273-8255
Website: www.suicidology.org

American Society of Addiction Medicine
4601 North Park Ave, Arcade Suite 101
Chevy Chase, MD 20815
Telephone 301/656-3920
Fax: 301/656-3815
Website: www.asam.org

Army Publishing Directorate
An excellent source of information related to the army, it's also linked to more general information on the Armed Services. Full text versions of army regulations, including those pertaining to separation (Army Regulation 635-200) from the army can be downloaded.
Website: www.usapa.army.mil

Child and Adolescent Bipolar Foundation
This is a web-based parent-run not-for-profit membership organization for families with children who have bipolar disorder or are at risk for developing it. The membership cost is $40 per year, but there is also much information available for free.
1000 Skokie Blvd.
Suite 570
Wilmette, IL 60091
Phone: (847) 256-8525
Fax: (847) 920-9498
Website: www.bpkids.org

Consumer Reports Best Buy Drugs
Website: www.crbestbuydrugs.org
Judge David L. Bazelon Center for Mental Health Law
1101 15th Street, NW, Suite 1212
Washington, DC 20005
Phone: (202)-467-5730
Fax: (202)-223-0409
Email: webmaster@bazelon.org
Website: www.bazelon.org

Mental Health America (Formerly known as the National Mental Health Association)
2000 N. Beauregard Street, 6th Floor
Alexandria, VA 22311
Main Switchboard: (703) 684-7722
Toll-free: (800) 969-6MHA (6642)
TTY: (800) 433-5959
Fax: (703) 684-5968
Website: www.nmha.org

National Alliance on Mental Illness (NAMI)
Colonial Place Three
2107 Wilson Blvd., Suite 300
Arlington, VA 22201-3042
Local: (703) 524-7600
Fax: (703) 524-9094
TDD: (703) 516-7227
Member Services: (888) 999-NAMI (6264)
Help line: (800)-950-NAMI (6264)
Website: www.nami.org

National Mental Health Association (NMHA)
2001 N. Beauregard Street, 12th floor
Alexandria, VA 22311
Local: (703) 684-7722
Toll-free: (800) 969-6642
TTY: (800) 433-5959
Website: www.nmha.org

National Mental Health Information Center
(SAMHSA)
Toll free: (800) 789-2647
TTY: (301) 443-8431
Website: www.healthfinder.gov

The National Suicide Prevention Lifeline
This is a federally funded network of crisis centers dedicated to
suicide prevention.
Tel: 800-273-TALK
TTY: 800-799-4TTY (4889)
Website: www.suicidepreventionlifeline.org

The Centers for Medicare and Medicaid Services (CMS)
7500 Security Boulevard
Baltimore, MD 21244
Toll-Free: 800-MEDICARE (800-633-4227) for general information
TTY Toll-free: 877-486-2048
Website: www.cms.hhs.gov

Depression and Bipolar Support Alliance
A not-for-profit consumer-run organization that includes support groups, advocacy and education among its objectives.
730 N. Franklin Street, Suite 501
Chicago, IL 60610-7224
Local (312) 642-0049
Toll free: (800) 826 -3632
Fax: (312) 642-7243
Website: www.dbsalliance.org

National Institute on Drug Addiction (NIDA)
Extensive online information and many publications that can be ordered at no cost, or at minimal cost (expense of production).
6001 Executive Boulevard, Room 5213
Bethesda, MD 20892-9561
Tel: (301) 443-1124
Website: www.nida.nih.gov

National Institute of Mental Health (NIMH)
This is the lead governmental agency that funds research on mental illness. There is extensive material available through their website and many free publications that can be ordered by topic.
Website: www.nimh.nih.gov

National Institutes of Health, DHHS
6001 Executive Blvd. Rm. 8184, MSC 9663
Bethesda, MD 20892-9663
Tel: (301) 443-4513/866-615-NIMH (6464)
TTY: (301) 443-8431 Fax: (301) 443-4279
Website: www.nimh.nih.gov

National Mental Health Consumers' Self-Help Clearinghouse
1211 Chestnut Street, Suite 1207
Philadelphia, PA 19107
Phone: (800) 553-4539
or (215) 751-1810
Fax: (215) 636-6312
Email: info@mhselfhelp.org

National Suicide Prevention Lifeline
This is a nationally funded network of crisis centers that offers
round-the-clock telephone support, crisis counseling, mental health
referrals, and crisis intervention.
Toll-free: (800) 273-TALK
Website: www.suicidepreventionlifeline.org

Substance Abuse and Mental Health Administration (SAMHSA)
Along with the extensive amount of information one can obtain
through the SAMHSA website, there are many free publications and
other materials, most available at no cost.
P.O. Box 42557
Washington, DC 20015
Tel:(800) 789-2647
Monday through Friday,
8:30 a.m. to 12:00 a.m., EST

TDD: 866-889-2647
Website: www.mentalhealth.samhsa.gov

The World Health Organization (WHO)
Website: www.who.int

Other online Sources of Information:

Mentalhelp.net
This is a well-organized site that contains topic-specific information on advances in the field of mental health.

PsychCentral.com Blog Community
Basic information organized by topic, with extensive blogs and chat sessions.

Healthy Skepticism
A non-profit organization dedicated to countering misleading pharmaceutical promotion.
Website: www.healthyskepticism.org

Appendix B

State by State Guide to Mental Health Agencies/Division/Bureaus
(Including District of Columbia and Puerto Rico)

STATE	AGENCY	ADDRESS	WEB SITE	TELEPHONE
Alabama	Alabama Department of Mental Health and Mental Retardation	1000 North Union St. PO Box 301410 Montgomery, AL 36130-1410	www.mh.alabama.gov	Tel: (800) 367-0955
Alaska	Division of Behavioral Health	3601 C Street, Ste 934, Anchorage, AK 99503	http://hss.state.ak.us/dbh	Tel: (907) 269-3410
Arizona	Arizona Department of Health Services/Division of Behavioral Health Services	150 N. 18th Avenue, 2nd Floor, Phoenix, AZ 85007	www.azdhs.gov/bhs	Tel: (602) 364-4558
Arkansas	Arkansas Department of Health and Human Services/Division of Behavioral Health	4313 West Markham, Little Rock, AR 72205	www.arkansas.gov/dhhs/dmhs	Tel: (501) 686-9164 TTD: (501) 686-9176
California	Department of Mental Health	1600 9th Street, Rm. 151, Sacramento, CA 95814	www.dmh.cahwnet.gov	Tel: (800) 896-4042 or (916) 654-3890 TTY: (800) 896-2512
Colorado	Colorado Division of Human Services/Division of Mental Health (DMH)	3824 W. Princeton Cir., Denver, CO 80236	www.cdhs.state.co.us/dmh	Tel: (302) 866-7400

(Continued on next page)

STATE	AGENCY	ADDRESS	WEB SITE	TELEPHONE
Colorado	Colorado Division of Human Services/Division of Mental Health (DMH)	3824 W. Princeton Cir., Denver, CO 80236	www.cdhs.state.co.us/dmh	Tel: (302) 866-7400
Connecticut	Department of Mental Health and Addiction Services (DMHAS)	410 Capitol Avenue, P.O. Box 341431 Hartford, CT 06134	www.dmhas.state.ct.us	Tel: (860) 418-7000; Toll Free: (800) 446-7348 TDD: (860) 418-6707; Toll Free: (888) 621-3551
Delaware	Delaware Health and Social Services/Division of Substance Abuse and Mental Health	1901 N. Du Pont Highway, Main Bldg. New Castle, DE 19720	www.dhss.delaware.gov/dhss/dsamh	Tel: (302) 255-9399 Fax: (302) 255-4428
District of Columbia	DC Department of Mental Health	64 New York Avenue, NE, 4th Floor Washington, DC 20002	http://dmh.dc.gov/dmh/site/default.asp	Tel: (202) 673-7440 Access HelpLine: (888) 793-4357 (7WE-HELP)
Florida	Florida Department of Children and Families/Mental Health Services	1317 Winewood Blvd. . Building 1, Room 202 Tallahassee, Florida 32399-0700	www.dcf.state.fl.us/mentalhealth	Tel: (850) 487-1111
Georgia	Division of Mental Health, Developmental Disabilities and Addictive Diseases	Two Peachtree Street, N.W. 22nd Floor Atlanta, Georgia 30303	http://mhddad.dhr.georgia.gov/portal/site/DHR-MHDDAD	Tel: (404) 657-5737
Hawaii	Hawaii State Department of Health/Adult Mental Health Division	1250 Punchbowl #256 Honolulu, HI 96813	www.hawaii.gov/health/mental-health	Tel: (808) 586-4686 Fax: (808) 586-4745

(Continued on next page)

Idaho	Idaho Department of Health and Welfare—Adult Mental Health Services		www.healthandwel-fare.idaho.gov/site/3341/default.aspx	Idaho Care line Dial: 211 or (800) 926-2588
Illinois	Illinois Department of Human Services	100 S. Grand Ave. E. Springfield, IL 62762	www.dhs.state.il.us/mhdd/mh/	Tel: (800) 843-6154 TTY: (800) 447-6404
Indiana	Indiana Family and Social Service Administration/ Division of Mental Health and Addiction	402 West Washington St. W353 Indianapolis, IN 46204	www.in.gov/fssa/mental	Tel: (800) 901-1133 TDD: (317) 232-7844
Iowa	Iowa Department of Human Services/Mental Health and Developmental Disabilities	Department of Human Services Division of BDPS 5th Floor Hoover Building 1305 East Walnut Des Moines, IA 50319-0114	www.dhs.state.ia.us/mhdd	Tel: (515) 281-5454
Kansas	Kansas Department of Social and Rehabilitation Services/Mental Health		www.srskansas.org/services/mhsatr_mental-health.htm	
Kentucky	Kentucky Department of Mental Health and Mental Retardation Services	100 Fair Oaks Lane 4E-B Frankfort, KY 40621	http://mhmr.ky.gov/kdmhmrs/default.asp	Tel: (502) 564-4527 TTY: (502) 564-5777 Fax: (502) 564-5478
Louisiana	Office of Mental Health	Bienville Building 628 North 4th Street Baton Rouge, LA 70802	www.dhh.louisiana.gov/offices/?ID=62	Tel: (225) 342-2540 Fax: (225) 342-5066

(Continued on next page)

Maine	Behavioral and Developmental Services	State House Station #11 Hospital Street Marquardt Building, 2nd Floor Augusta, ME 04333-0040	www.maine.gov/dhhs/bds	Crisis Services: (888) 568-1112
Maryland	Maryland Mental Hygiene Administration	Spring Grove Hospital Center 55 Wade Ave Dix Building Catonsville, MD 21228	www.dhmh.state.md.us/mha	Tel: (410) 402-8300 Fax: (410) 402-8301 TTY/MD Relay Number (800) 735-2258
Massachusetts	Massachusetts Department of Mental Health	Department of Mental Health Central Office 25 Staniford Street Boston, MA 02114	www.mass.gov/?pageID=eohhs2agency-landing&L=4&L0=Home&L1=Government&L2=Departments+and+Divisions&L3=Department+of+Mental+Health&sid=Eeohhs2 Email: dmhinfo@dmh.state.ma.us	Tel: (617) 626-8000 TTY: (617) 727-9842
Michigan	Michigan Department of Community Health/Mental Health and Substance Abuse	Capitol View Building 201 Townsend Street Lansing, MI 48913	www.michigan.gov/mdch/0,1607,7-132-2941_4868—,00.html	Tel: (517) 373-3740 TTY: (517) 373-3573
Minnesota	Minnesota Department of Human Services/Adult Mental Health Division		www.dhs.state.mn.us/main/idcplg?IdcService=GET_DYNAMIC_CONVER-SION&RevisionSelectionMethod=LatestReleased&dDocName=id_000085	Tel: (651) 431-2225.

(Continued on next page)

Mississippi	The Mississippi Department of Mental Health	1101 Robert E. Lee Building. 239 N. Lamar St. Jackson, MS 39201	www.dmh.state.ms. us	Tel: (601) 359-1288 Fax: (601) 359-6295 TTY: (601) 359-6230
Missouri	Missouri Department of Mental Health	1706 E. Elm St. Jefferson City, MO 65101	www.dmh.missouri. gov	Tel: (800)-364-9687
Montana	Department of Public Health and Human Services/Addictive and Mental Disorders Division	555 Fuller Avenue PO Box 202905 Helena, MT 59620	www.dphhs.mt.gov/amdd/index.shtml	Tel: (406) 444-3964
Nebraska	Nebraska Health and Human Services System/Division of Behavioral Health Services	P.O. Box 98925 Lincoln, NE 68509-8925	www.hhs.state.ne.us /beh/mh/mh.htm	Tel: (402) 471-7818
Nevada	Department of Health and Human Services/Division of Mental Health & Developmental Services	4126 Technology Way, Second Floor Carson City, NV 89706	http://mhds.state.nv .us	Tel: (775) 684-5943 Fax: (775) 684-5964 or (775) 684-5966
New Hampshire	Department of Health and Human Services/Bureau of Behavioral Health	105 Pleasant St. Concord, NH 03301	www.dhhs.state.nh. us/DHHS/BBH/def ault.htm	Tel (603) 271-5000 (800) 852-3345 ext 5000 TDD: (800) 735-2964

(Continued on next page)

New Jersey	Department of Human Services/Division of Mental Health	P.O. Box 700 Trenton, NJ 08625-0212	www.state.nj.us/humanservices/dmhs	Tel: 609-292-3717
New Mexico	Department of Health/Department of Behavioral Health	1190 S. St. Francis Dr. Santa Fe, NM 87502	www.bhd.state.nm.us	Tel: (505) 827-2658
New York	Office of Mental Health	44 Holland Avenue Albany, New York 12229	www.omh.state.ny.us	Tel: (800) 597-8481
North Carolina	North Carolina Division of Mental Health, Developmental Disabilities and Substance Abuse Services	NC Division of MH/DD/SAS, Section/Branch name *(4-digit MSC number)* Mail Service Center Raleigh, NC 27699-*(4-digit MSC number)* Attn: *(name of person you are mailing)*	www.dhhs.state.nc.us/mhddsas	Tel: (919) 733-7011 Fax: (919) 508-0951
North Dakota	North Dakota Department of Human Services: Mental Health and Substance Abuse Services	1237 W Divide Ave, Suite 1C Bismarck, ND 58501-1208	www.nd.gov/humanservices/services/mentalhealth	Tel: (701) 328-8920 Toll Free: (800) 755-2719 (ND only) Fax: (701) 328-8969
Ohio	Ohio Department of Mental Health	30 E. Broad Street, 8th floor Columbus, OH 43215-3430	www.mh.state.oh.us	Tel: (877) 275-6364 TTY: (888) 636-4889
Oklahoma	Oklahoma Department of Mental Health and Substance Abuse Services	1200 NE 13th St. P.O. Box 53277 OKC, OK 73152-3277	www.odmhsas.org	Tel: (800) 522-9054 (405) 522-3908 TDD: (405) 522-3851

(Continued on next page)

Oregon	Oregon Department of Human Services/Mental Health Division	Mental Health and Addiction Services 500 Summer Street NE E86 Salem, OR 97301	www.oregon.gov/DHS/mentalhealth/index.shtml	Tel: (503) 945-5763 Fax: (503) 378-8467 TTY: (503) 945-5895
Pennsylvania	Department of Public Welfare/ Office of Mental Health and Substance Abuse Services	P.O. Box 2675 Harrisburg, PA 17105	www.dpw.state.pa.us/Family/MentalHealthServ	Tel: (717) 787-6443 TDD: (800) 830-6252
Puerto Rico	Mental Health and Anti-Addiction Services Administration	Ave Barbosa 414 P.O. Box 21414 San Juan, PR 00928-1414	E-mail: jgalarza@assmca.gobierno.pr	Tel: (787) 764-3670 (787) 764-3795 Fax: (787) 765-5888
Rhode Island	Rhode Island Department of Mental Health, Retardation and Hospitals	14 Harrington Road Cranston, RI 02920	www.mhrh.ri.gov	Tel: (401) 462-3201
South Carolina	South Carolina Department of Mental Health	South Carolina Department of Mental Health Administration Building 2414 Bull Street Columbia, SC 29202	www.state.sc.us/dmh	Tel: (803) 898—8581 TTY : (864) 297-5130
South Dakota	South Dakota Division of Mental Health	Hillsview Plaza, E. Hwy 34 c/o 500 East Capitol Pierre, SD 57501-5070	http://dhs.sd.gov/dmh	Tel: (605) 773-5991 (800) 265-9684 Fax: (605) 773-7076

(Continued on next page)

Tennessee	Department of Mental Health and Developmental Disabilities	425 Fifth Avenue North 3rd Floor Cordell Hull Bldg Nashville, TN 37243-0675	www.state.tn.us/mental/index.html	Tel: (615) 532-6500 24 hour crisis line: (800) 809-9957
Texas	Texas Department of State Health Services/Mental Health and Substance Abuse			

Appendix C

CHAPTER NOTES AND REFERENCES

Chapter 1: Bipolar Basics

Charles Atkins, MD, "Chad," *Yale Psychiatry* 4 (1994): 19–21. Republished in *New England Writers Network* (1995): 11–12.

Ross Baldessarini, MD; Maruizio Pmpili, MD; Leonardo Tondo, MD; "Suicide in Bipolar Disorder: Risks and Management," *CNS Spectrum* (2006): 465–471.

Steven L. Dubovsky, MD, "Treatment of Bipolar Disorder," *Psychiatric Clinics of North America* 28 (2005): 349–370.

David A. Jobes, PhD, *Managing Suicidal Risk* (Guilford Press, 2006).,

Gary S. Sachs et al, "Integration of Suicide Prevention into Outpatient Management of Bipolar Disorder," *Journal of Clinical Psychiatry* 62, supplement 25 (2001): 3–11.

Roy H. Perlis, MD, et al, "Clinical Features of Bipolar Depression Versus Major Depressive Disorder in Large Multicenter Trials," *American Journal of Psychiatry*, 163 (2006): 225–231.

Melvin G. McInnis et al, *Emery and Rimoin's Principles and Practice of Medical Genetics, Fifth Edition* (Elsevier Press, 2007): 2615–2628.

Andrew W. Skodol, MD; Ross Baldessarini, MD; Maruizio Pmpili, MD; Leonardo Tondo, MD; "Suicide in Bipolar Disorder: Risks and Management," *CNS Spectrum* (2006): 465–471.

Psychopathology and Violent Crime (American Psychiatric Press, Inc.,1998).

Jeffrey W. Swanson, PhD, et al., "Violence and Psychiatric Disorder in the Community: Evidence from the Epidemiologic Catchment

Area Surveys," *Hospital and Community Psychiatry* (1990): 761–770.

"Practice Guideline for the Treatment of Patients with Bipolar Disorder," Second Edition, *American Journal of Psychiatry* 159, supplement 4 (2002): 1–50.

Practice Guidelines for the Assessment and Treatment of Patients with Suicidal Behaviors (American Psychiatric Association, 2003).

Chapter 2: The Bipolar Spectrum: One Size Does Not Fit All

Diagnostic and Statistical Manual of Mental Disorders, Fourth edition Text Revised DSM-IV-TR (American Psychiatric Association, 2000).

Malcolm Bowers, Jr., M.D., *Abetting Madness: The Role of Illicit and Prescribed Drugs in Promoting Psychotic and Manic Disorders* (Xlibris, 2003).

R.M.A. Hirschfeld, J.B. Williams, R.L. Spitzer, J.R. Calabrese, L. Flynn, P.E. Keck, Jr., L. Lewis, S.L. McElroy, R.M. Post, D.J. Rapport, J.M. Russell, G.S. Sachs, J. Zajecka, "Development and Validation of a Screening Instrument for Bipolar Spectrum Disorder: The Mood Disorder Questionnaire," *American Journal of Psychiatry* 157(2000): 1873–1875.

Roy H. Perlis, MD et al, "Clinical Features of Bipolar Depression Versus Major Depressive Disorder in Large Multicenter Trials," *American Journal of Psychiatry* (February 2006): 225–231.

S. Nassir Ghaemi, Christopher J. Miller, Douglas A. Berv, Jeffrey Klugman, Klara J. Rosenquist, Ronald W. Pies, *"Sensitivity and Specificity of a New Bipolar Spectrum Diagnostic Scale,"* Journal of *Affective Disorders* 84 (2005): 273–277.

Chapter 3: Getting into Treatment

Javier Amador, Ph.D, *I Am Not Sick I Don't Need Help!* Second Edition (Vida Press, 2007).

Charles Atkins, "Patients usually have reasons for being noncompliant," *American Medical News* (April 9, 2001).

Brandon Gaudiano and Ivan W. Miller, "Patients' Expectancies, the Alliance in Pharmachotherapy, and Treatment Outcomes in Bipolar Disorder," *Journal of Consulting and Clinical Psychology* 74:4 (2006): 671–676.

New York State, Office of Mental Health, *An Explanation of Kendra's Law*, revised 2006, available online at www.omh.state. ny.us/omhweb/Kendra_web/Ksummary.htm.

Martha Sajatovic, MD et al, "Self-Reported Medication Treatment Adherence Among Veterans with Bipolar Disorder," *Psychiatric Services* 57 (2006): 56–62.

Sajatovic M. Valenstein, et al, "Treatment Adherence with Antipsychotic Medications in Bipolar Disorder," *Bipolar Disorder* 8 (2006): 232–241.

Chapter 4: Medications: Useful Tools on the Road to Recovery

Charles L. Bowden, MD, "Treatment Options for Bipolar Disorder," *Journal of Clinical Psychiatry* 66, supplement 1 (2005): 3–7.

Consumer Reports/Best Buy Drugs, web site: www.crbestbuydrugs. org

Patricia E. Deegan, PhD, Robert E. Drake, MD, "Shared Decision Making and Medication Management in the Recovery Process," *Psychiatric Services* (2006): 1636–1639.

Paul E. Keck, Jr.,. MD, "Long-Term Management Strategies to Achieve Optimal Function in Patients with Bipolar Disorder," *Journal of Clinical Psychiatry* 67, supplement 9 (2006): 19–24.

Kim H. Lew, Pharm D. et al, "The Effect of Medication Adherence on Health Care Utilization in Bipolar Disorder," *Managed Care Interface* (2006): 41–46.

Pete Penna, Pharm D., "The Issue of Medication Adherence Raises More Questions than Answers," *Managed Care Interface* (September 2006): 37–38.

Robert Rosenheck, "The Growth of Psychopharmacology in the 1990's: Evidence-Based Practice or Irrational Exuberance," *International Journal of Law and Psychiatry* 28 (2005): 467–483.

The Medical Letter, Inc. (source of unbiased medication reviews and other publications) (800) 211-2769, http://www.medicalletter. org/

The Physician's Desk Reference, Edition 60 (Thomson/PDR, 2006).

Chapter 5: Mood Stabilizers

Joseph R. Calabrese, et al, "Recurrence in Bipolar I Disorder: A Post Hoc Analysis Excluding Relapses in Two Double-blind Maintenance Studies," *Biological Psychiatry* 59 (2006) 1061–1064.

David L. Dunner, MD, "Correlates of Suicidal Behavior and Lithium Treatment in Bipolar Disorder," *Journal of Clinical Psychiatry* 65, supplement 10 (2004): 5–10.

Lakshmi N. Yatham, MD, "Newer Anticonvulsants in the Treatment of Bipolar Disorder," *Journal of Clinical Psychiatry* 65, supplement 10 (2004) 28–35.

Chapter 6: Antipsychotic Medications

Alex Berenson, "Lily Settles with 18,000 over Zyprexa," *The New York Times* (January 5, 2007).

Philippe Damier, MD, PhD, et al, "Bilateral Deep Brain Stimulation of the Globus Pallidus to Treat Tardive Dyskinesia," *Archives of General Psychiatry* (February 2007): 170–176.

Kalyna Z. Bezchlibnyk-Butler and J. Joel Jeffries, *Clinical Handbook of Psychotropic Drugs*, Fifteenth Edition (Hogrefe and Huber Publishers, 2005).

Robert Rosenheck, MD, et al, "Cost-Effectiveness of Second-Generation Antipsychotics and Perphenazine in a Randomized Trial of Treatment for Chronic Schizophrenia," *American Journal of Psychiatry* 163:12 (2006): 2080–2089.

Stephen M. Stahl, *The Prescriber's Guide*, Revised and Updated Edition (Cambridge University Press, 2006).

Chapter 7: Antidepressants and Other Medications

Gabriele S. Leverich, MSW, LCSW, et al., "Risk of Switch in Mood Polarity to Hypomania or Mania in Patients with Bipolar Depression During Acute and Continuation Trials of Venlafaxine, Sertraline, and Buproprion as Adjunts to Mood Stabilizers," *American Journal of Psychiatry* 163 (2006): 232–239.

Chapter 8: Other Medical Therapies

Kitty Dukakis and Larry Tye, *Shock: The Healing Power of Electroconvulsive Therapy* (Avery, 2006).

Mark S. George, et al, "Vagus Nerve Stimulation: A New Tool for Brain Research and Therapy," *Biological Psychiatry* 47 (2000): 287–295.

Charles H. Kellner, MD, et al, *Handbook of ECT* (American Psychiatric Press, Inc., 1997).

Harold Sackeim, et al., "The Cognitive Effects of Electroconvulsive Therapy in Community Settings," *Neuropsychopharmacology* 32 (2007): 244–254.

Raj S. Shiwach, MD, MR, et al., "An Analysis of Reported Deaths Following Electroconvulsive Therapy in Texas, 1993-1998," *Psychiatric Services* 52(2001): 1095–1097.

Chapter 9: Psychotherapies and Supportive Strategies

Ellen Frank, PhD, *Treating Bipolar Disorder: A Clinician's Guide to Interpersonal and Social Rhythm Therapy* (The Guilford Press, 2005).

Ellen Frank PhD, "Two-Year Outcome for Interpersonal and Social Rhythm Therapy in Individuals with Bipolar I Disorder," *Archives of General Psychiatry* 62:9 (2005): 996–1004.

David J. Miklowitz, PhD, "A Review of Evidence-Based Psychosocial Interventions for Bipolar Disorder," *Journal of Clinical Psychiatry*, supplement 11 (2006): 28–33.

David J. Miklowitz, PhD and Michael J. Goldstein, *Bipolar Disorder: A Family-Focused Treatment Approach* (The Guilford Press, 1997). (This book outlines Family Focused Therapy, or FFT.)

David J. Miklowitz, PhD and Michael W. Otto, PhD, "New Psychosocial Interventions for Bipolar Disorder: A review of Literature and Introduction of the Systemic Treatment Enhancement Program," *Journal of Cognitive Psychotherapy* 20: 2 (2006): 215–230.

Jan Scott, MD and Francesc Colom, D. Clin Psych, PhD, "Psychosocial Treatments for Bipolar Disorder," *Psychiatric Clinics of North America* 28 (2005): 371–384.

Eduard Vieta, MD, PhD, "Improving Treatment Adherence in Bipolar Disorder Through Psychoeducation," *Journal of Clinical Psychiatry* 66, supplement 1 (2005): 24–29.

Chapter 10: Relapse Prevention Strategies

Ellen Frank, PhD, "The Importance of Routine for Preventing Recurrence in Bipolar Disorder," *The American Journal of Psychiatry* 163;6, (2006) 981–985.

Chapter 11: Bipolar Disorder and Substance Abuse and Chemical Dependency

Monika Kolodziej, et al., "Anxiety disorder among patients with co-occurring bipolar and substance use disorders," *Drug and Alcohol Dependence* 80 (2005): 251–257.

G. Alan Marlatt, et al., Harm Reduction: *Pragmatic Strategies for Managing High-Risk Behaviors* (The Guilford Press, 1998).

Lana A. Vornik, MS, and E. Sherwood Brown, MD, PhD, "Management of Comorbid Bipolar Disorder and Substance Abuse," *Journal of Clinical Psychiatry* 67, supplement 7 (2006): 24–30.

Chapter 12: Other Common Coexisting Psychiatric Disorders and Treatment Strategies

Mark S. Bauer, et al., "Prevalence and Distinct Correlates of Anxiety, Substance, and Combined Co-Morbidity in a Multi-Site Public Sector Sample with Bipolar Disorder," *Journal of Affective Disorders* 85 (2005): 301–315.

Sara Bolton, MD, and John G. Gunderson, MD, "Distinguishing Borderline Personality Disorder from Bipolar Disorder: Differential Diagnosis and Implications," *American Journal of Psychiatry* 153:9 (1996): 1202–1207.

Joseph F. Goldberg and Jessica L. Garno, "Development of posttraumatic stress disorder in adult patients with histories of severe childhood abuse," *Journal of Psychiatric Research* 39 (2005): 595–601.

Paul E. Keck, Jr., MD et al., "Pharmacologic Treatment Considerations in Co-Occurring Bipolar and Anxiety Disorders," *Journal of Clinical Psychiatry* 67, supplement 1 (2006): 8–15.

Martin B. Keller, "Prevalence and Impact of Comorbid Anxiety and Bipolar Disorder," *Journal of Clinical Psychiatry* 67, supplement 1 (2006): 5–7.

William R. Marchand, MD, et al., "Adverse Life Events and Pediatric Bipolar Disorder in a Community Mental Health Setting," *Community Mental Health Journal* 41: 1 (2005): 67–75.

Michael H. Stone, MD, "Relationship of Borderline Personality Disorder and Bipolar Disorder," *American Journal of Psychiatry* 163:7 (2006): 1126–1128.

Chapter 13: Age, Gender, and Culture Issues

Salvatore Gentile, "Prophylactic treatment of bipolar disorder in pregnancy and breastfeeding: focus on emerging mood stabilizers," *Bipolar Disorder:* 8 (2006): 207–220.

Nona S. Federenko, PhD, "Women's Mental Health During Pregnancy Influences Fetal and Infant Developmental and Health Outcomes," *CNS Spectrums* (March 2004): 198–206.

Susan Foster et al., *School Mental Health Services in the United States 2002-2003*, U.S. Department of Health and Human Services/ Substance Abuse and Mental Health Services Administration, 2005 (This is available for free through the SAMHSA website— www.samhsa.gov).

Richard Herrell, et al., "First Psychiatric Hospitalizations in the US Military: The National Collaborative Study of Early Psychosis and Suicide (NCEPS)," *Psychological Medicine* (2006): 1405– 1415.

Robert A. Kowatch et al. and The Child Psychiatric Workgroup on Bipolar Disorder, "Treatment Guidelines for Children and Adolescents with Bipolar Disorder," *Journal of the American Academy of Child and Adolescent Psychiatry* (March 2005): 213–235.

Robert A. Kowatch, MD, Melissa P. DelBello, MD, "Pediatric Bipolar Disorder: Emerging Diagnostic and Treatment Approaches,"

Child and Adolescent Psychiatry Clinics of North America 15 (2006): 73–108.

James F. Luebber, MD, et al., "Psychopharmacology, Disability Law and the Administration of Psychotropic Medication in the School Setting," *Psychiatric Services* (November 2000): 1369–1370.

Lee S. Cohen, MD, et al., "A Reevaluation of Risk of In Utero Exposure to Lithium," *Journal of the American Medical Association* (January 12, 1994): 146–149.

Pedro Ruiz, MD et al., "Ethnicity and Psychopharmacology," *Review of Psychiatry* Volume 19 (American Psychiatric Press, 2000).

Department of Defense Memorandum. Subject: *Policy Guidance for Deployment-Limiting Psychiatric Conditions and Medications*, November 7, 2006.

Kimberly Yonkers, MD et al., "Management of Bipolar Disorder During Pregnancy and the Postpartum Period," *American Journal of Psychiatry* (April 2004): 608–620.

Chapter 14: Living with Bipolar Disorder

Patty Duke and Gloria Hochman, *A Brilliant Madness: Living with Manic-Depressive Illness* (Bantam Books, 1992).

Kay Redfield Jamison, PhD, *Touched with Fire: Manic-Depressive Illness and the Artistic Temperament* (Free Press Paperbacks (a Division of Simon and Schuster, Inc.), 1993).

Chapter 15: Survival Tips for Family and Friends

Javier Amador, PhD, *I Am Not Sick I Don't Need Help!* Second Edition (Vida Press, 2007).

Chapter 16: Finding Resources: The Patchwork Quilt of Behavioral Healthcare in America

See Appendices A & B for pertinent organizations, websites, and state agencies.

Index

alcohol or sedative-hypnotic detoxification, 203–204
as cause of bipolar disorder, 25–26
DD treatment, 191–192, 201. *See also*
Dual Diagnosis (DD) Treatment
harm reduction model, 194–195, 196*f*
inpatient detoxification admissions,
199–200
inpatient rehabilitation program,
200–201
insurance, 202
motivational interviewing/enhance-
ment, 192–194. *See also*
Motivational Interviewing
occurrence in people, 188
opiates, 204–205
other medications, 206
self-medication, 189
substance dependence, 188–189
twelve-step groups, 197–198
Suicide and Bipolar Disorder, x, 12, 17,
31–32, 50, 57–58, 66, 72–74, 84, 88,
91, 105, 133, 208, 270
committing, 26–27, 269
decrease in risks, 28–30
depression and, 12
demographics, 29*f*
means of, 30*f*
risk factors for, 27–28

Supplemental Security Income (SSI),
278. *See also* Healthcare Resources in
Bipolar Disorder
Supportive Therapy, 169

T

Tactile Hallucinations, 17
Tardive Dyskinesia (TD), 100, 126–128,
130
Thyroid Hormone, 59, 61, 111
Topiramate (Topamax), 120, 234
Trans-Cranial Magnetic Stimulation
(TCMS), 138, 153
Treatment of Bipolar Disorder
anosognosia and, 68–69
behavioral crisis, 71–73. *See also*
Behavioral Crisis
continuation of, 97
ECT, 78. *See also* Electroconvulsive
Therapy
emergency rooms and crisis centers,
75. *See also* Emergency Rooms
less intensive, 83–84
inpatient hospitalizations, necessity of, 77
inpatient hospitalizations, procedure
followed in, 77–79
IOP, 83. *See also* Intensive Outpatient
Program
maintenance treatment. *See*
Maintenance Bipolar Disorder
Treatment

About the Author

Charles Atkins, MD, is a board-certified psychiatrist, author, and professional speaker. He is on the clinical faculty at Yale University and is an attending psychiatrist at Waterbury (Connecticut) Hospital. IIe has worked in both public (Regional Medical Director for the state of Connecticut) and private (hospital and clinic-based) settings.

He has published three psychological thrillers with St. Martin's Press as well as hundreds of articles, columns, and shorts stories in both professional and popular magazines, newspapers, and journals. His website is www.charlesatkins.com.